PEA... ...TRE
...'s Church
Princes Street, Edinburgh

Edinburgh Peace and Justice Education Centre Library

St John's Church, Princes Street, Edinburgh
EH2 4BJ

Please return by the following date either to
the Centre or to the Quaker Meeting House,
7 Victoria Terrace, Edinburgh (in an
addressed envelope, please)

PEACE AND JUSTICE RESOURCE CENTRE
St. John's Church
Princes Street

PEACE AND JUSTICE RESOURCE CENTRE
St. John's Church
Princes Street, Edinburgh
Tel.: 031-229 0993

341. 67

PEACE AND DISARMAMENT

documents of the

WORLD COUNCIL OF CHURCHES

Presented by the

Commission of the Churches on International Affairs

ROMAN CATHOLIC CHURCH

Presented by

The Pontifical Commission «Iustitia et Pax»

PREFACE

The second World War which ended in 1945 brought great destruction to much of Europe and several other regions, and directly or indirectly affected the whole world. Since that time, the spectre of war has not been banished. Instead, the world has witnessed a whole series of wars, more or less "contained" geographically and politically. Equally, it has seen the development and deployment of nuclear weapons of a variety and number that is astonishing and in many respects frightening.

In the spirit of the pastoral mission of Christianity, the Churches have been attentive to the threats to peace these phenomena have posed, and in a number of ways have tried to reflect on the significance of these developments and the challenges they pose ethically and morally to those who try to follow one whom we call the Prince of Peace.

The Roman Catholic Church, through the teaching of the Sovereign Pontiffs and the Second Vatican Council, has offered a consistent and constant reflection on the problem of peace and disarmament that has utilized the tools of theological tradition to proclaim the principles of its teaching, to re-assert the values that must be maintained, and to call people to a commitment that brings about a model of peace, justice and fraternity.

From its first General Assembly at Amsterdam in 1948, the World Council of Churches (WCC) has been sensitive to these same issues and has called the attention of its member churches and world leaders to the questions involved and the responsibility to bring about the necessary changes that will ensure a more peaceful world. This concern has not been limited only to the five General Assemblies. Meetings of the General Committee and the Executive Committee have been faced time and again with pressing situations that threaten peace and with new developments that fostered the spread of armaments both vertically and horizontally. In addition, the ongoing work of the Commission of the Churches on International Affairs (CCIA) and special meetings and studies have served to focus the attention of WCC Member Churches on problems and difficulties as they arose.

As a major part of their ecumenical collaboration, the Pontifical Commission "Iustitia et Pax" of the Holy See and the Commission of the Churches on International Affairs of the WCC offer this volume on Peace and Disarmament. The aim is to bring together the major — but not all — official statements and teachings of the World Council of Churches and of the Holy Father and the Vatican Council concerning disarmament, the arms race and the especially complex question of nuclear arms. The purpose is to put the reader into direct contact with the texts themselves as the bearers of the thought and teaching of the authors.

The texts are arranged chronologically. The documents of the World Council of Churches are introduced by an explanatory preface prepared by the CCIA. Similarly, the Pontifical Commission "Iustitia et Pax" (PCJP) has offered a presentation of the teachings of the Sovereign Pontiffs from Pius XII to John Paul II, along with the pertinent section of the Second Vatican Council's Pastoral Constitution on the Church in the Modern World, "Gaudium et Spes".

This volume purposely does not attempt a theological analysis of these texts. Neither is there any attempt to compare the teachings to point out possible convergences or divergences. The teaching of each body stands on its own merits, its own tradition, with its own history and its own integrity.

Of course, the reader will become aware of the extent to which the condemnation of hostility, war and the arms race and the yearning and striving for peace, true security, justice and disarmament have been central concerns of the worldwide Christian community in the entire post-World War II era. The documents assembled here bear witness to the extent to which the different Christian traditions have wrestled with concrete problems of humanity in a timely, relevant and realistic manner, attuned to critical historical events, yet at the same time drawing from their theological sources the insights necessary to cope with the current reality, which has made of peace and disarmament an elusive dream.

It is the earnest hope of both CCIA and PCJP that this volume will serve to inform Christians and others of the pastoral concern we share in these difficult problems and that it will help deepen reflection, instruct consciences and inspire actions that will contribute to making this a world in which peace is found by turning away from the arms race, by fostering meaningful disarmament and the peaceful solution of conflicts, by promoting justice, equality and human dignity, and by forging the bonds of mutual respect, confidence and responsibility among nations.

Jan P. Schotte, CICM
Secretary, Pontifical Commission
"Iustitia et Pax"

Ninan Koshy
Director, Commission of the
Churches on International Affairs

THE WORLD COUNCIL OF CHURCHES
ON
DISARMAMENT AND PEACE

The problems of arms and armament have been considered by the churches since the early Christians refused to serve in the Roman legions. *But disarmanent became a basic issue when the leaders of the churches and the ecumenical movement became aware of the dawn of the atomic age starting with the bombing of Hiroshima and Nagasaki by the USA in August 1945. The Provisional Committee of the WCC already recognized the fact by stating at its meeting in February 1946 that* "Man's triumph in the release of atomic energy threatens his destruction. Unless men's whole outlook is changed, our civilization will perish" *(The World Council of Churches : Its Process of Formation, Geneva 1946, pp. 71f). The General Assembly of the United Nations to whom this report referred also took up the armaments issue. Early in 1947 a Commission on Conventional Armaments was set up. Its Working Committee restricted its discussion on conventional arms, although the Soviet Union tried to combine conventional disarmament with the question of nuclear armament.*

THE FIRST ASSEMBLY PERIOD (1948 - 1953)

While these negotiations were still underway, the First Assembly of the World Council of Churches met at Amsterdam in September 1948. Its Section IV "The Church and the International Disorder" *recognized both the horror of nuclear power and the destructiveness of conventional armaments, condemned the whole conduct of modern warfare and asked the churches to support any effort dealing specifically with the use of atomic power and the multilateral reduction of armaments. The aim was established : The WCC did not consider nuclear and conventional weapons as separate problems. As was reiterated in a CCIA statement prepared in 1951 for the WCC Central Committee* 1) *on the Korean situation and World Order, it tried to overcome the dead-*

---

1) *According to the Constitution of the World Council of Churches (WCC) the Central Committee is responsible for implementing the policies adopted by the Assembly as the supreme legislative body governing the World Council of Churches. The Central Committee is also empowered to exercise the functions of the Assembly itself delegated to it by the Assembly between its meetings.*

lock of the UN negotiations caused by the contradictory proposals of the USA and the USSR. In another statement, CCIA expressed "strong agreement with the progressive reduction and eventual abolition of all national armaments, including atomic weapons and all weapons of mass destruction, and of all national armies, subject always to certain conditions which we put forward provisionally for consideration" *(CCIA, Annual Report 1950/51, p. 27). Together with a strong appeal for generous assistance by the rich nations to the poor countries of the world those conditions were spelled out in the statement of the CCIA Executive Committee, entitled* "Christians Stand for Peace" *and issued in August 1951.*

THE SECOND ASSEMBLY PERIOD (1954 - 1960)

Although the WCC General Assembly at Evanston in 1954 focused primarily on other international issues such as racism, the full Assembly adopted "An Appeal from the World Council of Churches" *urging the prohibition of all weapons of mass destruction under the provision of international inspection and control along with the reduction of all other types of armaments. It recognized that the first constructive step in helping to restore confidence would be the renunciation of the use of nuclear weapons or the threat of use. It also called for safeguards in the further testing of the hydrogen bomb after its invention and first test by the USA in October 1952.*

In an informal memorandum on 19 April 1954 the CCIA tried to press for agreement on a starting point for disarmament. It pointed out that it was possible, under the UN Charter, to outlaw any threat or use of force including nuclear, hydrogen and other devices of mass destruction against the territorial integrity of any member state and simultaneously to recognize the inherent right of self-defence against any armed attack. As often in the following years, the CCIA thus tried to anticipate possible lines for negotiations at the UN level. Inspired by the Geneva summit meeting apparently showing general acceptance of disarmament proposals, the CCIA Executive Committee 2) started an immediate follow-up by issuing a "Statement on Disarmament and Peaceful Change" *which was adopted by the WCC Central Committee. The statement linked the problem of disarmament to that of rectifying existing injustices by recognizing both processes as indispensable and complementary. The old concern was rephrased : the elimination and prohibition of all weapons of mass destruction had to be coupled with a reduction of conventional arms under a system of inspection and control acceptable both politically and technically. In order to identify a starting point, the statement recommended seeking ways of co-operation whereby compliance could be tested on a day-by-day performance. Thus, tensions could be further relaxed, and the*

---

2) *The CCIA Executive Committee acts on behalf of the Commission of the Churches on International Affairs itself which is composed of Commissioners elected by the Central Committee of the WCC.*

way paved for a kind of co-operation which might ultimately offer security to all people. As the statement says, this step-by-step approach has to be supported by the development of internationally accepted methods for peaceful settlement and change in order to rectify existing injustices.

The WCC itself was aware that these suggestions were running ahead of the political reality. Both the USA and the USSR continued their attempts to develop bigger and more sophisticated nuclear weapons with ongoing atmospheric testing, and the crises over Suez and Hungary distracted the world's attention from disarmament issues. Furthermore, the Twelfth Session of the UN General Assembly in 1957 is known as the last one until 1978 with "Regulation, Limitation and Balanced Reduction of all Armed Forces and all Armaments" as an item on its agenda. In the same year, however, the churches renewed their efforts and activities. The Prime Minister of Great Britain, as well as Albert Schweitzer and a group of German scientists, issued statements requesting the halt of nuclear testing. In a long and thorough statement "Atomic Tests and Disarmament" *the CCIA Executive Committee noted the dangerous aspects of the ongoing nuclear tests : the fear of the nuclear weapons themselves, the fear of the consequences of their use, and the fear of the unknown consequences of radiation both for the living generation and those yet to be born. The Executive Committee reiterated its conviction of an overall strategy to halt the nuclear build-up, renewed its plea for international co-operation in developing nuclear power for peaceful purposes, but was less than optimistic about any possible progress. So it asked Christians in the states conducting nuclear tests to urge their governments to unilaterally abstain from testing for a trial period in order to create the necessary confidence for an international agreement on this subject. The WCC Central Committee, in discussing the statement, was divided in its opinion.*

It appealed to the moral responsibility of the superpowers taking decisions which affect many people with no part at all in the decision making process in addition to the usual considerations of national defence and international security. As a follow-up, the texts were sent to all delegates at the Twelfth Session of the UN General Assembly, and CCIA representatives had many informal consultations on the statement with delegates at the latters' request. Furthermore, heads of governments such as General de Gaulle, Chancellor Adenauer and Prime Minister Grotewohl reacted formally to the documents submitted to them by the National Councils of Churches but without committing themselves. The Secretary of State of the USA, John Forster Dulles, reacted in a similar way. Although a petition signed by 9000 scientists from 43 countries was presented to the UN Secretary-General, urging an immediate cessation of nuclear testing, both these religious and secular activities failed to influence the development of events. On 26 March 1958 President Eisenhower announced that another series of tests was to be conducted and invited qualified experts under UN auspices to observe that scientists had succeeded in reducing the fall-out. The decision to hold these tests was maintained even though on 31 March 1958 the Supreme Soviet decided unilaterally to end their nuclear testing.

In order to overcome the strong objections from the USA regarding inspection and control, a Conference of Experts on Detection of Nuclear Tests, *was held in Geneva from 1 July to 21 August 1958 to consider the technical feasibility of detection of nuclear tests. The CCIA Executive Committee meeting immediately afterwards welcomed the agreement of the Conference seeing it as an approach which could be applied both for the cessation of the production of nuclear weapons and the danger of surprise attacks. Meanwhile, the Soviet Union, the United Kingdom, and the United States, had agreed to start a Conference on the Discontinuance of Nuclear Tests, scheduled for 31 October 1958. France abstained. The American and the British governments agreed to suspend their planned tests for the duration of the Conference and kept to their decision, although the Soviet Union carried out a short series of tests during the first days of the Conference. On the other hand, by early 1959 the USA seemed to be recalcitrant in insisting on special detection techniques. Therefore, the WCC Executive Committee, 3) in a statement adopted that February indicated that* "any agreement, however carefully framed, involves a measure of calculated risk for all parties" *and urged persistence and realism in attempting to achieve fraudproof means of inspection. In addition, since the WCC Central Committee was requested by the member churches from Africa and Asia to oppose the scheduled French testing, it urged, at its meeting in Rhodes in August 1959, that* "so long as international control is under discussion, powers which have not made tests as yet should not launch them anywhere for military purposes." *But this statement, as well as some other formal and informal interventions of CCIA representatives, failed. The nuclear power nations, now including France, resumed their testing programmes in the course of 1960.*

During the same period, the WCC Central Committee appointed a Commission to study the problem of "the prevention of war in the atomic age". The composition of this Commission was explicitly formed to bring together pacifists and non-pacifists in a time of anxiety with "much inarticulate fear and a great deal of inarticulate pacifism", as a member of the Commission put it in his presentation to the Central Committee. Following three years of discussion, from 1955 to 1958, the Commission's Report still reflected a division in its opinion. Dissension was primarily focused on Section V, dealing with proposals on how to limit war in the nuclear age. Thus, the statement of the majority of the Commission reflected basic considerations of a new concept, the "arms approach", including as one of its main subjects : how to end a war in the nuclear age if deterrence fails. Bearing in mind the firm condemnation of any war since the First WCC

---

3) *The WCC Executive Committee, elected from among the members of the WCC Central Committee, acts on behalf of the WCC Central Committee between its meetings.*

Assembly in Amsterdam, the Commission's majority tried to face the inherent dilemma. "It is not our purpose to preserve warfare. It is our purpose to limit war as a first step in getting rid of it. In this sense limited war can be used only for two reasons. First it can be used to prevent all out war. Second, it can be used to deter even limited war from breaking out, in the sense that a nation or group of nations known to be prepared and resolved to resort to limited war may thereby deter an aggressor. It should never be resorted to for the pursuit of merely nationalistic ends, but only as a last resort in order to preserve justice and order." (WCC, Division of Studies, A Provisional Study Document on "Christians and the Prevention of War in an Atomic Age — A Theological Discussion", 1958, p. 33). In trying to define "an absolute limit" to actions of warfare and "the stage at which all out war may be reached", the Commission was split. The majority believed in the development of a "discipline among the peoples and their leaders which will enable them to stop, even if necessary on the enemy's terms, rather than embark on all out war" (p. 34). Through education and training, an attitude "must be so firmly implanted in people's minds that it will not be easy to get a war going, difficult to expand it if it should start, and not impossible to cease fire before it develops into all out war", especially if "the aggressor is willing to negotiate" (p. 34). Certain members of the Commission had strong reservations at this point and expressed them in a dissenting vote. Nevertheless, all members of the Commission agreed on one point : "This is that Christians should openly declare that the all out use of these (nuclear) weapons should never be resorted to... Finally, if all out war should occur, Christians should urge a cease fire, if necessary on the enemy's terms, and resort to non-violent resistance" (p. 30). Faced with this situation, the WCC Central Committee was not in a position to adopt the report, but declared rather formally "that the Commission's statement... in no wise constitutes a formulation of World Council policy, whether in respect to war in general, limited war, megaton weapons, all out war, the problems of surrender and non-violent resistance, or any other matter" (Minutes of the WCC Central Committee, 1958, p. 55).

THE THIRD ASSEMBLY PERIOD (1961 - 1967)

The Third Assembly of the WCC, held in New Delhi from 19 November to 5 December 1961, still had to face the issue of a nuclear test ban. In the report of the Section on Service, the resumption of nuclear tests as well as any use of weapons which kill indiscriminately was condemned. In its paragraph on disarmament the churches were requested to fight the growing conviction that some day weapons of mass destruction would inevitably be used. "Christians must also maintain that the use of nuclear weapons, or other forms of major violence, against centres of population is in no circumstances reconciliable with the demands of the Christian Gospel." *Obviously, this was referring to the military strategy of "massive retaliation", at that time still emphasized by both the USA and the USSR.*

The "Appeal to all Governments and Peoples" *adopted by the Assembly which had just previously been enlarged by about 40 new member churches, reflected the concern of the delegates gathered from all parts of the world in facing the global political situation. There is a slight note of resignation in the statement that* "to halt the race in arms is imperative". *Complete and general disarmament was still the accepted goal, but it was realized that it had to be seen as a long term goal. Many small but concrete steps had to be taken to reach this goal. The verified cessation of nuclear tests was identified as a decisive first step despite all obstacles and setbacks. Referring to the objection of both sides, the* "Appeal" *concluded that to break through mutual distrust nations should be willing to run reasonable risks for peace. As a sign of hope, the* "Appeal" *recognized the* "struggle for world development" *as a* "great opportunity for constructive action", *thus becoming* "a moral equivalent for war". *Indeed, by linking disarmament and development, the* "Appeal" *set a new tone.*

As a rare occurence, the WCC Executive Committee, which met in Geneva from 28 to 31 March 1962, was ready to note with gratitude the reconvening of the Disarmament Conference and the resumption of the discussion on the cessation of nuclear weapons testing in its recently created Sub-Committee. Aware of the many failures of the past and the immense number of difficulties still remaining, the Executive Committee, with renewed hope, issued a statement on effective agreements for disarmament in the face of what it called "a highly precarious peace which rests on the formidable and unstable balance of terror". *The statement firmly emphasized it as the task of the worldwide Christian fellowship to urge all governments concerned* "to be ready to take, in their individual capacities, those calculated risks" *which would contribute to disarmament in such a way that they would neither betray governments responsibility for international security nor prejudice the requirements of information and verification.*

In fulfilment of a mandate given by the New Delhi General Assembly, a "Consultation on Peace and Disarmament" *was held in Geneva from 20 to 22 June 1962. On the first day, the heads of delegations of the UN Eighteen Nation Disarmament Committee (ENDC) were invited and in fact appeared, with the Swedish Ambassador speaking for the eight non-aligned members of the ENDC. The CCIA Executive Committee saw this event as an encouragement and issued a detailed* "Statement on Contemporary Problems of Peace" *at its meeting in Paris from 1 to 4 August 1962 which reiterated and reaffirmed the position of the churches but gave new emphasis to their opinion-shaping role and the direction that was to be pursued. The WCC Central Committee meeting in Paris the following week generally approved the statement, urging that the widest publicity be given to it. Although the Cuba missile crisis in September heightened the tensions between the big powers the meeting of the ENDC continued and, as it happened, the general relaxation after those days on the brink of a nuclear war promoted, after all the previous setbacks, an agreement on the principles of* a controlled halt to nuclear testing. In the early month of 1963 a treaty banning nuclear tests in the atmosphere, in outer space, and under water seemed to be imminent, and in fact it was signed as early as 5 August.

The WCC Central Committee, at its late August meeting in Rochester, USA, in 1963, addressed a letter of gratitude to the heads of the three signatory states. Nevertheless, it noted in an accompanying statement on "The Test Ban Treaty and the Next Steps : From Co-existence to Co-operation" that the Treaty did not at all slow down the arms race or prevent the spread of nuclear weapons to nations so far without them. The latter remark was obviously a suggestion for a non-proliferation treaty, in those days clearly again ahead of time. The mutual goodwill shown by the signing powers should be employed, it urged, to explore further co-operative steps like the inhibition of surprise attacks, the establishment of nuclear free zones, and the agreement on a non-aggression pact, thus opening the way for negotiations on general and complete disarmament. Despite its opposition to the proliferation of nuclear weapons, the WCC Central Committee considered with concern the concentration of ultimate military power in very few hands, recommending that this responsibility be shared within an alliance. Furthermore, it again asked for a halt to underground testing, including those for peaceful as well as for scientific purposes, and proposed that outer space be held free from military competition, a proposal which was subsequently included in a treaty in 1966.

Thus, the constant preoccupation of the WCC with this issue finally achieved its aim, however limited its political impact might have been in practice. Despite the daily Cold War news of the time, the WCC had made it its major task to make people aware of the desirability of such a treaty as a starting point and first step on the long way to disarmament. The attainment of this goal was seen as a sign of hope and encouragement to continue.

The WCC Executive Committee, meeting in Odessa, USSR, at the invitation of the Russian Orthodox Church, reviewed the global political situation in the midst of the sixties, stating that the precarious détente of that time needed to become more firmly established. It saw the danger that the growing number of local conflicts might tempt the powerful nations to seek ideological or territorial gains — whether by military aid, economic exploitation, or acts of subversion. Facing the possibility of escalation of those conflicts, general and comprehensive disarmament had to be the goal of international striving. However, one would fail to seize the opportunities at hand, the Executive Committee said, if there were the belief that an easy road would rapidly lead to that goal. Therefore, the WCC Executive Committee advocated unilateral measures such as the reduction of military budgets, the reshaping of military postures which clearly avoided impressions of aggressive intentions, and the reduction of standing armed forces in order to invite others to follow these examples and thus set the stage for more formal international actions and negotiations.

No significant progress in disarmament had been made when the WCC Central Committee met in Enugu, Eastern Nigeria, from 12 to 22 January 1965. Recognizing that there was little hope that the limited Test Ban Treaty could be extended to include underground testing it suggested steps for the limitation of nuclear striking and delivery power, simultaneously reiterating its plea to establish nuclear-free zones and to prevent the proliferation of nuclear weapons. Diverting the money now spent on arms production to the assistance of the developing countries, it added, was an additional incentive. Shortly after the reconvening of the UN Eighteen Nation Disarmament Committee in January 1966, a "Statement on Disarmament" *was adopted by the WCC Executive Committee. It supported the claim of the non-nuclear powers, in foregoing the possession of nuclear weapons, to be protected against the threat or use of nuclear weapons, and to avail themselves of nuclear power for peaceful purposes. The proposal of a World Disarmament Conference was welcomed although the Executive Committee expressed its awareness of the difficulties in holding such a conference and of the too great hopes it might raise.*

This line was then picked up by the World Conference of Church and Society *convened in Geneva from 12 to 26 July 1966. In its report* "Living together in Peace in a Pluralistic World", *Section III of the Conference concluded that* "we are in a passing moment of grace which may never recur and in which we were given the opportunity to act" *(Official Report, p. 125). Therefore,* "the churches must warn the nations that the balance of power requires ever-increasing defence budgets, keeps men in a condition of distrust and fear, and lessens the ability of the powers involved in it to act justly amidst the struggles for national liberation and social justice" *(Official Report, p. 128). The Section then requested* "a system to prevent the proliferation of nuclear weapons be established, in which all nations should co-operate" *(Official Report, p. 129), and which could guarantee smaller non-nuclear powers against nuclear blackmail. Subsequently, such a system should be* "jointly controlled, open and set up on a legal basis in order to pave the way for a new legal order in which the people of this world can learn to live with the new power which has been put into their hands" *(Official Report, p. 129). Thus, the Conference Report already contained most of the components of the later Non-Proliferation Treaty.*

In the statement "Limitation in Modern Warfare" *which was issued by the CCIA Executive Committee and firmly adopted by the WCC Central Committee at its meeting at Heraklion, Crete, from 15 to 26 August 1967, the title already indicated a shifting of emphasis. The reference to both the Geneva Convention of 1949 and the Declaration of the International Conference of the Red Cross of 1965 was clearly directed to outlawing new devastating devices such as napalm bombs, although the war in Vietnam was not mentioned. Obviously, because of the deep concern that war with new weapons of mass destruction might return as a political means, the CCIA and the Central Committee did not examine the ongoing non-proliferation talks.*

8

THE FOURTH ASSEMBLY PERIOD (1968 - 1974)

The Fourth General Assembly of the WCC, however, convened at Uppsala from 4 to 20 July 1968, took the recently concluded Non-Proliferation Treaty (NPT) as a basis for fundamental considerations about war, disarmament and peace. The report of Section IV, adopted by the Assembly, described the NPT as only one small step "towards justice and peace in international affairs", as can be seen from the title of the report. Reaffirming the declaration of the Amsterdam Assembly in 1948, it declared that it was a duty of the churches to press for the prevention of war, a halt to the arms race, the cessation of experiments concerned with mass destruction by chemical and biological means and the production of weapons for the same purpose as the first duty of govern-ments. It also advocated the abandonment of the initial use of nuclear weapons, probably referring to the then newly established NATO strategy "Flexibility in Response". As further steps to be taken, the General Assembly again requested the cessation of underground testing and added as a new suggestion the prohibition of anti-ballistic missile systems already established by the superpowers. Criticisms on an additional paragraph dealing with the special danger of wars by proxy through a competitive arms trade were voted down, whereas an amendment, stating that participation in the manufacture of nuclear or bacteriological weapons or the threat to use them was incompatible with Christian obedience, failed due to the absence of a seconder.

In 1969, the UN General Assembly unanimously passed a resolution declaring the 1970s to be the Disarmament Decade. Détente started to become a key issue both in politics and in the public. The United States and the Soviet Union began their Talks on Strategic Arms Limitation (SALT), in a way already suggested by the WCC Central Committee in its statement of 1965.

The CCIA, which had already submitted a summary of WCC pronouncements on disarmament to more than 1000 delegates of the 1968 UN General Assembly, provided a "Statement on European Security and Cooperation", *adopted by the WCC Central Committee at its meeting in Utrecht, from 13 to 23 August 1972. Obviously, the statement did not comment on the progress made in SALT and with the final agreement on the Convention on Prohibition of Development, Production and Stockpiling of Bacterio-logical and Toxic Weapons and their Destruction in April 1972 as well as the ratification of the Treaty on the Limitation of Anti-Ballistic Missile Systems in October 1972 but focused attention on the European Conference on Security and Cooperation and the proposed talks on Mutual Balanced Force Reduction (MBFR). Looking at it in a world-wide context, the statement viewed the ongoing talks and negotiations on different levels as part of the general mood of détente. However, with regard to world affairs the stance of Europe was seen as "the acid test". A stronger and more unified Europe, it was asserted, could constitute a new and dangerous factor, despite its immense value for justice, order and peace in the world. Therefore, it was urged, a stronger Europe should use the strength it might gain for attaining social justice through both trade and aid with the developing countries.*

The meeting of the CCIA Executive Committee in Visegrad, Hungary, from 14 to 19 June 1973, was an important turning point in the ecumenical debate on international affairs and, in particular, on disarmament. The statement, adopted by the CCIA Executive Committee, clearly reflected the new climate in international politics caused by the "oilshock" and made a new departure by reshaping the approach for disarmament. It dropped the traditional framework of the superpower confrontation by identifying the continuing arms race and the rapidly growing arms trade as only symptoms of a global structure of injustice. It recognized that the narrow concept of arms control was increasingly substituting the idea of general and comprehensive disarmament, and it analysed the growing militarism in highly industrialized countries as a result of the combination of political, industrial, scientific and cultural forces. It called, as the United Nations did later in the same year, for the global rechannelling of resources now committed to armament. Furthermore, the statement slightly shifted priorities by emphasizing that the efforts to promote general and controlled disarmament should not lead* "to blocking the necessary evolutions in the life of the people". *The statement noted the paradox of the situation that,* "the longer the liberation of peoples is denied, the more unrealistic it becomes to ignore the right of the oppressed to resort to arms." *Thus, Christians were confronted with a dilemma created by the concern for human dignity on the one hand and the need for disarmament on the other.* "Only a decisive and genuine change in the field of social justice and international relations," *the Executive Committee emphasized,* "can break the evil and escalating spiral of violence and counter-violence."

In its proposal for "Concrete Steps towards Disarmament" *the statement repeated the request for a comprehensive nuclear test ban and added a* "most urgent plea" *for an agreement to ban the production, possession and use of chemical weapons. The new line of moving beyond the more pragmatic approach to disarmament issues was the guiding principle behind the statements of the CCIA Executive Committee in the following two years. In the statement* "The Economic Threat to Peace" *of the CCIA Executive Committee which met in Berlin (West) from 11 to 18 August 1974, the developments in the arms control process were consequently disregarded, and attention was drawn to the fact that* "in a world of immense scientific knowledge and technical skill, millions are underfed, underprivileged, exploited, and denied human dignity, while resources and skill are lavished on the extravagant and lethal accumulation of weapons of destruction." *Besides the military threat to peace, the structural injustice of the international system regulating the economic, social and political relationships of nations and people, together with the ongoing environmental deterioration and depletion of natural resources were identified as symptoms of a* complex but real crisis which threatens the very future of the global society and even its actual survival. Therefore, the statement called upon the WCC Member Churches to fully support and work for the establishment of a New International Economic Order, solemnly proclaimed by the Sixth Special Session of the General Assembly of the United Nations.

"The Memorandum on Disarmament", issued by the CCIA Executive Committee at its meeting in Geneva, Switzerland, from 16 to 20 June 1975, underscored the wrong but overriding priority given by governments to defence and security. In particular, the Memorandum then gave some analytical indications of the driving forces behind the rapid expansion of armament spreading throughout the world. This global arms race propelled by a rapidly expanding arms trade, forced the churches "to press for an ethical code of restrictive criteria for the arms trade" in order to stop the distortion of social and economic priorities it had already caused especially in many of the developing countries. Bearing in mind all those hundreds of thousands of innocent people who have been killed in the approximately 130 so-called "small" wars since 1945, the statement finally called for an absolute ban on both the use and the production of new and even more sophisticated means of indiscriminate destruction, however nominally conventional.

THE FIFTH ASSEMBLY PERIOD (1975 - 1982)

The Fifth General Assembly of the WCC, convened in Nairobi, Kenya, from 23 November to 10 December 1975, based its statement "The World Armaments Situation" on those insights. Seeing that humankind is armed to levels unequalled in history, the Assembly alarmed the churches into an awareness of a growing militarization provoked not only by an increasing number of military regimes but also by the preponderance of military considerations both in national and international politics especially in the Third World countries. In its Appeal to the Churches, the Assembly asked the churches to stimulate public discussion and initiate research on the root causes and driving forces behind both militarism and the armament dynamics.

In his address to the United Nations First Special Session on Disarmament, the General Secretary of the WCC emphasized the need for new perspectives in the disarmament debate by spelling out the qualitatively new elements of the situation. The General Secretary referred to the findings of two WCC consultations, one on militarism and one on disarmament, held previous to the UN Special Session. He in particular challenged the prevalence of the concept of national security identifying it as a main source of fear and mistrust between nations and peoples. Finally, the General Secretary reaffirmed the pledge of the WCC to support the UN in its efforts to promote peace and justice.

At its meeting in Kingston, Jamaica, from 1 to 11 January 1979, the WCC Central Committee received a CCIA report, which was a first attempt to shape the Programme on Militarism and the Arms Race *with regard to the new mandate given by the Nairobi Assembly. Based on the findings of the consultations mentioned above, the report dealt with two basic factors promoting militarism : the competition of the superpowers and the prevalence of the doctrin of national security. The report noted the close interrelation between the dynamics of militarism and that of the arms race and the distorting consequence it has on the social, economic, and political priorities. The report asked that special attention be given to the function of advanced technology in becoming the focus of the continuing expansion of armament both nuclear and conventional.*

The WCC Executive Committee, meeting in Liebfrauenberg, France, from 11 to 15 February 1980, was confronted with a tendency to revert back to the cold-war mentality, fueled by the military action of the USSR in Afghanistan and the decision of NATO to deploy an additional 572 nuclear weapons in Europe. In facing the increasing deterioration of international relations on almost all levels, the Executive Committee recognized a basic change in the power relations among nations at the beginning of the eighties heightened by the increasing world poverty and exacerbated by the significantly increased arms race. The accumulation of a number of developments rather than one single event had created a situation where war seemed to be more likely than before. The Executive Committee therefore reminded the ecumenical fellowship of its bridge-building capacity, urging the churches "to inject a note of sanity and sobriety into an atmosphere charged with tension, fear, irrationality, and mutual distrust."

The WCC Central Committee, which met in Geneva, from 14 to 22 August 1980, supported the concern of the Executive Committee and adopted a shorter statement of its own, particularly emphasizing the need "to initiate and encourage innovative measures for peaceful resolutions of conflicts". *In an additional* Statement on Nuclear Disarmament, *adopted at the same meeting the Central Committee spoke of* "a great sense of urgency" *after having received reports from two major WCC Conferences (World Conference on Mission and Evangelism; Conference on Faith, Science and the Future). Deeply concerned about the official announcement of the USA of a new policy which considered the strategic option of a* "limited nuclear war", *the Central Committee asked in particular the nuclear powers for an immediate freeze of all nuclear weapons and delivery systems designed to carry nuclear weapons.*

When the WCC Central Committee met in Dresden, from 16 to 26 August 1981, it recognized that the international situation had become even more dangerous during the previous year. In the adopted statement "Increased Threats to Peace and the Task of the Churches" *the Central Committee listed the trends and events which had intensified the already existing tensions, giving again special attention to the concerted attempts of new strategies dealing with the feasibility of nuclear war. Aware that urgent steps were needed, the Central Committee then appealed to the political leaders to consider unilateral steps for disarmament and nuclear free zones. Furthermore, the political leaders were urged to start negotiations for a more just relationship between North and South in order to close the widening economic gap and to support the right of people everywhere to seek to change exploitative and unjust conditions. In addressing the churches, the Central Committee then reiterated it as a main task of the churches* "to call attention to the root causes of war, mainly to economic injustice, oppression and exploitation and to the consequences of increasing tensions including further restriction of human rights". *Finally, the scheduled* International Public Hearing on Nuclear Weapons and Disarmament *was especially commended to the attention of the churches.*

This Hearing, jointly organized by the WCC Sub-unit on Church and Society and the CCIA, took place in Amsterdam, in November 1981. The report of this Hearing, submitted to the General Secretary of the WCC, provides a great amount of information and analysis based on the testimony of a number of witnesses of international standing. One of the urgent tasks for the churches identified by the Hearing group draws particular attention to the following :

"We believe that the time has come when the churches must unequivocally declare that the production, deployment and use of nuclear weapons is a crime against humanity and that such activities must be condemned on ethical and theological grounds." *(Report of the Public Hearing on Nuclear Weapons and Disarmament)*

Friedhelm Solms

THE FIRST ASSEMBLY PERIOD

WAR IS CONTRARY TO THE WILL OF GOD
September 1948

"War as a method of settling disputes is incompatible with the teaching and example of our Lord Jesus Christ. The part which war plays in our present international life is a sin against God and a degradation of man. We recognize that the problem of war raises especially acute issues for Christians today. Warfare has greatly changed. War is now total, and every man and woman is called for mobilisation in war service. Moreover, the immense use of air forces and the discovery of atomic and other new weapons render widespread and indiscriminate destruction inherent in the whole conduct of modern war in a sense never experienced in past conflicts. In these circumstances the tradition of a just war, requiring a just cause and the use of just means, is now challenged. Law may require the sanction of force, but when war breaks out, force is used on a scale which tends to destroy the basis on which law exists.

Therefore the inescapable question arises — can war now be an act of justice ? We cannot answer this question unanimously... Three broad positions are maintained :

(1) There are those who hold that, even though entering a war may be a Christian's duty in particular circumstances, modern warfare, with its mass destruction, can never be an act of justice.

(2) In the absence of impartial supra-national institutions, there are those who hold that military action is the ultimate sanction of the rule of law, and that citizens must be distinctly taught that it is their duty to defend the law by force if necessary.

15

(3) Others, again, refuse military service of all kinds, convinced that an absolute witness against war and for peace is for them the will of God, and they desire that the Church should speak to the same effect.

We must frankly acknowledge our deep sense of perplexity in face of these conflicting opinions..."

(Report of the WCC I. Assembly meeting in Amsterdam, Netherlands, 22 August - 4 September 1948)

CHRISTIANS STAND FOR PEACE
August 1951

"1. As Christians it is our duty to seek both peace and justice. We no less than others detest war and we shall do everything in our power to prevent present tensions and limited conflicts from leading to a third world war. Yet we must neither purchase peace at the price of tyranny nor in the name of justice look on war as a way to justice or as a ground of hope.

2. We stand opposed to every form of oppression and aggression. We condemn any extension of oppression, carried on behind a façade of propaganda for peace. We condemn equally the proposal of a preventive war, or the use for aggressive purposes of atomic weapons.

3. We do not believe that peace will come merely by new pacts or disarmament. There must first be sufficient mutual trust and good faith between nations to ensure that agreements will be honoured. Peace and disarmament will follow from mutual trust; they will not automatically create it.

4. In present world conditions peace and justice require international organs of law and order. We therefore fully support all forms of cooperation between the nations which will serve this purpose. Believing that the United Nations and its agencies present now the best means to develop the rule of law over the nations, we condemn unilateral military action in defiance of decisions under the Charter of the United Nations.

5. We press urgently for the most generous assistance by the wealthier to the poorer nations of the world in their economic and social development, and for the immediate sharing by all nations in responsibility for the millions of refugees.

6. We believe that it is the duty of all governments and of the United Nations to recognize the dignity of man as a child of God, and to protect the rights of the individual. Every denial of fundamental rights should be made known and resisted.

7. Christians can witness convincingly to peace only if they and their churches, in their relations with one another across all frontiers, put loyalty to their common Lord above any other loyalty."

(Statement of the CCIA Executive Committee at its meeting in Rolle, Switzerland, 30 July - 1 August 1951)

RESOLUTION ON DISARMAMENT
July 1952

The CCIA Executive Committee,

Recognizing the urgent importance of achieving the progressive reduction and eventual abolition of all national armaments including atomic weapons and all weapons of mass destruction and all national arms except for mutually agreed weapons required for internal police purposes;

Welcomes the action of the United Nations General Assembly at its Sixth Session to establish under the Security Council a Disarmament Commission;

Considers that the Disarmament Commission in seeking to fulfil its assignments must, *inter alia*, provide for

(a) An assessment by international inspection under the United Nations of weapons and fighting forces maintained by the different nations;

(b) An adequate system of safeguards including provision for effective and continuous inspection and control, to ensure compliance with the arrangements for progressive reduction of all armaments and armed forces;

(c) A schedule to fix the stages by which the reduction of all armaments and armed forces can be effected as speedily as possible;

Believes that a system of guaranteed disarmament can be put into effect only to the extent that sufficient mutual confidence has been attained and that international institutions are adequate for regulating the common interests of nations;

Urges the necessity of considering political and moral factors along with the mathematical and mechanical approach to the reduction of armaments;

Recognizes the importance — both as an aid to reduction of armaments and as a step toward a real international police force — of military contingents, made available by governments on an individual or regional basis, over which national or regional jurisdiction is retained until they are called to act under the United Nations;

Requests its officers and the co-operating National Commissions to work along these lines towards an alleviation of the burden of armaments with its dangerous consequences for the international and social situation.

(Adopted by the CCIA Executive Committee at its meeting in Willingen, Federal Republic of Germany, 22 - 24 July 1952)

THE SECOND ASSEMBLY PERIOD

CHRISTIANS IN THE STRUGGLE
FOR WORLD COMMUNITY
August 1954

... "12. It is not enough for the churches to proclaim that war is evil. They must study afresh the Christian approaches to peace, taking into account both Christian pacifism as a mode of witness and the conviction of Christians that in certain circumstances military action is justifiable.

Whatever views Christians hold in respect of these approaches, they must seek out, analyse, and help to remove the psychological and social, the political and economic causes of war. Without forsaking their conviction that all weapons of war are evil, the churches should press for restraint on their use. Christians in all lands must plead with their governments to be patient and persistent in their search for means to limit weapons and advance disarmament.

13. But even this is not enough. An international order of truth and peace would require :

(a) under effective international inspection and control and in such a way that no state would have cause to fear that its security was endangered, the elimination and prohibition of atomic, hydrogen and all other weapons of mass destruction, as well as the reduction of all armaments to a minimum;

(b) the development and acceptance of methods for peaceful change to rectify existing injustices.

14. However, it must be recognized that on the basis of current suspicions and distrust the nations at the moment have reached a stalemate on the issue of

control of atomic and nuclear weapons, either through international inspection or by mere resolution. What constructive steps can be proposed in this impasse?

15. We first of all call upon the nations to pledge that they will refrain from the threat or the use of hydrogen, atomic, and all other weapons of mass destruction as well as any other means of force against the territorial integrity or political independence of any state.

16. If this pledge should be broken, the Charter of the United Nations provides for collective action and, pending such international action, recognizes the right of national self-defence. We believe that any measures to deter or combat aggression should conform to the requirements of the United Nations Charter, and Christians should urge that both the United Nations and their own governments limit military action strictly to the necessities of international security.

17. Yet even this is not enough. The churches must condemn the deliberate mass destruction of civilians in open cities by whatever means and for whatever purpose. The churches should press through CCIA and other channels for the automatic stationing of UN Peace Commission teams in areas of tension to identify any aggression if it takes place. Christians must continue to press for social, political and economic measures to prevent war. Among these should be the giving of strong moral support for the positive use of atomic power for the benefit of mankind.

18. We must also see that experimental tests of hydrogen bombs have raised issues of human rights, causing suffering and imposed an additional strain on human relations between nations. Among safeguards against the aggravation of these international tensions is the insistence that nations carry on tests only within their respective territories or, if elsewhere, only by international clearance and agreement.

19. Above all, Christians must witness to a dynamic hope in God, in whose hands lie the destinies of nations, and, in this confidence, be untiring in their efforts to create and maintain an international climate favourable for reconciliation and goodwill. The specific problems and tasks will vary in each country according to circumstances. Civil authorities may be hostile to the Church or even avowed enemies of Christ. We know that the power of the Holy Spirit does work effectively through the witness of faithful and obedient and suffering Christians, and the purposes of God will not be denied but will be fulfilled in His time."

2. AN APPEAL FROM THE WORLD COUNCIL OF CHURCHES

"God is the God of justice and peace, and the Lord of history. He calls us all to repentance. It is in obedience to Him, and through the eyes of our Christian faith that we look at the problems of this troubled world.

It is not our purpose in the present statement to pass judgement on past actions. We seek rather to contribute to a new spiritual climate in which a fresh start can be made by all governments and peoples.

The world is so broken up and divided that international agreement seems remote at the moment. Everywhere fear and mistrust prevail. The very possibility of good-neighbourly relations between nations is denied.

We believe that there are two conditions of crucial importance which must be met, if catastrophe is to be avoided :

(1) The prohibition of all weapons of mass destruction, including atomic and hydrogen bombs, with provision for international inspection and control, such as would safeguard the security of all nations, together with the drastic reduction of all other armaments.

(2) The certain assurance that no country will engage in or support aggressive subversive acts in other countries.

We believe that a sound international order is possible only to the extent that peace, justice, freedom and truth are assured.

We are convinced that peace will be gravely endangered so long as the armaments race continues, and so long as any nation seeks to extend its power by the threat or use of military force.

To meet the demands of justice, whether in a particular nation, or in the assistance of peoples in under-developed countries, is our moral duty. We recognize that progress in raising the standard of living in under-developed countries is discouragingly slow; and that increasing sacrifice on the part of richer nations is essential. Freedom means man's opportunity to realize his worth in God's sight, and to fulfil his God-given destiny. All nations have a duty to secure for their citizens the right to criticize or approve, as conscience dictates. Moreover fear and suspicion cannot be replaced by respect and trust unless powerful nations remove the yoke which now prevents other nations and peoples from freely determining their own government and form of society. Freedom and justice in their turn depend upon the steady proclamation of truth. False propaganda, whether to defend a national policy or to criticize the practice of another government, will increase international tension and may contribute to war.

The World Council of Churches bears witness to Christ as the Hope of the World. In the strength of that hope, and impelled by the desire to help in the relief of present tensions, it makes the following appeal :

1. We appeal to the governments and the peoples to continue to speak to one another, to avoid rancour and malice, and to look for ways by which fear and suspicion may be removed.

2. We appeal to the governments and the peoples also to devote their strength and their resources to meeting the peaceful needs of the citizens of their countries, and above all to a determined common effort to secure a decent standard of living among the poorer and under-developed countries.

3. We appeal to the statesmen, and the leaders of public opinion, and the press, to refrain from words and actions which are designed to inflame enmity and hatred.

4. We appeal to the representatives of the churches in those countries between which tension exists to visit one another, so that they may gain a better understanding of one another and of the countries in which they live, and thus strengthen the bonds of fellowship, and promote the reconciliation of the nations.

5. We appeal to the churches to bid their members to recognize their political responsibilities, and also to ask Christian technicians and administrators to find a vocation in the service of UN Agencies engaged in meeting the needs of economically and technically under-developed countries, thus bringing a Christian temper of love and understanding to bear upon the immensely difficult task of mutual assistance in the encounter of different cultures.

6. We appeal to all members of all churches to unite in a common ministry of reconciliation in proclaiming Christ as the Hope of the World, in intercession for one another, and in mutual service.

7. Finally, we call upon all Christians everywhere to join in prayer to Almighty God, that He will guide the governments and the peoples in the ways of justice and peace."

(Report of the Section "International Affairs" to the WCC II. Assembly meeting in Evanston, USA, 15 - 31 August 1954)

DISARMAMENT AND PEACEFUL CHANGE
August 1955

"The CCIA has consistently advanced the thesis that both moral and political factors must be taken into consideration, as well as the mathematical and mechanical approach to the reduction of armaments. These factors apply to two indispensable and complementary processes :

(1) The process whereby all armaments will be progressively reduced under adequate international inspection and control; and

(2) The process of developing and securing international acceptance of methods for peaceful settlement and change to rectify existing injustices, particularly in situations where military conflict has arisen.

Progress in these complementary approaches is dependent upon the extent to which mutual confidence has been attained. Every genuine agreement strengthens confidence and provides the basis for more significant agreements. Therefore, we are encouraged by the willingness of representatives of governments to talk together, and we urge that such exchanges be continued in order that mutual trust may be further developed and the area of agreement progressively expanded.

PEACEFUL USE OF ATOMIC ENERGY

The prospect of the benefits which can come to mankind from the discovery of atomic energy is dimmed by the fear that its military use may lead to catastrophic destruction. As Christians we consider it the responsibility of all men to see to it that this power is used solely for positive and constructive purposes.

We therefore welcome the expressed desire of the United Nations General Assembly "to promote energetically the use of atomic energy to the end that it will serve only the peaceful pursuits of mankind..." We support the proposal to establish an International Atomic Energy Agency, and believe that it should be constituted within the framework of the United Nations. We commend the decision to convene the International Conference on Peaceful Uses of Atomic Energy to study "the development of atomic power and... consider other technical areas — such as biology, medicine, radiation, protection, and fundamental science — in which international cooperation might most effectively be accomplished." We are encouraged by the manifest concern and diligent participation of highly competent scientists from many nations.

The present effort to place the benefits of atomic energy at the service of mankind is little hampered by the necessity of controversial provisions for inspection and control. There is thus offered an opportunity for nations to work together constructively and to remove some of the suspicions which have hitherto divided them.

REDUCTION OF ARMAMENTS

In face of difficulties that may at times seem insuperable, we urge unwavering effort to devise and put into effect, under adequate inspection and control, a system for the elimination and prohibition of atomic, hydrogen and all other weapons of mass destruction, as well as the reduction of all armaments to a minimum. At the same time we caution against oversimplified formulas which are pressed merely to secure propaganda advantage or superficial agreements. Reliance on such formulas could subsequently expose an unprepared world to greater danger.

Two tasks appear especially urgent :

(1) To devise a system of inspection and control;

(2) To find a starting point for the reduction of armaments.

Any system of inspection and control must be technically adequate and politically workable, so as to provide warning for other nations if any nation violates its treaty commitment. Since there is so much incertainty as to what is scientifically necessary for reliable inspection and control, we suggest that the United Nations establish an international commission of scientists and technicians to identify the essential scientific requirements for an adequate system. Members of the Commission should be selected from a panel named by governments, but should serve in their individual capacity. Their findings would be indispensable to trustworthy and politically acceptable arrangements. They would also provide a basis for testing the readiness of governments to cooperate in the elimination and prohibition of all weapons of mass destruction under trustworthy international control, and in the reduction of all other armaments to a minimum.

The starting point for reduction of armaments must be both equitable and mutually acceptable. The prospect of finding such a starting point for successive stages is becoming progressively brighter. At various times since the Disarmament Commission was established in 1951, we have called attention to the fact that member governments of the United Nations have committed themselves in the Charter to abstain from the threat or use of force for aggressive ends. The implicit commitment not to use atomic or hydrogen or any other weapons for aggressive purpose should be made explicit as a possible first step toward a trustworthy system to control all weapons of mass destruction.

As the nations proceed to devise an adequate system, they should meanwhile seek ways whereby they can cooperate voluntarily and whereby compliance of all parties can be tested by day-to-day performance. These could include exchange of military information and various types of inspection. Tensions could thus be further relaxed, the threat military action eased, and the way paved for the kind of inspection and control which will ultimately offer the greatest security to all peoples.

PEACEFUL CHANGE AND PEACEFUL SETTLEMENT

If any disarmament plan is to be successful, the effort to remove the occasion or purported justification for military action must keep pace with it. So far as possible, injustices should be prevented from arising and, if they do occur, measures should be promptly taken to rectify them. This is, in the first instance, the responsibility of national governments in all their territory. It is also the responsibility of the United Nations and the Specialized Agencies, and of Regional Organizations.

When situations involving real or alleged injustices create tensions or disputes between nations, every effort should be made to reach agreements on necessary changes by peaceful means which include accurate analysis, negotiation, arbitration, and the like. Such preventive and constructive measures are of the highest importance.

In the past military action has been initiated to remedy real or alleged injustices, or to pursue aggressive or subversive ends, and we cannot ignore the possibility that similar situations will appear. The international community, through the United Nations, should be prepared to cope with any such emergency and should seek international acceptance of measures which will both prevent the enlargement of any conflict and help to rectify such existing injustices as may have given rise to it.

We suggest for consideration a series of steps which, by previous special agreement of member governments, should be taken when conflict breaks out anywhere in the world. Decision on each step should be reached by an agreed majority without the right of veto by any Government. We do not here deal with technical details, nor do we specify the agency in which authority should be vested. Fully aware of difficulties in winning international acceptance for such a procedure, our primary purpose is to stimulate governments to develop methods which will better assure peaceful settlement in the common interest of mankind when international peace is endangered. Toward this end existing international institutions must be more effectively utilized or new institutions established.

1. Upon request by a government in accordance with the provisions of the Charter, decision should be reached whether or not to consider a reportedly critical situation.

2. If the situation is considered, its critical aspects should be determined on the basis of the danger of international involvement.

3. If the conclusion is reached that such danger of international involvement exists, a cease-fire should promptly be recommended.

4. A unit of the Peace Observation Commission should immediately be sent to see to it that the terms of the cease-fire are complied with.

5. An impartial agency should identify causes for the conflict and ascertain possible approaches for rectifying existing injustices.

6. The findings of such inquiry should be submitted to the government or governments directly concerned, and, if necessary, thereafter to the International Court of Justice for legal decision or advisory opinion, and to other appropriate organs of the United Nations for recommendation or necessary action.

We have emphasized the importance of the complementary processes for the reduction of armaments under international inspection and control and for the development of internationally accepted methods for peaceful settlement or peaceful change to rectify existing injustices. Such a two-fold approach will give necessary weight to the moral and political factors which are essential ingredients of peace with justice and freedom."

(Statement of the CCIA Executive Committee, adopted by the WCC Central Committee at its meeting in Davos, Switzerland, 2 - 8 August 1955)

ATOMIC TESTS AND DISARMAMENT
August 1957

"The Central Committee expresses its gratitude to the Commission of the Churches on International Affairs for the Statement on "Atomic Tests and Disarmament" and desires for it the widest distribution. In commending it to the attention of the member churches, we address this special appeal to our Christian brethren about our common responsibility at the present time :

Beginning with the stepping up of the atomic armaments race and the start of development of hydrogen bombs, the World Council of Churches has shown its deep concern in this whole field. It has done this in many ways, through statements and actions by the Central Committee, its Executive Committee, the Assembly at Evanston, as well as through the CCIA.

Within the last year, public apprehension has grown as to the effects of nuclear tests, and there have been intensified warnings from responsible groups of scientists. In particular, the fact that these tests contain a threat to generations yet unborn rouses us to a more acute awareness than ever of the moral responsibility which must be upon the conscience of the present generation.

We recognize that the question of stopping the testing of nuclear weapons has to be considered in the wide extent which is set out in the CCIA Statement. We agree that it is not possible to deal with one part of the interrelated disarmament problem without risks.

There are, however, certain moral principles affecting the whole issue of atomic warfare which we desire to emphasize. The Central Committee re-affirms the conviction expressed at its Toronto meeting in 1950 that "such methods of modern warfare as the use of atomic and bacteriological weapons and obliteration bombing involve force and destruction of life on so terrible a scale as to imperil the very basis on which law and civilization can exist." The condemnation of such methods finds broad support in the fact that total war, in the sense of warfare without any limitation in the methods employed, is universally in conflict with the conscience of mankind. We also believe that the use of such methods of warfare inevitably involves spiritual degradation for any nation that uses them.

We are bound to ask whether any nation is justified in continuing the testing of nuclear weapons while the magnitude of the dangers is so little known and while effective means of production against these dangers are lacking. We must ask further whether any nation is justified in deciding on its own responsibility to conduct such tests, when the people of other nations in all parts of the world who have not agreed may have to bear the consequences. Therefore, we call upon each nation conducting tests to give full recognition to this moral responsibility as well as to consideration of national defence and international security.

Nothing less than the abolition of war itself should be the goal of the nations and their leaders and of all citizens. The attainment of this goal constitutes a solemn challenge to our particular generation. We welcome and support every honest effort now being made to limit and control armaments of all kinds and to establish conditions for a secure peace. We repeat the Evanston appeal for prohibition of all weapons of mass destruction, including atomic and hydrogen bombs, with provision for international inspection and control.

We know that a comprehensive programme for disarmament must proceed by stages, and we realize how much depends upon the deepening of confidence between the nations. But we urge that as a first step governments conducting tests should forego them, at least for a trial period, either together, or individually in the hope that the others will do the same, a new confidence be born, and foundation be laid for reliable agreements.

We therefore appeal to all our brothers to act with Christian courage, and to pray to Almighty God to guide the peoples and their governments aright."

(Adopted by the WCC Central Committee at its meeting in New Haven, USA, 30 July - 7 August 1957)

DISARMAMENT AND ATOMIC TESTS
August 1958

"In the year since we last met, nations have not made decisive progress towards disarmament, although recent developments afford ground for hope. Many grave problems of peaceful change and settlement still remain unsolved.

At our Yale meetings (WCC Central Committee Meeting, 1957), three significant principles were emphasized :

1. The main concern must always be the prevention of war itself, for the evil of war is an offence to the spiritual nature of man.

2. The objectives of a strategy to combat the menace of atomic war are inter-related and inter-dependent, such as ceasing tests, halting production, reducing existing armaments with provision for warning against surprise attacks, the peaceful uses of atomic energy, peaceful settlement and peaceful change.

3. If persistent efforts bring no sufficient agreement on any of the inter-related objectives, partial agreements should be seriously explored and, if need be, reasonable risks should be taken to advance the objectives which must continue to stand as inter-dependent.

Under the third principle, the proposal that governments should forego testing for a trial period was advanced as a recognized and reasonable risk.

The Yale statements were used all over the world and in many lands churches pressed them on the attention of governments. The suspension of tests seems more and more justified for these reasons : (a) to prevent the increase of radio-activity in the atmosphere; (b) to get started on mutual inspection which will be needed in other areas of disarmament, and (c) to limit the danger of an un-controlled spread of atomic armaments.

Both the strategy of governments and the universal conscience repudiate the senseless and fatal havoc of megaton war. There is thus a more vivid awareness of the universal dilemma of the nations and a consequent demand for more flexible policies to which governments are now responding.

Is there then prudent ground for constructive hope ? In some ways, yes. The conference of technicians* by reaching agreement on the detection of tests has not only made some clear advances, but is an approach which might well be applied to such fields as cessation of production and the danger of surprise attacks. Again the Russian offer to suspend tests, albeit conditional, stands : like all such offers from any side it must be judged by its contribution to mutual trust and sound agreement. The USA and UK have now made their offers and the fact that they have been made although in different circumstances and with different conditons, encourages us to hope that agreement on this important question may at last be reached, and may lead to further attempts to achieve similar accords on subsequent steps in disarmament to which the suspension of tests will be a welcome prelude. And again the second conference on the peaceful uses of atomic energy opens in September 1958.

Yet Christians through the very earnestness of their desire for peace, must not oversimplify these tortuous questions, since this needlessly opens the door to violation of justice and the reign of force. What then shall we do ? An "open society" is one key to peace, and first steps may well lie in making more friendships and contacts between peoples. When by agreement armament control comes with its teams of inspectors, we shall need to understand one another better. Inspection and control are so important that a start at any one point where it is possible should be welcomed, provided the essential requirements of security are not endangered.

And for these and other reasons we have continued to advocate, as we did at Yale, the suspension of tests at least for a trial period so that a new hope may be built on truly secure foundations. But we must not deceive ourselves by resting content with suspension if it comes, for the subsequent steps in disarmament are at least as urgent and may well be more difficult. If we are to avoid the nuclear holocaust and move forward, then day by day, month by month, we must be vigilant in study, steadfast in action, and ceaseless in prayer."

---

* This Conference of Experts on the Detection of Nuclear Tests met in Geneva from 1 July to 21 August 1958 by invitation of the CCIA to consider the technical feasibility of detection.

(Statement of the CCIA Executive Committee received and approved by the WCC Central Committee at its meeting in Nyborg Strand, Denmark, 21 - 29 August 1958)

DISARMAMENT AND ATOMIC TESTS
August 1958

"The governments producing atomic weapons have taken a first step towards bringing the testing of those weapons under international control. We welcome this evidence of the beginning of a better understanding among the nations. At the same time we solemnly urge the statesmen of the world not to rest content with this beginning, but to show courage in pressing forward along the way now opened.

The cessation of atomic testing which we advocated a year ago should lead to diligent efforts to halt the production of nuclear weapons and to reduce existing armaments.

The achievement of these ends requires friendship and confidence between the nations. We need an "open society" where people may meet freely and learn to understand and trust one another. We appeal to the churches to help prepare the way for such an open society.

We know the great difficulties that must be overcome. Yet what appears to be impossible with men, is surely possible with God. To Him we pray that He who has taken upon Himself the burdens and sorrows of mankind, may guide and strengthen our work for peace on earth."

(Adopted by the WCC Central Committee at its meeting in Nyborg Strand, Denmark, 21 - 29 August 1958)

THE CESSATION OF NUCLEAR WEAPONS TESTING
February 1960

"In response to expressions of profound concern by Christians in many lands, the World Council of Churches has in recent years urged the cessation of nuclear weapons testing with provision for international inspection and control. Its basic position was set forth in Statements on Atomic Tests and Disarmament, adopted at New Haven in 1957, and subsequent statements were more explicitly directed to the problems which emerged in the process of negotiating an international treaty. Church leaders in various countries have brought these views to the attention of highest government officials. Officers of the Commission of the Churches on International Affairs have communicated them to the representatives of all states members of the United Nations and, more particularly, have interpreted them in personal consultations with the heads of the delegations at the Geneva Conference representing the United Kingdom, the USSR and the United States.

The Executive Committee of the World Council of Churches, in session at Buenos Aires, expresses appreciation of such progress as has resulted from persistent effort at the Geneva Conference, but cannot avoid uneasiness over the failure thus far to have resolved the differences which prevent the conclusion of a treaty. The importance of adequate inspection provisions, whether to ensure compliance with treaty commitments or to point the way to verified disarmament, must be recognized, and the present inability to distinguish the underground explosions of smaller nuclear weapons from natural disturbances ought not to be ignored. Nevertheless, the difficulties here encountered cannot and must not be regarded as insuperable. As members of the Executive Committee, we therefore express our views on the kind of action which is demanded in the present situation.

We urge the governments concerned to continue to commit themselves to the objective of a comprehensive treaty which will include the cessation of all forms of nuclear weapons testing — atmosphere, space, underwater and underground. This commitment will become more meaningful when it is uniformly supported in each government and fortified by an informed and vocal public opinion.

34

In order to honour such a commitment, we believe that governments should demonstrate their readiness promptly to negotiate a treaty covering all forms of testing which can now be detected. These would apparently include the larger underground explosions as well as these in atmosphere, space and underwater. Yet, this is not enough. A formal agreement ought also to be concluded to ban the underground testing of smaller nuclear weapons, at least for a specified period of time, on condition that arrangements be made for international cooperation in devising more adequate means of detection and for international inspection of explosions for peaceful purposes.

The concessions which will thus be required of both sides are in our judgement justifiable and imperative, if man is to act responsibly in this nuclear space age.

We welcome the apparent relaxation of international tensions, although we recognize the basic causes of suspicion and distrust have not been removed. The conclusion of a treaty to cease nuclear weapons testing, as we have here conceived it, would contribute to greater confidence and provide for the forthcoming meeting of the Committee of Ten on Disarmament both a healthy climate and an agreed start on procedures for international inspection."

RESOLUTION ON THE SAHARA TEST

"Noting public announcements that the government of France is proceeding with nuclear testing in the Sahara, the Executive Committee reaffirms the position that, so long as international control is under discussion, powers which have not made tests as yet should not launch them anywhere for military purposes."

(Adopted by the WCC Executive Committee at its meeting in Buenos Aires, Argentina, 8 - 12 February 1960)

THE THIRD ASSEMBLY PERIOD

THE APPEAL TO ALL GOVERNMENTS AND PEOPLES
December 1961

"1. The Third Assembly of the World Council of Churches, at which are gathered Christians from all parts of the world, addresses this Appeal to the government and people of every nation.

2. Today, war itself is a common enemy. War is an offence to the nature of man. The future of many generations and the heritage of ages past hang in the balance. They are now easy to destroy, since the actions or miscalculations of a few can bring about a holocaust. They are harder to safeguard and advance, for that requires the dedicated action of all. Let there be restraint and self-denial in the things which divide, and boldness and courage in grasping the things which make for peace.

3. To turn back from the road towards war into the paths of peace, all must renounce the threat of force. This calls for an end to the war of nerves, to pressures on small countries, to the rattling of bombs. It is not possible to follow at the same time policies of menace and of mutual disarmament.

4. To halt the race in arms is imperative. Complete and general disarmament is the accepted goal, and concrete steps must be taken to reach it. Meanwhile, the search for a decisive first step, such as the verified cessation of nuclear tests, should be pressed forward despite all obstacles and setbacks.

5. To substitute reason for force and undergird the will to disarm, institutions of peace and orderly methods to effect change and to settle disputes are essential. This imposes a duty to strengthen the United Nations within the framework and spirit of the Charter. All countries share this duty, whether aligned with the major power blocs or independent of them. The non-aligned can contribute

through their impartiality; with others they can be champions of the principles of the Charter.

6. To build peace with justice, barriers of mutual distrust must be attacked at every level. Mutual confidence is the most precious resource in the world today : none should be wasted, more must be found. The fundamentals of an open society are essential so that contacts may freely develop, person to person, and people to people. Barriers to communication must go, not least where they divide peoples, churches, even families. Freedom of human contact, information and cultural exchange is essential for the building of peace.

7. To enhance mutual trust, nations should be willing to run reasonable risks for peace. For example, an equitable basis for disarmament involves, on the one hand, an acceptance of risks in an inspection and control which cannot be foolproof, and, on the other, the danger that inspection may exceed its stated duties. Those who would break through the vicious circle of suspicion must dare to pioneer.

8. There is a great opportunity for constructive action in the struggle for world development. To share the benefits of civilization with the whole of humanity is a noble and attainable objective. To press the war against poverty, disease, exploitation, and ignorance calls for greater sacrifice and for a far greater commitment of scientific, educational, and material resources than hitherto. In this common task, let the peoples find a positive programme for peace, a moral equivalent for war.

9. A creative strategy for peace with justice requires universal recognition of the claims of humanity — of all people whatever their status, race, sex, or creed. Lest man's new powers be used to degrade his human freedom and dignity, governments must remember that they are the servants of their citizens and respect the worth of each individual human being. The supreme achievement for a government is to enhance the dignity of man, and free him for the creative exercise of his higher powers.

10. In making this Appeal to all governments and peoples, we are constrained by obedience to Jesus Christ, the Lord of history, who demands righteousness and mercy and is a light unto the nations and the hearts of men. For the achievement of peace with justice, we pledge our unremitting efforts and call upon the Churches for their support in action and in prayer."

_____

(Issued by the WCC III. Assembly at its meeting in New Delhi, India, 19 November - 5 December 1961)

STATEMENT ON DISARMAMENT
March 1962

"As members of the Executive Committee of the World Council of Churches, we note with gratitude that the Disarmament Conference has convened in Geneva, the three powers concerned have resumed their discussions on the cessation of nuclear weapon testing, and the USA and USSR have reached a better understanding on the peaceful uses of outer space. We have therefore examined, once again, the crucial question of peace and war in a world in which a highly precarious peace rests on the formidable and unstable balance of terror. Well aware of the many failures of the past and the immense difficulties yet to be overcome, we nevertheless press with renewed hope for effective agreements.

We believe that nations are accountable to God for their use of power. Moved by our common Christian faith we who are bound together in a worldwide Christian fellowship which transcends nation and race, urge all Governments concerned :

I. (a) Not to continue or resume the testing of nuclear weapons and, as a warrant of their good faith, to agree on a system of information and verification which will assure all parties that Treaty commitments are being honoured.

(b) To continue to press for positive agreements on the specific areas of international friction, and on the broad questions immediately related to disarmament as well as the peaceful uses of outer space for the advancement of scientific gains to the benefit of all.

(c) To be ready to take, in their individual capacities, calculated risks which will contribute to disarmament and at the same time will not betray their responsibility for international security, nor prejudice the requirements of information and verification.

(d) To search for and seize any possible starting point of disarmament while recognizing that the cessation of tests by verifiable agreements, if it can be obtained, seems now to offer the best base from which to advance.

II. Accordingly, we urge the member churches of the World Council of Churches to seize and use every opportunity to press these policies on their Governments, persistently to advocate the continuation of negotiations; and, using the resources of the ecumenical fellowship, to help allay what bedevils contemporary negotiations, namely the tragic lack of mutual trust amounting to profound mutual suspicion.

III. And we invite all Christians to fight frustration and defeatism; to persevere in patience and hope in spite of all setbacks; and to support by their prayers, attitudes and actions the endeavours of their Churches in ecumenical fellowship to advance peace, freedom, and justice between and among all nations and their anxious peoples."

(Adopted by the WCC Executive Committee at its meeting in Geneva, Switzerland, 28 - 31 March 1962)

STATEMENT ON CONTEMPORARY
PROBLEMS OF PEACE

August 1962

I.

"New and imaginative approaches to the problem of peace are essential if the voice of the churches is to be heard in these dangerous times.

The Third Assembly of the World Council of Churches suggested that a conference composed of Christians from various countries be held on the issues of disarmament and nuclear tests, with specialists present from the countries most involved, to explain their governments' policies.

Such a consultation was held in June 1962, and this unique and important experiment in ecumenical discussion is welcomed.

Church representatives came face to face with diplomats from the UK, the USA, the USSR, and one of the non-Aligned Powers, and began to understand the complexities and difficulties of their task and its highly technical nature. In their fellowship with one another, the members of the Consultation were able to dispel many of the misunderstandings and fears on these issues which have clouded even the ecumenical fellowship. The substantive conclusions which were published in the Statement issued by the Consultation are reflected in this document.

Though recognizing that the nations are continuing to negotiate, the view of the Consultation that there is need for a deeper dialogue in all problems dividing the great powers must be endorsed.

II.

NUCLEAR TESTS

Nuclear weapons testing can be stopped, and it must be stopped if mankind is to be spared the threat to health and even more the increased danger of war created by this unholy competition. An agreement by the United States, the USSR, and the United Kingdom to cease tests would decrease the likelihood of others entering the field, but would be properly effective only if France and other governments capable of testing signed it as well.

Scientific discoveries have apparently made it possible to identify, by national detecting posts, testing in the atmosphere, in space, underwater, and the larger underground explosions. Nations need demand only that minimum of verification which is shown to be scientifically necessary. In so far as smaller underground tests cannot be distinguished at a distance from natural disturbances, an international system of verification is still required to make the distinction. Furthermore, if a substantial number of national detection posts under an international system indicate that a nuclear explosion of any kind has occurred, the government of the territory concerned would be expected to invite international verification. Refusal to do so would be regarded as evidence that a nuclear test had in fact occurred.

There is a vicious circle wherein each side seeks to be the last to test. If there is no better way out, a future date may well be specified on which a treaty would go into effect after which tests would cease altogether.

The main sanction to enforce an agreement lies in the knowledge that, if one party breaks its treaty obligations, other parties will consider themselves free to resume tests. In such a lamentable eventuality, resumption should be delayed at least long enough to permit study of evidence of a breach, and to seek remedial action through an expression of world opinion and the operation of international diplomacy.

III.

DISARMAMENT

Mutual fear and the military logic of both parties have so far prevented any real progress towards disarmament.

Governments, it must be recognized, are faced with tremendous difficulties, and all parties are convinced of their fundamental obligation to carry out their defence programmes. So they feel bound to prepare for war at the very time they seek to disarm. In this process there is the danger that the very systems of defence they favour themselves create new and avoidable obstacles to disarmament. If a way out of this dilemma is to be found, defence and disarmament policies must be more closely harmonized in the interests of peace. All parties must recognize that, in a world of highly developed technology, mankind is involved in a common fate made more terrible by profound ideological distrust.

General and complete disarmament is the goal in the agreed principles accepted by all parties as the basis for disarmament negotiations. This goal has little meaning as long as agreement cannot be reached on even the first steps towards disarmament. Accordingly, in order to pave the way for more comprehensive agreements, there should be constant readiness to modify previously held positions in the light of new scientific evidence or political circumstances, and to accept provisional and partial settlements where final solutions cannot be achieved. In this process, the great powers ought to accept, under international control and verification, a progressively lower level of armaments without disturbing the equilibrium of power. The trend is virtually as important as the immediate result.

Disarmament is not merely a technical matter. It is a political and moral issue of the first order. Politically it requires the readiness to abate local tensions, and for this purpose it is essential to develop more reliable, more objective and automatic international procedures and institutions to settle disputes and to remedy injustice by peaceful means. Moreover, such procedures and institutions must be readily available. Morally, agreements on disarmament will rely heavily on the profound conviction that it is humanely intolerable to continue the present unbridled armaments competition. Disarmament obviously involves certain risks. Yet the continuation or acceleration of the armaments race carries with it a risk far more dangerous and threatening. A choice of risk is inescapable, and the obligation on mankind is to choose that risk which best promises to break the present impasse...

IV.

The Churches throughout the world are called at this time to contribute more adequately to an enlightened public opinion on disarmament. What is required is not simply a greater volume of hasty criticism. The aim should be to produce a public opinion sufficiently alert and informed to support policies which are constructive, to be patient in the face of genuine difficulties, but impatient of half-truths and culpable hesitancy. For example, the assumption that in the "East-West" conflict one side is wholly right and the other wholly wrong is misleading and dangerous. Variations of history and geographical situation give rise to natural differences in outlook. Disarmament proposals are shaped by many factors including constructive desires and genuine fears. To succomb to automatic suspicion or uncritical condemnation can only widen the breach further. Where public opinion is sceptical or passive, the churches should emphasize that real progress may depend on its alertness. Where it is uncritical, the churches should stress that national interests cannot be determinative at a time when the unity of the world becomes ever more imperative. Where the complexity of the question facing governments is not appreciated, the churches should seek to promote understanding of the issue.

Above all, the churches should keep on reminding public opinion of the spiritual and moral aspects of the present situation. The mounting armament spiral, the continued threat of nuclear destruction and the undiminished "East-West" distrust and suspicion are a sad commentary on the present human predicament. They constitute a challenge concerning the nature of man which must be wrestled with ceaselessly, and which can only be overcome on a spiritual level."

(Adopted by the CCIA Executive Committee at its meeting in Paris, France, 1 - 4 August 1962 and generally approved by the WCC Central Committee at its meeting in Paris, France, 7 - 16 August 1962)

LETTER FROM THE OFFICERS OF THE WCC CENTRAL COMMITTEE ADDRESSED TO THE PRIME MINISTER OF THE UNITED KINGDOM, THE CHAIRMAN OF THE USSR AND THE PRESIDENT OF THE UNITED STATES
August 1963

August 31, 1963

"Dear Mr. Prime Minister,
Dear Chairman Khrushchev,
Dear Mr. President,

The Central Committee of the World Council of Churches, with representatives from churches around the world, is now in session, and has reviewed current progress towards peace and order. We have been very conscious of the hopes raised by the recent signing of the Treaty Banning Nuclear Weapons Tests in Atmosphere, in Outer Space and Underwater.

The Central Committee has unanimously bidden us to inform you of their profound gratitude for this first step in breaking the nuclear impasse. In saying this, we are confident that we reflect the aspirations of millions of Christians in the churches of all continents.

The Officers of the Commission of the Churches on International Affairs issued a statement on the day the Treaty was initialled, of which we enclose a copy. The Executive Committee of the Commission also prepared a more detailed statement, "The Test Ban Treaty and the Next Steps", which was adopted by the Central Committee and which we now remit for your information.

In sending you this message of appreciation, we hardly need to emphasize that much remains to be done before the achievement of that world order for which our churches work and pray. We assure you of our continuing prayers that you and all statesmen on whose shoulders lie the burdens of decision will find it possible in this new atmosphere to move from an era of co-existence to one of co-operation for the benefit of mankind.

Yours sincerely,

W.A. Vissert't Hooft   Ernest A. Payne   Franklin Clark Fry
General Secretary   Vice-Chairman   Chairman"

THE TEST BAN TREATY AND THE NEXT STEPS:
FROM CO-EXISTENCE TO CO-OPERATION
September 1963

"1. The Central Committee of the World Council of Churches welcomes the Treaty Banning Nuclear Weapons Tests in the Atmosphere, in Outer Space and Underwater as the first constructive international agreement in the current nuclear stalemate.

2. The Treaty is a first step. It does not halt production or reduce existing stockpiles of nuclear weapons; but it may slow up the nuclear arms race and will diminish the health hazards from radioactive fall-out to this and future generations. Of itself it does not prevent the spread of nuclear weapons to nations now without them; but it does prohibit assistance to other nations in making tests in the environments which it specifically proscribes. It does not end the threat of nuclear war or outlaw the use of nuclear weapons; but it opens the way to further agreements and thereby reduces the threat of war.

3. The nations must therefore seize every opportunity to capture the advantages of this moment, and to explore the possibilities of advancing from co-existence to the beginning of co-operation. General and complete disarmament is the declared goal. In whatever way the ultimate aim is defined, the following next steps towards establishing world peace merit both serious consideration and every effort for their achievement.

4. The immediate requirement is that public opinion should fully and urgently support governments which have advanced in this direction. The treaty should be ratified not only by formal signatures but in the wills of whole nations.

5. The full value of the Treaty depends on the adherence of all the nations in the world. In the nuclear age, to withhold assent on grounds of national influence or ideological doctrine is irresponsible. Ways must be found whereby France and China can associate themselves with the Treaty.

6. The Test Ban Treaty underlines the tendency for ultimate military power to be concentrated in a very few hands. This calls for new discipline and experiments in the sharing of international decisions and for the consideration of how the responsibility for nuclear defence can be shared within an alliance. In any case, the answer cannot be found in the possession by every nation of its own nuclear defence.

7. The Test Ban Treaty must be interpreted and applied not only in the letter but also in the spirit of its provisions. There is a grave responsibility on all parties not to invoke the right to withdraw from the treaty except in most extreme circumstances.

8. Co-operation in devising means of identifying underground testing should be vigorously pursued, so that in this environment also, nuclear weapons testing will be halted; and explosions for peaceful purposes including testing for scientific reasons should be undertaken only under international agreement and control.

9. The penetration of outer space opens a new area of high military consequence. If in this field mankind is not to face dangers equivalent to those he now seeks to escape from, co-operation of the parties to the present treaty is urgent.

10. Moreover, the parties should now explore with an open mind further co-operative steps, such as the use of mutual inspection teams to inhibit surprise attack and the establishment of nuclear free zones.

11. A non-aggression pact could well constitute a symbol of a new relationship. Its political implications should be carefully considered. If current proposals for such a pact are found unacceptable, a reasonable alternative to accomplish similar purposes should be diligently sought.

12. To bring about a durable peace to which the Test Ban Treaty may open the way, a lasting solution must be found for those great political problems and conflicts which still divide the world community and are a cause of insecurity and unrest.

13. The latest developments relating to the Test Ban Treaty inevitably isolate China more than ever from the rest of the world. This isolation in itself can be a new source of danger and suffering to China's neighbours as exemplified by her recent actions. Every opportunity should be seized to keep open channels of

contact with China, and to bring her into the family of nations, so that she may accept the responsibilities and disciplines of its institutions.

14. New hopes for peace have stirred in men's hearts in these days. It is supremely the task of the churches to strive that these hopes be not betrayed. So they have the duty to press upon the attention of governments the considerations outlined herein which express in practical terms the aspirations of millions of our fellow men. They can urge the nations to accept reasonable risks in seizing every opportunity opened up by the agreement on the Test Ban Treaty, and, while prudently alert to any threat of hostility, to be equally alive to the possibilities of co-operation in goodwill."

(Adopted by the WCC Central Committee at its meeting in Rochester, USA, 26 August - 2 September 1963)

PROBLEMS AND OPPORTUNITIES TODAY
February 1964

"... We welcome the relaxation of tensions between the major powers following the conclusion of the Limited Test Ban Treaty at Moscow last summer. Every opportunity should be seized to advance from competition in armaments to co-operation in disarmament. If the precarious détente of the moment is to become more firmly established and further agreements reached, serious obstacles must be overcome...

The effort to gain military advantage by steps toward disarmament carries with it the threat of war, and nations should seek agreement on measures which preserve reasonable parity since peace still rests tenuously on a balance of power. Local conflicts multiply, and this confronts powerful nations with the temptation to seek ideological or territorial gains — whether by military aid, economic exploitation, or acts of subversion. If this temptation is not resisted, the danger of enlarged conflict will continue to plague mankind. The lingering imposition of foreign controls which prevent peoples from freely choosing their own form of government and representatives perpetuates an uneasy international situation.

Notwithstanding lack of confidence, and in spite of the suspicion which survives so long as obstacles such as these remain, general comprehensive disarmament must be the goal of international striving. However, if we were to believe that an easy road will rapidly lead us to it, we would delude ourselves and would fail to seize the opportunities at hand — opportunities which seem to permit some quicker advance toward a world of peace with justice and freedom consistent with the dignity of man.

Proposals recently made by both sides can have vital meaning for international security. Among them are : to negotiate a non-aggression pact; to conclude an international agreement on the repudiation by all states of the use of force in solving territorial disputes and questions involving frontiers; to conclude an international agreement on the repudiation by all states of direct and indirect forms of the threat or use of force in their selfish political or economic interests and of aggression, subversion, or the secret supply of arms; to halt the production of fissionable material for military purposes and to direct nuclear production to peaceful uses; to establish inspection posts to safeguard against surprise attack; to limit nuclear striking capacity or nuclear delivery systems; to prevent proliferation of nuclear military power; to establish nuclear free zones; to cease underground testing for military purposes. In a number of instances, the proposals are sufficiently similar that agreement is possible and should be reached.

As the effort to bring progressive disarmament through multilateral arrangements go forward, nations should be mindful of the part they can play by unilateral action. Reduction of military budgets, responsible military posture which clearly avoids the impression of aggressive intent, reduction of standing armed forces, restraint in face of political tension, increased contribution of fissionable material to peaceful purposes — measures such as these ought to serve as an example and invitation to others, and thus set the stage for more formal international action.

The intermediate and smaller powers, whether they be in some manner identified with the major blocs or avowedly non-aligned, have their part to play. It is for them to press upon the great powers the need for such concessions as will advance agreement without endangering international security. In the process, they will remember that they themselves have a responsibility for disarmament and will meticulously avoid increasing their own military strength through the acquisition of armaments discarded by others. Their contribution can in some instances be determining and at all times highly significant.

(Issued by the WCC Executive Committee at its meeting in Odessa, USSR, 10 - 15 February 1964)

STATEMENT ON CURRENT INTERNATIONAL ISSUES
OF PEACE, JUSTICE AND FREEDOM
January 1965

DISARMAMENT

Progress towards disarmament must be recognized as a major obligation of all governments and especially of those who possess nuclear weapons. While some encouraging developments have taken place, including the limited Test Ban Treaty of 1963, the armaments race in fact continues unabated. We are convinced that more can and ought to be done. France and China ought to be brought into the disarmament negotiations and agreements. The Test Ban Treaty ought to be extended to include underground testing. Other possibilities are the limitation of nuclear striking and delivery power, and the establishment of nuclear free zones as is currently proposed for Africa by the Organization for African Unity. It is of highest importance that defence arrangements as long as they are needed, whether national or regional, will be so fashioned as not to impede, but to facilitate progress towards disarmament. This holds true for conventional weapons but has special relevance in the nuclear field. It is in the interest of all nations, and not least of the nuclear powers themselves, to prevent the proliferation of nuclear armaments. In this connection, the arguments for and against the multilateral force as originally conceived were taken into consideration. The constructive possibility of diverting money now spent for the manufacture of destructive weapons to the assistance of the developing countries is an additional incentive.

PEACE-KEEPING

Disarmament will become more readily possible and justice more fully served if international provisions are made to cope with the many problems that have arisen and will continue to arise in a world of constant change. Whether through the United Nations or by agreement between the nations directly concerned, arrangements ought to be made on a permanent basis for enquiry, conciliation, mediation, and an international peace-keeping "presence" whether political or military.

A solution of the United Nations current constitutional and financial crisis is urgently needed and must depend for its achievement not only on ingenuity but also on good will by all parties now in disagreement. If a final solution cannot be reached immediately, some temporizing agreement ought certainly to be possible without yielding basic positions and yet providing sufficient facilities and resources for the United Nations to move forward with its work.

(Resolved by the WCC Central Committee at its meeting in Enugu, Eastern Nigeria, 12 - 21 January 1965)

STATEMENT ON DISARMAMENT
February 1966

"The Central Committee and the World Council of Churches' Commission on International Affairs (CCIA) have been continuously concerned with the intricate and difficult field of disarmament, peace and security in a nuclear age. We have expressed our gratitude for such progress as has been made, however limited, and particularly for the treaty concluded at Moscow in 1963 banning nuclear tests in the atmosphere, in outer space, and underwater. Yet we must voice our deep concern that so much has been left undone, especially at a time when international controls are still possible but when the opportunity to achieve them seems to be rapidly diminishing. We appeal to the nations which have not yet acceded to the partial Test Ban Treaty to join the rest of the community of nations to make this treaty universally applicable.

Convinced of the urgency which characterizes the present situation, we address ourselves to three measures which can, if men will, be taken now. The first two relate to the work of the Conference of Eighteen-Nations Committee on Disarmament which resumed its session here at Geneva, 27 January 1966. The third has to do with the World Disarmament Conference. We have spoken of them before, but consider re-emphasis now particularly timely. We address our member churches, but also in thus speaking, seek to encourage governments to press forward in this task upon which the fate of mankind may hang.

The Limited Test Ban Treaty of 1963 ought to be expanded to include underground tests. This may require a limited number of on-site inspections, or it may be possible to ban at least those tests which it is agreed can be detected and identified without on-site inspections. In the latter instance, scientific studies ought to be pursued under international auspices so that, as means of detection and identification improve, the threshold may be progressively lowered. Mankind expects and awaits progress in this area.

While the expansion of the Limited Test Ban Treaty would in itself deter the spread of nuclear weapons, there is need to set up special safeguards against proliferation. Here there must be greater readiness to think objectively, not only of the responsibilities upon the nuclear powers, but also of ways of meeting the reasonable expectations of the non-nuclear powers. This will require that the non-nuclear powers will be assured of protection against the threat or use of nuclear weapons, whether by informal or formal agreements; and that the non-nuclear powers, denying themselves the advantages of nuclear possession, will nevertheless have the benefits of the nuclear powers, whether political or in terms of prestige, as well as those which involve peaceful uses of nuclear energy. The nuclear powers, on their part, must reverse the trend of nuclear weapons building and place at the disposal of all mankind greater nuclear resources for peaceful uses.

In July 1965, the CCIA Executive Committee welcomed the proposal of the United Nations Disarmament Commission to convene a World Disarmament Conference to include all countries and saw in it a particular advantage in opening a possible way, perhaps initially through preparatory steps, for bringing the People's Republic of China into disarmament negotiations. The Twentieth Session of the UN General Assembly has now endorsed that proposal. All countries are to be invited, a representative preparatory committee set up, and the Conference actually held not later than 1967. Aware of the difficulties in a Conference of this kind and of the too high hopes of it which some may entertain, we nevertheless believe that it merits fullest support both in its preparatory stages and when it is actually convened.

The situation is so urgent as to require renewed and unflagging effort to press for these, as well as other, disarmament measures. Towards these ends we call once more for the prayers of Christians and churches, and for co-operation in good will across all ideological and political barriers."

(Adopted by the WCC Central Committee at its meeting in Geneva, Switzerland, 8 - 17 February 1966)

STRUCTURES OF INTERNATIONAL COOPERATION-LIVING TOGETHER IN PEACE IN A PLURALISTIC WORLD SOCIETY : CONCLUSIONS ON NUCLEAR WAR

July 1966

LIVING TOGETHER IN PEACE IN A PLURALISTIC WORLD SOCIETY

"The development of military technology, and especially of atomic, radiological, biological and chemical arms and the means to deliver them, marks a decisive turning point in the history of mankind, of states and their wars. The frightful possibilities of indiscriminate war exterminating not only combatants but civilian populations as well, the impossibility of self-defence by smaller nations, the danger of annihilation of human cultures, the continuing danger for future generations from radiation — all this radically changes the situation of the states and their relations with one another.

This new and terrible situation forces Christians to reexamine previous thinking in the churches concerning war and the function of the state in relation to it. In Amsterdam in 1948, the First Assembly of the WCC declared, "War is contrary to the will of God". At the same time it acknowledged three attitudes towards the participation by Christians in the evil of war, one of the three attitudes being that war might at times be a lesser evil. Today the situation has changed. Christians still differ as to whether military means can be legitimately used to achieve objectives which are necessary to justice. But nuclear war goes beyond all bounds. Mutual nuclear annihilation can never establish justice because it destroys all that justice seeks to defend or to achieve. We now say to all governments and peoples that nuclear war is against God's will and the greatest of evils. Therefore we affirm that it is the first duty of governments and their officials to prevent nuclear war...

The real problem is how the supreme task, to avoid nuclear war, can be carried out. The following measures would help :

- the changing of a mere balance of power into a community with institutions for the prevention of escalation of conflict between the main powers;

- the embodiment in a code of conduct of the discipline necessary to prevent war; step-by-step agreements concerning limitations on the use of war; the development of a new international law for the nuclear dimension;

- control and inspection of armaments by international agencies to ensure an equilibrium of power and regulate the different phases of disarmament;

- an increasing role for the smaller powers in depolarizing international affairs.

The nuclear powers have a great common interest in not letting their precarious balance escalate into nuclear war. They also have a common interest in preventing nuclear proliferation and the escalation of local conflict.

The churches should add that they have something more in common : the duty to preserve the life of the people of this world, and to work for a world order which will transcend the present uneasy peace of the equilibrium of power. It is intolerable for the peace of the world to depend on a precarious nuclear balance.

Such disarmament measures as might be immediately implemented should be vigorously pursued in order to sustain the present armistice and release resources for the urgent task of economic development in the rest of the world. Patient and persistent negotiations on all these matters are the way to wider possibilities for settling outstanding questions between the blocs.

International agreements in this field should be honoured, brought up to date, and extended.

The United Nations is the best structure now available through which to pursue the goals of international peace and justice. Like all institutions, it is not sacrosanct, and many changes in its Charter are necessary to meet the needs of the world today. Nevertheless we call upon the churches of the world to defend it against all attacks which would weaken or destroy it, and to seek out and advocate ways in which it can be transformed into an instrument fully capable of ensuring the peace and guaranteeing justice on a worldwide scale.

The United Nations has obvious limitations :

- it can exercise little influence in conflicts between the great powers;

- the process of decision-making in the General Assembly is weakened by lack of agreement.

But the United Nations has resources which should be more fully used :

- UN debates offer a corrective for national self-righteousness and unilateral action in world affairs;

- the UN offers a forum for continuous diplomacy, conciliation and mediation;

- the UN can contribute to peace-keeping operations and the elimination of local conflict;

- the UN machinery can be used as an instrument for the promotion of dynamic justice;

- the work done by the UN and its specialized agencies in the fields of human rights, labour relations, and social and economic conditions may form the basis for an international ethos in these fields;

- the churches should make use of their consultative status with the UN to bring their influence to bear.

We urge Christians and the churches, by every means at their disposal, to join those who seek to rouse the conscience of their fellow men concerning peace and justice. The life of the churches itself is the principal means but others will also be needed. These will vary : patient political effort and impatient protest, advocacy of feasible measures and projection of long-range goals, the creation of greater order and the transformation of existing orders will all be involved. Whatever the means, Christians must help to bear one another's burdens of loneliness and weakness, and support one another in their common witness.

A system to prevent the proliferation of nuclear weapons should be established in which all nations should cooperate; such a system should also be jointly controlled, open, and on a legal basis.

In this situation the churches, especially as an ecumenical community, can help. Real dialogue is needed; the tendency to absolutize ideologies must be challenged; an example of true community transcending the nations must be manifested; every conceivable means must be used to create a climate of confidence. We have not been able to explore these possibilities in detail. They represent urgent agenda for the churches of the World Council of Churches and the Commission of the Churches on International Affairs.

In the atomic stalemate, small nations enjoy greater liberty to act for good or evil than before. A new world order will be impossible without their full co-operation, their willingness to renounce nuclear weapons and their discipline in the prevention of local conflict..."

(Approved by the WCC World Conference on Church and Society at its meeting in Geneva, Switzerland, 12 - 26 July 1966)

LIMITATIONS IN MODERN WARFARE
August 1967

The WCC and its Commission on International Affairs have sought to encourage the solution of international disputes by methods other than war. They continue to encourage progress toward disarmament or the international control of armaments and to support the development of institutionalized measures for peaceful change, peace-keeping and peaceful settlement.

These objectives have not yet been attained. Wars continue to plague mankind and modern warfare becomes increasingly devastating and indiscriminate.

We commend to governments for their urgent and positive action the declaration of the International Conference of the Red Cross at Vienna in 1965 :

"All governments and other authorities responsible for action in armed conflicts should conform at least to the following principles :

- that the right of the parties to a conflict to adopt means of injuring the enemy is not unlimited;

- that it is prohibited to launch attacks against the civilian populations as such;

- that distinction must be made at all times between persons taking part in the hostilities and members of civilian population to the effect that the latter be spared as much as possible;

- that the general principles of the Law of War apply to nuclear and similar weapons."

Governments who have not become parties to the Geneva Conventions of 1949 should do so, and those who have become parties should honour their commitment. Furthermore, all governments should be aware that they are bound by such laws of warfare as have grown into general rules of customary international law (e.g. the prohibition of chemical and biological warfare).

In addition, we urge that the laws of warfare be expanded to include more recently developed weapons which produce new horrors of human suffering, such as napalm bombs.

We support the initiative of the International Committee of the Red Cross in urging governments to seek agreement on a more comprehensive international instrument. Meanwhile pending the development of a more comprehensive international instrument, we urge appropriate action by the UN General Assembly to secure these ends during an intermediate period.

(Adopted by the CCIA Executive Committee at its meeting in Geneva, Switzerland, 7 August 1967 and adopted by the WCC Central Committee at its meeting in Heraklion, Crete, 15 - 26 August 1967)

THE FOURTH ASSEMBLY PERIOD

TOWARDS JUSTICE AND PEACE
IN INTERNATIONAL AFFAIRS
July 1968

... 11. The World Council of Churches reaffirms its declarations at the Amsterdam Assembly in 1948 : "War as a method of settling disputes is incompatible with the teachings and example of our Lord Jesus Christ." Of all forms of war, nuclear war presents the gravest affront to the conscience of man. The avoidance of atomic, biological or chemical war has become a condition of human survival. This is true, not only because it would be suicidally destructive, but because, unlike "conventional" war, nuclear war would inflict lasting genetic damage. The churches must insist that it is the first duty of governments to prevent such a war : to halt the present arms race, agree never to initiate the use of nuclear weapons, stop experiments concerned with, and the production of weapons of mass human destruction by chemical and biological means and move away from the balance of terror towards disarmament.

12. In no way can the present nuclear stalemate be accepted as a lasting solution or as a justification for maintaining nuclear armaments. The churches should welcome agreement among the great powers in the non-proliferation treaty as an important step towards averting nuclear disasters and all nations (including China and France) should be urged to sign it. Further steps will be needed, especially the extension of the test-ban to underground tests, and the prevention of the establishment of anti-ballistic missile systems by agreement between the USA and the USSR.

The concentration of nuclear weapons in the hands of a few nations presents the world with serious problems :

a) how to guarantee the security of the non-nuclear nations;

b) how to enable these nations to play their part in preventing war; and

c) how to prevent the nuclear powers from freezing the existing order at the expense of changes needed for social and political justice.

13. Since smaller nations are expected to accept the discipline of nuclear abstinence, the nuclear powers should accept the discipline of phased disarmament in all categories of weapons. At the same time, the nuclear nations should accept the right and responsibility of the non-nuclear nations to their share in vital decisions regarding their own security and the peace of the world.

14. Non-nuclear wars with all their cruelty have the additional danger of escalating into uncontrolled violence. In a world that regrettably still resorts to the use of arms, there are those who hold that absolute pacifism is the true Christian response. For them, and also for those who do not share this conviction, there is the old problem of limiting the use of force. Such limitation involves the attempt to preserve the social fabric of the enemy, to spare non-combatants, to lessen human suffering and to recognize that military force alone never ensures the emergence of a new order and may even prevent it.

15. A special danger today is the encouragement of wars by proxy through the competitive delivery of armaments, so aggravating the dangers in many explosive situations. This constitutes an international scandal which governments must no longer tolerate or permit.

16. The churches are urged to support contemporary work in the field of peace research. They should also encourage educational programmes in the service of peace.

(Report of the Committee on Church and Society, adopted by the IV. Assembly at its meeting in Uppsala, Sweden, 4 - 20 July 1968)

STATEMENT ON EUROPEAN SECURITY
AND COOPERATION
August 1972

A. 1. The Central Committee of the WCC, meeting in Utrecht, Netherlands, 13 - 23 August 1972, welcomes the evident signs of the relaxation of tension in Europe indicated by such developments as :

a) the treaties of the Federal Republic of Germany with the Soviet Union and Poland,

b) the Four Power Agreement on Berlin,

c) the agreement on traffic control between the two German states,

d) the progress made in the Strategic Arms Limitation Talks (SALT),

e) the negotiations currently under way between the CSSR and the Federal German Republic for whose successful outcome the World Council is praying.

2. As a next step in the relaxation of tension, the Central Committee welcomes the proposals for an all-European conference which would genuinely seek to facilitate security and cooperation.

3. The importance of solid agreements that would lessen the danger of war within and originating in Europe is obvious and not for Europe only.

B. 1. *Within Europe* the proposed conference has been understood to involve the following significant aims :

a) the maintenance of the present political balance in Europe,

b) mutually balanced force reduction,

c) recognition of the territorial *status quo*,

d) elimination of political tensions,

e) examination of possible fields of cooperation.

2. Progress towards these aims would encourage the transition from the military confrontation of NATO and the Warsaw Pact countries to new forms of cooperation. Depending on vigour and sincerity in the search for such cooperation, new and more hopeful patterns of relationship could emerge.

3. The cooperation that would be essential should include, *inter alia* :

a) agreement on an acceptable method of supervision of military forces,

b) agreement on the rights and obligations of European states under international law,

c) agreement on cultural exchanges to improve mutual understanding,

d) agreement on the understanding and implementation of civil and religious rights.

C. 1. *Outside Europe* Christians affirm the desirability of progress in understanding within Europe, believing that peaceful security in Europe is essential to world security.

But, as a representative and worldwide body of Christians, we would insist that European security and cooperation must be seen in a global context. There is widespread and understandable fear, especially within the developing nations, that if the major purpose of European détente is to secure an even more powerful Europe there could follow, in a new guise, new attempts at still further increasing European domination in other areas of the world.

2. The acid test is the stance of Europe with regard to world affairs. A stronger, more united Europe could be of immense value for justice, order and peace in the world — or it could introduce a new and dangerous factor.

3. Even in the contemporary situation, both possibilities are present. The World Council of Churches has consistently appealed for more generous support, both by trade and aid, for the developing nations. It has

emphasized the necessity for equal partnership between nations. A stronger Europe could accept more readily these positive responsibilities. Fear of potential dangers should not hide from us the great potentiality for good. Nor is this simply an appeal to the "benevolence" of Europe. Without social justice in the world, there is no lasting security for Europe.

4. European security must be understood in the context of the collective security of all nations. It implies the cessation of the export of European problems and tensions to other parts of the world as this would threaten the security of other countries. It shall include the control of the trade in arms and in strategic materials, so as not to perpetuate an unjust international system which both generates and maintains poverty and insecurity.

D. The churches in Europe should continue to give serious and informed consideration to these questions being assured of the full cooperation of the WCC and its Commission of the Churches on International Affairs. But the churches have an additional responsibility and opportunity : to develop between themselves models of cooperation and understanding.

(Adopted by the WCC Central Committee at its meeting in Utrecht, Netherlands, 13 - 23 August 1972)

MEMORANDUM ON DISARMAMENT
June 1973

"I. ARMAMENT AND SOCIETY

The militarization of the World continues unabated. One Research Institute — Stockholm International Peace Research Institute (SIPRI) — estimates that :

1. Global military expenditure reached 190 billion dollars in 1971.

2. Much of the information about the ongoing strategic arms race comes from reconnaissance satellites. Of the total of 1,268 satellites launched by the United States and the Soviet Union since 1957, 47 per cent have been reconnaissance satellites.

3. Since the signing of the SALT I agreements in May 1972, the number of nuclear warheads deployed on operational strategic weapons has increased from 5,890 to 7,040 in the United States, and from 2,170 to 2,260 in the Soviet Union.

4. Major weapon imports to the Third World have increased by 10 per cent per year since 1950, more than twice as fast as their GNP. Thirty-five Third World countries now possess supersonic or trans-sonic fighter aircraft. Estimates like these lead us to ask the question : What reasons compel the different systems and states to increase their armament to such a tremendous extent ?

At the outset the distinction must be made between arming for self-defence and arming beyond such requirements.

Armament above the requirements of self-defence can be geared towards external aggression or the maintenance of domination over other peoples, or towards the internal purpose of keeping a ruling minority in power. Such armament is frequently related to the denial of freedom and justice not only within nations but also worldwide.

In all parts of the world, the fear of neighbouring states frequently stimulates the arms race and tends to give an exaggerated value to consideration of national interests. Armament policy may become the expression of a nation's fascination with the material means of power which negates the deepest sense of life and the true values of civilization.

In highly industrialized societies, militarism has resulted in a combination of political, industrial, scientific and cultural forces which has developed a dynamic influence pervading the whole society.

As a result there is always the danger that special or even broad sectors of the society will resist disarmament measures for mainly economic reasons.

The urgent need is for a deep change of social values. The mortal danger of continued armament in itself requires this change. However, the adverse effects of arms' manufacture upon the environment and the wasteful use of scarce natural resources give further impetus to the need for change.

A beginning in the achievement of greater freedom and justice for the peoples of the world can result from the rechannelling of resources now committed to armament. These resources should be directed both towards neglected communities in the developed countries and towards developing nations primarily with a view to contributing to their self-reliance.

II. DISARMAMENT AND CHANGE

The efforts aiming at reaching a general and controlled disarmament have to be actively pursued, since without such disarmament there can be no durable peace in the future. However, these efforts should not lead to blocking the necessary evolutions in the life of the people. It would be inadmissible, in particular, that, under the guise of disarmament, the dependence of the poor on the powerful should be forever maintained, and that those who have the terrible stocks of arms — even if they would limit the possession and use thereof — should continue to impose upon those who do not have them, their social, economic, political and cultural systems, their revolutions and counter-revolutions.

The paradox of the present situation is that, the longer the liberation of peoples deprived of their freedom is denied, the more unrealistic it becomes to deny their right to resort to arms. Although we cannot ignore the tradition of pacifism and the voices of those who warn of the dangers of recourse to violence, it is important to recognize that the armed violence of the oppressed is often a natural response to the structural violence of which they are victims. No proper analysis of "terrorism" can ignore this factor.

The dilemma for Christians faced with such situations arises from concern for human dignity on the one hand and a desire for disarmament on the other. Only decisive and genuine change in the field of social justice and international relations can break the evil and escalating spiral of violence and counter-violence.

III. CONCRETE STEPS TOWARDS DISARMAMENT

1. The churches have a special responsibility to help develop public opinion, so that each measure of arms control and disarmament is seen as a useful but limited step towards a world in which armed force would not be used except under strict international control.

   In particular the churches should be encouraged to press for support for the forthcoming World Conference on Disarmament.

2. The will to disarm hinges in large part on the ready availability of reliable alternatives to military power in the pursuit of legitimate claims. The UN should give, and be enabled by the member states to give, high priority to a persistent search for generally acceptable and effective machinery for the peaceful change of unjust relations, the peaceful settlement of international disputes, as well as the maintenance of order in the process. A similar search should be pursued at the regional level. The temptations of unilateral military power must increasingly be curbed by the development of genuine collective security.

3. We welcome the positive efforts in the field of limitations of arms and international security which have taken place during the recent period, both within the framework of UN and bilateral relations between USA and USSR. Negotiations for an effective Comprehensive Nuclear Test Ban, the logical supplement to the SALT agreement, must be pursued. The obstacles to agreement on a complete system of verification should not be allowed to block such a treaty. Meanwhile, a moratorium on all testing, including the testing of new categories of nuclear weapons, should be worked out in which all nuclear powers, including China and France, should be urged to participate. An immediate consideration is the protection of populations from the effects of testing nuclear devices.

4. Attention should be drawn to the potential release of resources for peaceful uses of particular significance in view of the world energy shortage.

5. The ratification of the Non-Proliferation Treaty, particularly by those states who are on the threshold of nuclear arms possession, should be urged and supported.

6. The signing of the 1972 Biological Weapons Treaty is to be welcomed; but the most urgent plea must be made for progress in agreement to ban the production, possession or use of chemical means of warfare. In the interim, states should be urged to observe strictly the Geneva Protocol 1925.

7. In recent years the arms trade has increased alarmingly; the greater the quantity and the more sophisticated the quality of military weapons, the greater the danger to peace. With progress in disarmament, a system should be developed to ensure that the production, sale, transfer, acquisition, and possession of arms should be registered and reported by each nation to the UN.

8. Rules of international humanitarian law and warfare established over a century are no longer adequate to safeguard the victims of modern warfare, especially the civilian population, nor are they relevant to situations of guerilla warfare.

The International Red Cross has proposed new rules and measures of implementation of the Geneva Conventions, 1948, to be discussed by a Diplomatic Conference in 1974.

It is important that the WCC and its member churches should study these questions and support measures concerning the prohibition of the production and use of anti-personnel weapons, the elimination of starvation as a weapon of war, the use of environmental warfare and indiscriminate weapons, the prohibition of torture of both combatants and non-combatants and restriction on military reprisals.

IV. AN APPEAL

1. While the struggle for disarmament needs the support of all peoples and all men of goodwill, we make a special appeal to the member churches, and indeed to all Christians, to deepen their concern and to take a more active part in this great struggle. Christians should never weary in efforts to come

closer to the time proclaimed by the prophet Isaiah, when "nation shall not lift up sword against nation, neither shall they learn war any more" (Isa. 2:4). We and all mankind have been warned by the fore-knowledge that the bombs, if allowed to pile up, will sometime go off, producing tragedy and suffering on a scale as yet unknown. Therefore both faith and knowledge call us to do what we can do for world disarmament.

2. One contribution Christians have to make is to help combat the apathy and hopelessness which tend to undermine the struggle for genuine world disarmament. We can be sure that mankind is not fated to lose this essential cause if the will to succeed can be made strong enough. Our Lord is the Prince of Peace. In obedience to Him, Christians are committed to the ministry of reconciliation (II Cor. 5:18). And this calls for uniting our efforts to achieve universal and full disarmament. The lessons of history teach us not to delude ourselves with hopes of easy success. Yet we can be strong in heart and of good courage, for we are called to peace by our Lord, and our Lord is the God of Hope (Rom. 15:13).

3. Another contribution Christians should make is to help their societies and international society become more sensitive to the claims of justice and liberation for the disadvantaged, the exploited, the powerless. The struggle for justice and freedom is essential to the cause of disarmament, since a true peace requires both justice and liberty.

4. Finally, Christians knowing that God continues to hold the world in His hands, should be in the forefront of those supporting the willingness of their governments to take certain reasonable risks for peace and a disarmed world. The vicious circle of distrust, which inspires the fatal spiral of the arms race, cannot be broken until leaders and nations are prepared to make a new venture of confidence. Since the failure to accept justified risks means certain disaster, the courage essential to successful step-by-step disarmament is really not great. Christians, followers of one who rules the whole world, must serve as champions of a new birth of trust among men and nations.

(Memorandum of the CCIA Executive Committee, meeting in Visegrad, Hungary, 14 - 19 June 1973)

THE ECONOMIC THREAT TO PEACE
August 1974

1. The world faces a real crisis which threatens the very future of international society. "Crisis" is a word that has been too much used to dramatize emergency situations — the "oil crisis", the "financial crisis" — but its true and original meaning is both "burning point in history" and "judgement".

At this present time there has been a convergence of so many interrelated acute emergencies that to use the description "crisis" in its true meaning is no exaggeration.

2. The human race lives on a small planet with large but finite resources. It has lived here for a long time, but all at once it has been alerted to the serious danger of pollution of the environment, of a world food shortage and possible famine, of the consequences of a rapidly increasing world population, of the possible exhaustion or insufficiency of many natural resources, and of the threat posed by the proliferation of more deadly weapons of war. All these are in the context of the increasing political tensions caused by the widening gap between the wealth of the rich nations and the poverty of the poor. It is no accident that these tremendous problems have become inescapably evident at the same moment of time.

3. Using the religious interpretation of crisis — which is a realistic interpretation — these agonizing situations are an expression of judgement. Human beings are stewards in the world which God created; a world therefore in which harmony and peace are possible only in obedience to his will in the relationship between individuals, groups, and nations, and between mankind and the world of nature. The stewards have been disobedient. The manysided crisis is the consequence.

4. Such language may sound remote and abstract. The secular interpretation — which is often theological in meaning if not in language — is that through indifference, greed, envy, fear, love of power, and short-sighted stupidity, men have created, or allowed to develop, a demonstrably unjust economic order. For too many the result is pain, misery and oppression. In a world of immense scientific knowledge and technical skill, millions are underfed, underprivileged,

exploited, and denied human dignity, while resources and skill are lavished on the extravagant and lethal accumulation of weapons of destruction.

5. Every generation in human history has been confronted by injustice in the systems regulating the economic, social and political relationships of individuals. Today we face an unjust international system regulating the economic relationships of nations and peoples. This system is dominated by a minority composed of highly developed countries who control the world market and determine the allocation of world resources in accordance with their own order of priorities. But this system has been challenged by a majority of nations in the world. The awareness of injustice, and the demand for strategies for change, have been clearly articulated in the proceedings of the Sixth Special Session of the General Assembly of the United Nations.

6. The Session, convened to study the problems of raw materials and development, probed deeply into causes and remedies. The Assembly resolved :

"We, the members of the United Nations, having convened in a special session of the General Assembly for the first time to study the problems of raw materials and development, devoted to the consideration of the most important economic problems facing the world community, bearing in mind the spirit, purposes and principles of the Charter of the United Nations to promote the economic advancement and social progress of all peoples, solemnly proclaim our united determination to work urgently for

THE ESTABLISHMENT OF A NEW INTERNATIONAL ECONOMIC ORDER

based on equity, sovereign equality, interdependence, common interest and co-operation among all States, irrespective of their economic and social systems, which shall correct inequalities and redress existing injustices, make it possible to eliminate the widening gap between the developed and the developing countries, and ensure steadily accelerating economic and social development in peace and justice for present and future generations."

7. The Executive Committee of the CCIA draws the special attention of the Churches to this "Declaration" because there is a temptation, when confronted by such immense and apparently insoluble problems, to relapse into pessimistic or fatalistic resignation. To revert to the language of theology, judgement is a warning that is also a call to repentance. In secular language, but saying the same thing, the realization that mankind is nearing the end of a road that leads to disaster is a challenge to find a better road. We believe that the "Declaration"

indicates the way, though we cannot fully endorse the total approval of "steadily accelerating economic growth".

The need of the developing nations is evident, and their steadily accelerating development must be encouraged — with the warning, of which they are well aware, that "development" must be understood as progress towards a just and humanly satisfying social system, appropriate to the needs and aspirations of each developing country, and not crudely as growth only in gross national product. But it is also evident that some of the factors in the present crisis, e.g. the pollution of the environment, the wasteful use of natural resources, have followed from the activities of developed, highly industrialized nations. Overdevelopment should not be approved. On the contrary, wherever waste of food, energy, and natural resources occurs as a consequence of over-consumption, it should be condemned.

8.   The new way will be long and not easy. Those who survey it are not so deluded as to think that it will lead to a perfect ideal society. But it is better than the present way. The "Declaration" and the UN Programme of Action for the establishment of a new international economic order list some practical steps forward. They include, for example :

a) Sovereign equality of States, self-determination of all peoples, inadmissibility of the acquisition of territories by force, territorial integrity and non-interference in the internal affairs of other States.

b) The broadest cooperation of all the States members of the international community, based on equity, whereby the prevailing disparities in the world may be banished, and prosperity for all.

c) Full and effective participation on the basis of equality of all countries in the solving of world economic problems in the common interest of all countries, bearing in mind the necessity to ensure the accelerated development of all the developing countries, while devoting particular attention to the adoption of special measures in favour of the least developed, land-locked and island developing countries as well as those developing countries most seriously affected by economic crisis and natural calamities, without losing sight of the interests of other developing countries.

d) The right to every country to adopt the economic and social system that it deems to be the most appropriate for its own development and not to be subjected to discrimination of any kind as a result.

e) Full permanent sovereignty of every State over its natural resources and all economic activities. In order to safeguard these resources, each State is entitled to exercise effective control over them and their exploitation with means suitable to its own situation, including the right to nationalization or transfer of ownership to its nationals, this right being an expression of the full permanent sovereignty of the State. No State may be subjected to economic, political or any other type of coercion to prevent the free and full exercise of this inalienable right.

f) The right of all States, territories and peoples under foreign occupation, alien and colonial domination or apartheid to restitution and full compensation for the exploitation and depletion of, and damages to, the natural resources and all other resources of those States, territories and peoples.

g) Regulation and supervision of the activities of transnational corporations by taking measures in the interest of the national economies of the countries where such transnational corporations operate on the basis of the full sovereignty of those countries.

h) The right of the developing countries and the peoples of territories under colonial and racial domination and foreign occupation to achieve their liberation and to regain effective control over their natural resources and economic activities.

i) The extending of assistance to developing countries, peoples and territories which are under colonial and alien domination, foreign occupation, racial discrimination or apartheid or are subjected to economic, political or any other type of coercive measures to obtain from them the subordination of the exercise of their sovereign rights and to secure from them advantages of any kind, and to neo-colonialism in all its forms, and which have established or are endeavouring to establish effective control over their natural resources and economic activities that have been or are still under foreign control.

j) Just and equitable relationship between the prices of raw materials, primary products, manufactured and semi-manufactured goods exported by developing countries and the prices of raw materials, primary commodities manufactures, capital goods and equipment imported by them with the aim of bringing about sustained improvement in their unsatisfactory terms of trade and the expansion of the world economy.

k) Extension of active assistance to developing countries by the whole international community, free of any political or military conditions.

74

9. These are illustrative examples of steps that could be taken, of modifications that could lead to a transformation of existing economic relations. The goal is an international society in which there are no longer "developed" and "developing" nations, but one in which all are equal, cooperative, interdependent partners. The transformation demanded goes beyond modification of existing international economic structures, which perpetuate underdevelopment and intensify the threat of peace, to the establishment of a new, just, alternative system. But the decisions which could initiate this process are political. The "Declaration" emphasizes, for example, both the sovereign equality of States and their cooperation; a sharing by equals of opportunities and responsibilities. In this connection CCIA would underline the danger of a self-regarding "economic nationalism" of the type exemplified by the reaction of many developed nations to the current "energy crisis". The nationalism commended by the Special Session is a genuine national sovereignty, having authority to protect the nation from economic domination or manipulation by external states or multinational corporations. But such nationalism is not a sufficient end in itself. The next stage is voluntary cooperation as an expression of genuine interdependence; a relationship which ensures the participation of equal partners.

10. The points noted relate to action between nations, which is the proper field of concern of CCIA. We recognize that for many people the suffering most acutely felt is caused by injustice, oppression, discrimination, and inequality within the nation, and that the issues of economic and social justice between nations and within nations are intimately related.

11. In the final analysis these complex and technical questions are concerned with the quality of life for people; with human dignity and human opportunity. The solutions demand the specialized skills of economists and politicians. But there will be no urgency to find the solutions if the will is lacking. We therefore appeal to the member Churches of the WCC, and to all people of goodwill, to make widely known the problems and the challenges, and to urge on their governments' support of initiatives so to change the existing international economic structures that priority is given to the most deprived. If concern for the welfare of the poor and the oppressed is not enough — though it should be — perhaps the warning given by our time of crisis that we are on the road to catastrophe will stir statesmen and people to action.

(Statement by CCIA Executive Committee presented to the WCC Central Committee at its meeting in Berlin (West), 11 - 18 August 1974)

MEMORANDUM ON DISARMAMENT
June 1975

"One hard fact must be stated bluntly : the arms race goes on. Thirty years after the delivery of the first two atomic bombs, there has been an enormous increase in the weapons of total destruction. According to the reliable calculations of the Stockholm International Peace Research Institute (SIPRI), world expenditure on arms in 1974 totalled more than 210,000 million dollars, a sum roughly equal to the entire income of the poorer half of the human race.

Twenty years ago, the combined military expenditure of the US, the USSR, Britain and France amounted to 82 per cent of the world total : last year, this percentage fell to about 70. This is not a hopeful reduction : it merely means that there has been a rapid expansion in the level of armaments in other countries. What was once the prerogative of major powers has now spread, like an infection, throughout the rest of the world.

WRONG PRIORITIES

Such expenditure on weapons of destruction means a distortion, on an immense scale, of what most people, certainly all Christians, would regard as the true priorities in national budgeting. Food, health, social services, education — these are vital to the welfare of a nation. Yet all are constantly under attack because of the overriding priority by governments to what they call "defence".

WHY DO THEY DO IT ?

It may be asked what reasons motivate those who produce and sell armaments, whether they are governments or private industry acting with the approval of governments, and those nations which buy such goods.

The sellers' most obvious incentive is simply that in many cases arms are an extremely profitable business. There are indications that certain defence budgets are being deliberately expanded to boost the economy. Political and strategic considerations also prompt some nations to provide arms, thus ensuring a continued sphere of influence and a possible site for military bases.

Moreover, a market for such exports exists, or can be stimulated; if there were no market, the arms would not be manufactured on the present scale. It is also true that scientists and engineers want to use their talents to achieve technological breakthroughs in the work in which they are expert. There should be an ongoing dialogue between churches and scientists, and we should demand of governments that the cost of scientific research for military purposes should be clearly identified. Indeed, the entire defence budget of the nations should be published in a standard form which would make it possible for all peoples to know the size of the expenditure to which they were forced to contribute, so that they could demand reductions in this burden.

The buyers' motives are varied. Sometimes, no doubt, a developing country genuinely believes it necessary to strengthen its defences against a powerful and hostile neighbour. Sometimes, it may be a question of prestige, of "keeping up with the Joneses". Governments of various kinds, democratic and authoritarian, buy arms to protect themselves against external or internal threats; or simply to improve their own export trade.

A CODE FOR CONTROL ?

It is possible that the control of this lethal trade should be undertaken at the point of production rather than at the point of sale : what is certain is that it cannot continue uncontrolled without great dangers to peace and to the world's economic balance. The present volume of arms sales seems to be unrelated to any responsible and coherent international policy at all. The attention of governments should be called to the following points :

(1) the manufacture of arms occupies an excessive proportion of the economy of certain industrial nations, which are under strong pressure from a military-industrial complex.

(2) the uncontrolled sale of arms to countries situated in areas where there is a threat of war can intensify this danger.

(3) the purchases of modern arms places too heavy a load on the economies of many countries and delays their development.

(4) the seller of arms to countries in which the people suffer oppression shares in the guilt of the oppressors.

The Churches should press for an ethical code of restrictive criteria for the arms trade, bearing in mind the experience acquired by means of legislation by such governments as those of Sweden and Switzerland, which have already enacted such codes.

Different types of control are needed for two main categories of weapons : nuclear weapons, with their "Doomsday" potential, which no one dares to use; and "conventional" weapons, with which the trade in arms is mostly concerned. The experience of Vietnam and other "small" wars has illustrated the urgent necessity of agreement to outlaw many weapons of indiscriminate destruction, however nominally conventional, such as napalm, and many other devices, such as defoliants, which are tried out in Vietnam. Hundreds of thousands of innocent people have been killed in this way. There are already too many of these so-called conventional weapons : we call for an absolute ban on the production and use of new and even more sophisticated means of destruction.

THE HOPES THAT FAILED

Over the years, many attempts have been made to check the arms race : the most important of them were the test-ban treaty and the non-proliferation treaty. They have failed, or been only partially successful, because there were loopholes through which the nations could escape from their obligations, or because there was no real will to make agreements work. The non-proliferation treaty, for instance, was resented by some nations other than the original signatories because it seemed to them discriminatory.

In international affairs, mutual understanding and a readiness to cooperate must replace confrontation. We hope that the European Security Conference will succeed in bringing about a general agreement on conditions for security in Europe. However, the powers concerned seem unable to make progress towards a mutual and balanced reduction of forces; it is essential that negotiations for such a reduction should be successsful. We also hope that the SALT talks will lead to a real disarmament agreement.

A WARNING UNHEEDED

There is an increasing danger in the proliferation of military bases. One zone which should have been free from conflict and confrontation is the Indian Ocean. Two years ago, meeting at Visegrad, we stressed the dangers attending "the escalation and expansion of the military presence in the Ocean" of certain powers and called on the member churches of the WCC to urge those powers "to begin consultation with a view to demilitarising the Indian Ocean".

Like the UN General Assembly resolution, which it was designed to support, our warning was ignored. Instead, there is a massive build-up of bases throughout the area.

It may now be too late to demilitarise the Indian Ocean, but we should not abandon our efforts to do so; and we note that voices for peace in the Ocean are raised in various political quarters.

Not far from the Indian Ocean is another potentially explosive area, South Africa; and we note with regret that even some of those nations which condemn the evil of apartheid do not hesitate to profit by the sale of arms to South Africa — an action which must trouble consciences of Christians in the countries concerned. The US, Britain and France have defied the arms embargo imposed by the UN Security Council; and it has now been reported — and not denied — that South Africa has bought advanced military communications material from some of these countries.

Churches, individual Christians and the general public in all countries involved should question their governments about this matter.

A CALL TO CHRISTIANS

What can be done ? What, in particular, should Christians do in the present crisis ?

We believe that there is much to be said for consultation on a regional basis, sponsored by the churches, where possible in collaboration with people of good will, including those of other faiths, in which they can be involved with those who make national and international policy.

Some urge the calling of a World Disarmament Conference. Member churches of the WCC, and individual Christians everywhere, can help to create the climate of opinion in which, at last, such a conference might have some hope of success. In such a climate, the stereotypes of old "enemies" can be discarded.

Peace — by which we mean always peace with justice — is not dependent only on arms control or disarmament : it depends both on the prevention of war and on mutual respect between nations for each others' vital interests. "Détente" should be a continuing exercise in political and diplomatic negotiation, in which the Super-Powers must be involved, since the heaviest responsibility for avoiding conflict is theirs.

To such ends all Christians should work, think and pray."

(Adopted by the CCIA Executive Committee at its meeting in Geneva, Switzerland, 16 - 20 June 1975)

THE FIFTH ASSEMBLY PERIOD

THE WORLD ARMAMENTS SITUATION
December 1975

"1.   Three decades after World War II, humankind is again armed to levels unequalled in history. According to reliable calculations (from Stockholm International Peace Research Institute) world expenditure on arms in 1974 totalled more than 220 billion US dollars. Thus, actual world military spending is about equal to the national income of more than a billion people in the developing countries of South Asia, the Far East, and Africa. The bulk of this expenditure — 82 per cent in 1973 — is shared by NATO and Warsaw Pact nations. China accounts for about 5 per cent. In addition to the monetary expenditures, the figures represent a tremendous waste of the world's natural resources.

2.   The increased expenditure on arms is surpassed only by advances in military technology. Modern nuclear warheads have an explosive power of several millions of tons of TNT. Of equal importance are the improvements in speed and accuracy of delivery vehicles of nuclear weapons. In addition to the strategic nuclear weapons designed for intercontinental exchanges, the superpowers have developed a large arsenal of tactical nuclear weapons, thus reducing the potential importance of a threshold between conventional and nuclear warfare.

3.   The cancerous growth of military research and development in the post-World War II period reflects the shift in the arms race from competition in quantity to a race for "quality" in both conventional and nuclear weapons. In the conventional field, out of the testing grounds of Indochina and the Middle East has come a "quiet revolution" in modern warfare, new generations of planes, helicopters, gunships, and bombs. The modern arsenals include among other things electronic tools, guided projectiles, sensors, and a diverse assortment of anti-personnel fragmentation bombs.

4.   There is an increasing danger in the proliferation of military bases. The presence of foreign military bases represents a threat to the independence and integrity of many nations. In one zone which so far has been relatively free from conflict and confrontation, the Indian Ocean, a massive build-up of bases has lately taken place.

5.   Another alarming development is the increasing militarization of the Third World. The Third World, China excluded, accounts for 7-9 per cent of world military expenditure, nearly three times the level of official foreign development assistance. In general, the military expenditure of developing countries increases relatively faster than the equivalent expenditure of industrialized nations. Most of the Third World weapons come from developed countries. However, some Third World countries have plans for an armament industry of their own. Armament and militarization have in many cases contributed to shifting development priorities, to weaken and stifle economic growth and to check socio-political strength.

6.   The relationship between the world's two main military blocs is based on the idea of mutual deterrence. However, the dynamics of deterrence tends to accelerate rather than to restrain the arms race. Peace and stability, naturally, cannot be attained by a policy based on threats. The calculation in terms of the worst possible case, and the propensity to over-perception, over-reaction, and over-design escalate the arms race.

7.   However, the armament dynamics seem to be rooted not only in external, but also internal forces nowadays. The growing military-industrial-bureaucratic complexes play an important role in speeding up the arms race. In addition, the arms dynamics are propelled by the race in technology, each side trying to maximize its capabilities. Military research and development, as a rule, do not wait for reactions from the other side, but react rather in a continuous process to their own achievements.

8.   In the past 25-30 years, several attempts to reduce the arms race have been made. Multiple UN resolutions calling for disarmament notwithstanding, only bacteriological weapons have been destroyed as a result of disarmament negotiations.

9.   The interest for disarmament has been replaced by a concentration around the notion of arms control, i.e. controlling the advance in armaments. The Antarctic Treaty, the Outer Space Treaty, and the Seabed Treaty, as well as the Partial Test Ban Treaty, could be mentioned in this connection. Most notable is

the five-year-old nuclear Non-Proliferation Treaty to prevent the spreading of nuclear weapons. This Treaty also provides for the control of peaceful use of nuclear energy. Regrettably, several important nations have not signed or ratified the Treaty.

10. The SALT negotiations and agreements between the Soviet Union and the United States represent an effort of the two super-powers to accommodate each other in questions of quantities in lines of upward parity. The negotiations may have contributed to a better political atmosphere between the two countries, but have also channelled the strategic arms race primarily in the direction of improved qualities.

11. Although there has been no direct military confrontation between the super-powers, since World War II some hundred wars have been fought, causing the deaths of more than ten million people in about sixty countries. There are limits to how far the great powers, in accordance with the Helsinki Declaration, can develop relationships of partnership and cooperation, under conditions where weapons of massive destruction could be used."

AN APPEAL TO THE CHURCHES

1. The above analysis is recommended to the churches for study.

2. Christians must resist the temptation to resign themselves to a false sense of impotence or security. The churches should emphasize their readiness to live without the protection of armaments, and take a significant initiative in pressing for effective disarmament. Churches, individual Christians, and members of the public in all countries should press their governments to ensure national security without resorting to the use of weapons of mass destruction.

3. We call upon the new Central Committee to initiate steps to organize a consultation on disarmament. This consultation should investigate and compare available material on the factors producing the present arms race and the technological, economic, environmental, and military implications. The consultation should aim at proposing a strategy, at national and international levels, to prevent further increased military expenditure. This strategy should include, among others, the following points :

(a) Prepare educational programmes for the use of the churches.

(b) Stimulate public discussion on the matter.

(c) Study the questions of war and peace in a theological perspective.

(d) Share the experience of the historic Peace Churches.

(e) Investigate the involvement of the churches in arms production and trade.

(f) Call for a World Disarmament Conference under UN auspices.

(g) Stress the need for retraining and re-employment of those who now make their living through the arms production industry.

4. The Central Committee should ensure that disarmament is a major concern of the WCC.

5. We appeal to all Christians to think, work, and pray for a disarmed world.

(Statement by the WCC V. Assembly, Nairobi, Kenya, 23 November - 10 December 1975)

ADDRESS OF Dr. PHILIP POTTER, GENERAL SECRETARY OF THE WORLD COUNCIL OF CHURCHES, TO THE UNITED NATIONS FIRST SPECIAL SESSION ON DISARMAMENT

June 1978

12 June 1978

"Mr. Chairman, Distinguished Delegates :

It is a great privilege for me, on behalf of the World Council of Chuches, to address you. The World Council of Churches is a fellowship of 293 Orthodox and Protestant churches in over 100 countries. They comprise hundreds of millions of believers who live in East and West and North and South who find themselves caught up in all the ideological, political, economic, social, racial and cultural conflicts of our time. One of the main functions of the Council is "to express the common concern of the churches in the service of human need, the breaking down of barriers between people, and the promotion of one human family in justice and peace".

The barriers caused by war and armaments race have been a major pre-occupation of the Council from its inception thirty years ago. The First Assembly of the Council in 1948 declared :

> "The Churches must also attack the causes of war by promoting peaceful change and the pursuit of justice. They must stand for the maintenance of good faith and the honouring of the pledged word, resist the pretensions of imperialist power, promote the multilateral reduction of armaments, and combat indifference and despair in the face of the futility of war; they must point Christians to that spiritual resistance which grows from settled convictions widely held, themselves a powerful deterrent to war. A moral vacuum inevitably invites an aggressor."

Through its Commission of the Churches on International Affairs, which has consultative status with various UN bodies, the Council has indefatigably represented the churches in the concern for disarmament and has constantly sought to rouse the conscience of Christians to throw their weight with people of goodwill and governments in working for peace and justice.

Christians, expert in the field of disarmament, have been mobilized and valuable contributions have been made. The Fifth Assembly, at Nairobi, of the World Council of Churches in 1975 called for studies in depth on militarism and disarmament. Since then consultations have been held and their findings have been shared with delegates at this Special Session of the UN. I may also mention that on Sunday, May 21, on the eve of your special session, churches throughout the world remembered you in their prayers to the God of Peace.

Qualitatively new elements

As Christians have grappled with the issues of disarmament, they have been painfully aware of the qualitatively new elements in the situation during this Disarmament Decade. The world has in fact become more insecure in these years.

First, considerably more material and human resources are being concentrated on the production of armaments. Science and technology, the preserve of an intellectual elite in both rich and poor countries, are now deployed by the alliance of those involved in the business, bureaucratic, political and military sectors to produce new and ever more lethal weapons at a prodigious rate. This is often done secretly in the corridors of power and beyond social control. Moreover, the dramatic increase in the number, variety, destructive power and cost of these armaments frustrates disarmament negotiations more than ever before because they change the nature of the problems which have to be faced.

Secondly, arms production and sale have become part of the national economic policy of the rich developed world, and therefore dictates political and foreign policies. Weapons-producing national and transnational corporations have exacerbated this trend. This has meant a marked increase in the flow of arms to the poorer, developing countries which in the process become dependent clients of the powerful states and potentially widen the scope of armed conflict. For example, it is known that of the over 130 armed conflicts which have taken place since World War II nearly all have been in the Third World, and the powerful nations of the rich world have been involved in those conflicts. Disarmament has therefore become a truly global concern. Hence the necessity and timeliness of this Special Session of the UN.

Thirdly, national security should be the instrument for promoting the social, economic and political rights of all peoples within the nation state, however in a growing number of countries, it has become a doctrine which is used to justify military take-overs, the suppression of civilian political institutions and the violation of basic human rights. In the defence of "law and order", sinister instruments of torture, police and prison hardware, and sophisticated means of intelligence gathering have been produced and sold to minority and un-democratic regimes especially in the Third World. We are witnessing the increasing militarization of many of our societies and the tendency to extend a country's military, ideological and economic frontiers far beyond its national borders, all of which leads to greater insecurity. Moreover, in the name of national security, the mass media and educational institutions are frequently misused to foster a psychosis of fear and mistrust and to prevent any other way of looking at the resolution of conflicts than in military terms.

Fourthly, overshadowing all these dangerous tendencies is the development of new generations of even more destructive conventional and nuclear weapons. There is a growing danger of nuclear proliferation and of lowering the nuclear threshold. The deployment of weapons through missiles, submarines and long-range bombers has enabled striking capability to reach all nations and peoples. Furthermore, the super-powers are now seeking to create an atmosphere in which "first strike" capability will sooner or later be turned to reality, and thus hasten the annihilation of the human race.

The need for new perspectives

In face of this catalogue of accelerated insecutity, the churches cannot remain spectators and inactive. On the basis of their faith in a God who in Jesus Christ wills that we should have life and have it in all its fullness, and in his purpose that the earth should be replenished and used for the well-being of all, Christians are called to bring new perspectives to bear on the issues of militarism and the arms race. I only have time to mention in a general way a few of these perspectives.

1. Disarmament is an integral part of the struggle for a just, participatory and sustainable society. The threat to peace of the arms race is inextricably related to the other prevailing threats to human survival — poverty, hunger, racial, political and economic oppression, the suppression of human rights, the despoiling of the environment and the wanton wastage of the resources of the earth. Disarmament and the search for a New International Economic Order are inseparable efforts towards peace with justice. Thus disarmament is not a technical, but a political and moral concern. A global approach to disarmament is needed. Everything which is done to achieve a more just economic order, to share material and human resources in an equitably way, and to facilitate the participation of all in the life of society is bound to contribute to eliminating the arms race and the militarization of society.

2. We must challenge the idol of a distorted concept of national security which is directed to encouraging fear and mistrust resulting in greater insecurity. The only security worthy of its name lies in enabling people to participate fully in the life of their nation and to establish relations of trust between peoples of different nations. It is only when there is a real dialogue — a sharing life with life in mutual trust and respect — that there can be true security.

3. Christians are pledged to work for creating those structures and mechanisms by which disarmament can be sought boldly and imaginatively. The UN is the most effective forum for enabling the nations to work for that international security which will ensure national security, for the rule of law through covenants freely entered into and maintained by mutually agreed peaceful methods. Therefore, it is imperative that the role of the UN be extended and strengthened in the search for disarmament and for a New International Economic Order. One of the tragedies of our time is the way in which member states and the mass media which support them ignore and denigrate the work of the UN. The World Council of Churches and its member churches stand pledged, as they always have done, to support the UN in all its efforts to promote peace and justice in our troubled, tortured world.

4. Disarmament is not the affair of statesmen and experts only, but of every man and woman of every nation. We are dealing here with the issues of life and death for humankind. They are not technical, but human and therefore political issues. This means that every effort must be made to dispel the ignorance, complacency and fear which prevail. Political decisions can only be made when people are fully aware of the facts and are enabled to discern the options before them. This is a necessary function which non-governmental organizations can perform. The churches have a very distinctive role to play because they have the criterion of faith in the God of hope whose purpose is that all should be responsible for each other in justice and peace. Therefore they will continue to rouse the conscience of people and encourage them to demonstrate by attitude, word and act that peace and justice are not ideals to be cherished but realities to be achieved. The arms race is the decision and creation of human beings. Disarmament must also be willed and won by human beings.

The churches do not approach their task with any self-righteousness or naivete. They are well aware that throughout their history they have often been so allied to the forces of disorder and oppression that they have promoted or connived in wars and in the war psychosis. They know that their own divisions are symptoms and signs of the divisions in our world. To be instruments of reconciliation they are in fact endeavouring to become reconciled to each other.

It is in humility and hope that the churches participate in the efforts towards disarmament and a just society. They do so with the vision of the prophet, whose words are engraved on the Isaiah Wall just across the street from this building :

"They shall beat their swords into plowshares
 and their spears into pruning-hooks :
Nation shall not lift sword against nation,
 neither shall they learn war any more."

It is this vision of the conversion of the tools of death into the tools of life which inspires and activates the churches today. Our prayer is that this vision will inspire you in your deliberations and your peoples in the pursuit of peace and justice."

THE PROGRAMME ON MILITARISM AND ARMAMENTS RACE

January 1979

"ii. PART I – NEW PERSPECTIVES

5. The two major meetings held recently — the Consultation on Militarism and the Conference on Disarmament — have given new perspectives on the issues to the ecumenical movement. They have identified the qualitatively new elements in militarism and armaments race and have underlined the close inter-relation between the two. The armaments race is intimately interlinked to issues of development, justice and human rights. It is only natural therefore that the WCC's programme emphasis on a just participatory and sustainable society has provided the overall framework and rationale for the programme on militarism and armaments race.

MILITARISM — QUALITATIVELY NEW ELEMENTS

6. The contemporary phenomenon of militarism has qualitatively new elements. The nature of contemporary militarism differs from the previous manifestations of militarism mainly in its current global reach, the controlling position of the super-powers, the dominance-dependence relationship between the great powers and the developing nations, the socio-economic predicament of most of the Third World countries and the impact of the technological revolution. *Militarization* should be understood as the process whereby military values, ideology and patterns of behaviour achieve a dominating influence of the political, social, economic and external affairs of the state and as a consequence the structural, ideological and behavioural patterns of both the society and the government are "militarized". *Militarism* should be seen as one of the more perturbing results of this process. It must be noted that militarism is multi-dimensional and varied with different manifestations in various circumstances, dependent on historical background, national traditions, class structures, social conditions, economic strength, etc.

Today the problems of militarism have become more serious than ever. This is due to a number of factors, including advances in technology, which have greatly enhanced the effectiveness and power of military and police forces; a growing integration of military and civilian sectors; a widespread promotion of psychological insecurity leading people to seek refuge in the further acquisition of arms; and the increasing interdependence between the various dimensions and manifestations of militarism in different parts of the world.

EXTERNAL FACTORS THAT PROMOTE MILITARISM

7. The competition of the two super-powers to gain quantitative and techno-logical arms superiority is a major factor in the promotion of militarism. The increasing coordination of policy, standardization, military equipment and co-production schemes within the two major alliances tend to strengthen each of them internally and facilitate intervention in the domestic affairs of members as well as opponents of the particular alliance. Another factor which promotes militarism is the creation and maintenance of spheres of influence by many major developed nations and some Third World countries. This has led the major blocs, and in particular the super-powers to confront one another by proxy in local and international conflicts far from their own borders. These locals conflicts are very often testing grounds for new generations of weapons from arms producing countries and new techniques of warfare and internal re-pression. The steep increase in the flow of armaments to the developing countries particularly fuelled by economic and political competition between the arms producing nations, constitutes a form of intervention, creates and maintains dominance-dependence relationship and often encourages internal repression in the recipient countries. Often the support of repressive regimes is motivated by economic concerns, particularly the protection and advancement of the trans-national corporations. For this to happen efforts are promoted to ensure conditions of "law and order", a task generally entrusted to the military and police apparatus of the underdeveloped country, most often closely allied with the national elites.

INTERNAL FACTORS THAT PROMOTE MILITARISM

8. One of the most important contributing factors internally to militarism is the prevalence of new doctrines of national security. While there is legitimacy for national security there is an increasing tendency for new doctrines of national security which encompass all spheres of national activity. These doctrines have led to militarization of a large number of countries. The military-industrial-

technological complex represents a powerful political force in the determination of national and foreign policies of industrialized nations. Unjust class and racial structures tend to promote militarism and are maintained by militarism. There are ideological factors which contribute towards militarization. Political, economic and social factors are often made use of to promote militarization. It should be a matter of particular concern to the churches that religious factors contribute in important ways to the development of militarism.

SOCIAL CONSEQUENCES OF MILITARISM

9. The most serious social consequence of militarism is that of repression and authoritarian control of society. So-called "emergency" measures become normalized in the name of protecting people against threats from within and without but in effect they are mostly intended to protect the power and interests of the ruling groups. The trend towards suppression of dissent and the general erosion of civil liberties which characterize militarization is also evident, if less openly brutal, in several of the industrialized countries. Another consequence of militarism is the distortion of social and economic priorities. This involves not only a diversion of resources but the creation of economic systems based on wrong concepts of development. While the immediate effects may be more easily perceivable in the developing countries this is a definite trend in industrialized nations also. The results are "industrial militarism" in developing nations. Militarism has impact on values, norms and ideas and is increasingly reflected in the educational system in many countries. Many educational systems glorify combat and use of force, exalt patriotism and national chauvinism and military values of hierarchisation and strict conformity.

THE LINKAGES

10. The dynamics of militarism and that of armaments race are closely interrelated. No military regime can survive long without the supply of arms and no military establishment can flourish in an environment without arms. And vice versa the threat system established by the arms race and the violence in international relations serve to promote the interests of the military and to encourage militaristic tendencies. Factors like arms trade and transfer, research and development, military technology, ideologies, national and international political instability, exploitative economic systems, etc. provide the linkages between militarism dynamics and armaments dynamics.

TOWARDS INCREASING INSECURITY

11. In today's world the expansion of armed forces has gone far beyond the reasonable requirements of security. This is due to a number of factors among which the following may be mentioned :

- the influence of the military whose function as the defenders of the nation and symbol of its sovereignty may give them a priviliged role in society and a decisive voice in policy.

- other sectors of society, notably the managers, workers and in some instances shareholders in armaments industries may be influential in expanding a country's military effort.

- these military and other interests are supported by fear which may begin as a reasonable anxiety about the intentions of a potential enemy but can be played upon so that it no longer has any rational basis.

QUALITATIVELY NEW ELEMENTS

12. The arms race today is no longer a competition in quantities only, but predominantly a race in modern technology — in product improvements and sophistication. New weapons appear at a prodigious rate frustrating disarmament negotiations by changing the nature of the problem to be solved. Most of this work is conducted in secrecy beyond social control, and adds an important new element to the military, industrial and bureaucratic interests which favour the continued expansion of armaments. With technology becoming the focal point in armaments, the dynamics of the arms race has changed profoundly. The socio-political and economic motives and driving forces behind the arms race have grown greatly in influence and power. Parallel to the vertical escalation in weapon modernization and destructive capabilities we are witnessing a horizontal proliferation of arms of global dimensions. Armaments have become a status symbol, an indication of rank, power and authority in the international community. They are widely used as instruments of politics and diplomacy.

CONVENTIONAL WEAPONS

13. The cost of procuring conventional weapons and of training and maintaining the men who operate them accounts for more than 80% of current

world military expenditure now amounting to $ 1 billion per day. It must also be borne in mind that conventional weapons have been used — and are still being used — in the numerous armed conflicts which have occured since 1945 and that during that period they have claimed almost as many victims as did the Second World War. There is a dramatic increase in the number, variety and lethal power and cost of the conventional weapons deployed in all parts of the world. An active and expanding trade in conventional weapons has stimulated the arms race in both industrialized and developing countries. The increasing power of modern conventional weapons is blurring the distinctions between conventional and nuclear weapons thus facilitating the transition from conventional to nuclear warfare.

NUCLEAR WEAPONS

14. The nuclear arms race between the USA and the USSR has already produced a sufficient quantity of weapons to enable each side to destroy the other side many times over. The race has now become one for superior quality and if continued will lead to the acquisition of a first-strike capability making full-scale nuclear war a probability. Other recent developments notably the miniaturization of nuclear weapons — the neutron bomb being an example — have increased the likelihood of nuclear war which might also be provoked by accident.

DISARMAMENT AND DEVELOPMENT

15. There is a clear relationship between the armaments race and the socio-economic order. The armaments competition of the super-powers as well as of other nations involved in the arms race and the development of military weapons fosters the present economic order and prevents the principles of a new economic order from being put into practice. The interlocking relationship between the existing world economic order and the military-industrialized-bureaucratic-technological complex hinders the proper utilization of available resources and distorts developmental priorities. Disarmament is therefore essential for the proper utilization of the human and material resources available for social development and for the creation of a new international economic order. The armaments race has further detrimental effects on national and international development in that it has caused military research and development to predominate in science and technology.

PEACEFUL RESOLUTION OF CONFLICTS

16. The peaceful settlement of all international conflicts as the only alternative to avoid war or use of force must be generally recognized and accepted. The principles and treaties of international law, intended to preclude violence and war as means of national policy should be recognized as having continuing validity, requiring governments to submit themselves to peaceful settlement. The existing machinery provided by the UN and other institutions for peaceful resolution of conflicts should be strengthened. It is important to identify the typology of disputes in various areas and to utilize and activate the already existing institutional machinery at the regional level to resolve regional and inter-state disputes. It must be recognized that in an increasing number of instances the origins and causes of inter-state disputes are found outside the regions and nations concerned, who are now being used as proxies in conflicts between the super-powers and their allies.

THEOLOGICAL ISSUES

17. The two meetings — the Consultation on Militarism and the Conference on Disarmament — have underlined the need for more substantial work on the theological issues involved. They have posed questions rather than providing answers. This denotes a gap in theological exploration in the area and also challenges posed by the qualitatively new features of militarism and armaments race. It is necessary to formulate some basic affirmations which break the circle of anxiety and hopelessness.

18. It is evident that religious factors and theological interpretations also have contributed to the growth of militarism. Within the Christian church we recognize that we have nurtured and continue to nurture ideas and institutions which either promote or condone the growth of militarism.

19. Christians have a prophetic task to denounce both the structures of injustice which promote and sustain militarism in our world and those who misuse the power they have acquired to maintain these structures. We must be bold enough to imagine new forms of struggle against the evils of militarism, and new alternatives to replace the perverse options for security and peace offered to us by a militaristic system. In this renewed struggle and vision for a new society for which we labour there is no place for a militarism which claims to defend the "true faith", there is no justification for the distorted concepts of national security, there is no place for trade in arms or techniques in repression. The complex and disturbing subject of militarism requires of Christians a fresh and so far as

humanly possible, an unfettered approach to a theological understanding and critique of the nature of militarism and its relation to Christian faith and tradition.

20. Security for humanity has its true basis in the loving will of God who desires that none shall perish and that all His creations should enjoy the fullness of life. False notions of security blind the nations and they should be challenged. The peace we seek is a "warm peace", not merely the absence of war, but a peace best defined in the Biblical word "shalom" which expresses a positive state of justice, mutual respect for differences, welfare, health, security and a community embracing all humanity, in which there is loving concern for all. It is the prophetic duty of Christians to unmask and challenge idols of military doctrine and technology in the light of the Christian vision of justice and peace. Such idols include

- the doctrine of "deterrence" which holds millions of hostages to the threat of nuclear terror and has led to the development of still more terrifying weapons of mass destruction;

- any doctrine of national security that is used to justify militarism and arms race;

- the doctrine that "qualitative improvements" in military technology will result in a reduction of arms." . . .

(Report received by the WCC Central Committee at its meeting in Kingston, Jamaica, 1 - 11 January 1979)

THREATS TO PEACE
February 1980

"1. The Executive Committee of the World Council of Churches meeting in February 1980 at Liebfrauenberg, Woerth, France, gave attention to the disturbing trends and developments in international relations, including a sharp deterioration in the relations between the USA and the USSR and the growing threats to peace. Several member churches have already expressed their concern over the matter.

. . .

3. The present tensions need to be seen in the context of profound changes in the power relations among nations. Increasing world poverty, exacerbated by an arms race of almost unbelievable proportions, and energy crisis with heightened concern to control oil fields constitute continuing threats to world peace.

4. The Executive Committee recognizes that new threats which heighten possibilities of war in certain regions should be seen along with the fact that during the period after the Second World War, more than one hundred wars, many of them fuelled by conflicts of major powers, have claimed the lives of millions of people in the developing regions and that several such military conflicts still continue. These may further escalate in the context of the deterioration in the relations between the two super-powers, with very high rate of escalation of the arms race and race for military bases in these areas. Mention may be made of South-East Asia, especially Indochina, South Asia, Indian Ocean, Middle East and Iran, and Southern Africa.

5. The Executive Committee, recognizing that no single event should be seen in isolation and drawing the attention of the churches to a number of developments that have cumulatively contributed to the new situation that the world faces at the beginning of the eighties, expresses its serious concern about :

(a) The military action by the USSR in Afghanistan as constituting the latest direct, armed intervention in one country by another. This has heightened tension especially in and around the area of this development.

(b) The alarming frequency with which traditionally respected international laws are flouted. The number of armed interventions by foreign powers substantially increased in 1979.

(c) The decision of the NATO countries to deploy more than 500 "theatre nuclear weapons" in Europe, representing attempts at counterforce capability.

(d) The growing delusion that any nuclear war — albeit "limited" or "contained" — can be fought and won, which needs to be countered and condemned in the strongest terms.

(e) The worsening of the economic relations between developed and developing nations, and the military undergirding of the economic domination of the majority of countries by a few major powers.

(f) Tendencies on the part of certain nations to be militarily the most powerful have created a new sense of insecurity in other nations.

(g) Religious factors which in some regions have had a negative impact heightening tension.

6.   The Executive Committee believes that the present situation poses a serious challenge to the churches in their witness for peace. As the CCIA report to the Central Committee in 1979 stated, "The peace we seek is a 'warm peace', not merely the absence of war, but a peace best defined in the Biblical word 'shalom' which expresses a positive state of justice, mutual respect for differences, welfare, health, security and a community embracing all humanity, in which there is loving concern for all." The ecumenical fellowship should put its bridge-building capability to the utmost use. Therefore the churches should take initiatives to inject a note of sanity and sobriety into an atmosphere charged with tension, fear, irrationality and mutual distrust.

7.   The churches must speak out against the tendency to resume the perilous tactics of brinkmanship. Claims by any nation to become the strongest at any cost should be deplored. The churches should make clear in no uncertain terms that perspectives of foreign policy can no longer be seen in terms of "liquidating the enemy" (be it politically, militarily or through economic and cultural pressure). Peace requires willingness on the part of differing political and social systems to coexist and cooperate with each other. The churches have also the responsibility to call attention to the root causes of war, mainly to economic injustice, oppression and exploitation and to consequences of increasing tension including further restriction on human rights.

8. The Executive Committee calls upon the member churches :

(a) to intensify their engagement in efforts for peace and to collaborate with others working for peace in mobilizing public opinion and promoting education and actions for peace;

(b) to examine critically national policies and to challenge them if seen to be contributing to the increase of international tensions;

(c) to follow up urgently recommendations made by the Central Committee in 1979 under the Programme for Disarmament and Against Militarism and Arms Race;

(d) to initiate and encourage innovative measures for peaceful resolutions of conflicts.

9. The Executive Committee appeals to all people of goodwill and to all political leaders

(a) to avoid actions and policies that would further increase international tensions;

(b) to continue and promote détente and to resume negotiations on arms limitations including SALT;

(c) to strengthen the instruments and promote possibilities within the UN system and regional organizations for confidence-building measures and peaceful settlement of disputes;

(d) to take active steps for the de-escalation of regional conflicts and for their peaceful settlement.

10. Christians who put their trust in the Lord of history should be bearers of the light of hope amidst the prevailing gloom of despondency."

(Adopted by the WCC Executive Committee at its meeting in Liebfrauenberg, France, 11 - 15 February 1980)

THREATS TO PEACE
August 1980

"The WCC Central Committee, in the light of the statement THREATS TO PEACE adopted by the Executive Committee of the WCC in Liebfrauenberg, France, in February 1980, expresses its continuing concern regarding prevailing threats to peace, including those mentioned in the statement, and urges that peaceful solutions be sought through negotiations involving the participation of all parties concerned and with all states observing the principles of sovereign equality, mutual security, territorial integrity, respect for the lawful interests of each party, and non-interference in the internal affairs of other countries.

The Central Committee again calls upon the member churches :

1. To intensify their engagement in efforts for peace and to collaborate with others working for peace in mobilizing public opinion and promoting education and actions for peace;

2. to examine critically national policies and to challenge them if seen to be contributing to the increase of international tensions;

3. to follow up urgently recommendations made by the Central Committee in 1979 under the Programme for Disarmament and Against Militarism and Arms Race;

4. to initiate and encourage innovative measures for peaceful resolutions of conflicts."

(Adopted by the WCC Central Committee at its meeting in Geneva, Switzerland, 14 - 22 August 1980)

STATEMENT ON NUCLEAR DISARMAMENT
August 1980

"The Central Committee heard the message from the Melbourne Conference * which spoke of the "clouds of nuclear threat and annihilation" and that from the Conference on Faith, Science and the Future ** which reminded it that the gravest danger that humanity faces today is a nuclear holocaust. It is with a great sense of urgency that the Central Committee makes this statement.

Developments in the recent period have brought the world closer to the brink of a nuclear war. Unless the present trends are reserved or immediately halted, a nuclear war is now a distinct possibility. Many scientists are convinced that in the past year the hands of the clock have moved closer to the midnight of nuclear war.

The tension between the USA and the USSR has increased. They have each developed and continue to develop new generations of ever-more devastating nuclear weapons. The dangers inherent in the deployment ot these weapons within Europe have been heightened by the NATO decision to base new missiles possessing counterforce qualities and exceptional accuracy.

In August 1980 the United States officially announced a new policy which contemplates a "limited" nuclear war. This has further raised the anxieties about a nuclear holocaust. The current weapon programme of the major powers, if not stopped, will pull the nuclear trip-wire tighter. The development of "nuclear war-fighting capabilities" will increase the hair-trigger readiness for massive nuclear exchange at a time when political tensions are increasing all over the world.

Many years ago the USA, the UK and the USSR agreed to negotiate a treaty banning all nuclear tests. Regrettably no draft of such a comprehensive test ban treaty has been presented. Neither China nor France has indicated willingness to enter into such an agreement.

---

* World Conference on Mission and Evangelism, held at Melbourne, Australia, 12 - 25 May 1980, by invitation of the WCC Commission on World Mission and Evangelism.

** World Council of Churches' Conference on Faith, Science and the Future, held at the Massachusetts Institute of Technology, Cambridge, USA, 12 - 24 July 1979.

The deliberations at the Second Review Conference on Non-Proliferation Treaty currently being held in Geneva have highlighted the fact that the nuclear weapon states which have signed the treaty have failed to fulfil their obligations under the treaty to start nuclear disarmament, thus undermining the credibility of the non-proliferation regime.

The Central Committee urges all nuclear powers to :

(a) freeze immediately all further testing, production and deployment of nuclear weapons and of missiles and new aircraft designed primarily to deliver nuclear weapons;

(b) start immediately discussions with a view to making agreements not to enhance the existing nuclear potentials and progressively reducing the overall number of nuclear weapons and a speedy conclusion of a comprehensive test ban treaty.

The Central Committee also urges an early ratification of the SALT II agreement.

In view of the possibility of nuclear war, the Central Committee urges the Madrid Conference (on European Security and Cooperation) to decide to start negotiations on nuclear disarmament."

(Adopted by the WCC Central Committee at its meeting in Geneva, Switzerland, 14 - 22 August 1980)

INCREASED THREATS TO PEACE AND THE TASK
OF THE CHURCHES
August 1981

"1.   The Central Committee of the World Council of Churches in August 1980 expressed its concern that "the gravest danger that humanity faces today is a nuclear holocaust". The Central Committee, meeting in Dresden in August 1981, painfully aware of the devastation caused by bombing during World War II as tragically evidenced in this city and the continuing need to curb violence as a means of resolving international conflict, notes that international relations have deteriorated during the past year and have become even more dangerous. There has been intensification of tension and the emergence of disquieting trends :

a) Concerted attempts to make acceptable new strategies concerning the feasibility of nuclear war, and tendencies to consider the possibility of a limited nuclear conflict in which victory is assumed to be possible. In particular we are disturbed by the development and production in various countries of new dehumanizing weapons. The neutron weapon is the most recent and obvious example. It is a tremendous threat because it makes the use of nuclear weapons more likely, even against less developed countries. It is a further incentive to escalate the arms race and therefore makes disarmament negotiations more difficult. Even at this stage we urge that the manufacture of this and any other such weapons be stopped, that those already produced be eliminated and that no other nation decide to manufacture them;

b) The inability, so far, to reach a positive conclusion to the post-Helsinki talks in Madrid on European Security and Cooperation reflects a deterioration in East-West relations which constitutes a setback to détente and a further obstacle to disarmament;

c) The continuation of violent conflicts in areas mentioned in earlier statements of the Central Committee;

d) The worsening economic crisis throughout the world with graver consequences for the poor nations resulting in tensions within and among nations;

e) The continuing stalemate in the North-South discussions on global economic issues leading to confrontation and the reduction in aid to developing nations in contrast with the scandalous increase of expenditures on the arms race.

2. The Central Committee of the World Council of Churches, recognizing that urgent steps are needed for the prevention of a nuclear war and for the de-escalation of regional conflicts, appeals to all political leaders in the following terms :

a) The leaders of the two military blocs should meet at the earliest possible time to begin serious negotiations aimed at disarmament, both nuclear and conventional. To facilitate this process they and other national leaders should consider what unilateral steps for disarmament could responsibly be taken;

b) The peace-keeping machinery of the United Nations and of regional organizations should be strengthened in the interest of confidence building and the settlement of disputes. Existing disarmament negotiations should be reactivated and intensified;

c) In order to ease tension and build confidence among the nations, the nuclear powers should jointly propose a resolution in the United Nations Security Council which would give guarantees to countries which decide to create nuclear free zones that these will be fully respected;

d) Adequate preparation at national and international levels to ensure the success of the second special session on disarmament of the United Nations General Assembly scheduled for mid-1982 is of the greatest importance;

e) The widening economic gulf between developed and developing countries undermines confidence and is a threat to peace and cooperation. The industrialized nations should fulfil the United Nations goal for international development assistance and should start to negotiate in good faith for a more just relationship between the North and the South;

f) The rights of people everywhere to seek changes in social, economic and political exploitative and unjust conditions must be supported.

3. The Central Committee has in the past recommended to the churches a number of concrete actions for disarmament and against militarism and the

arms race. In the light of the current, most dangerous situation, the Central Committee :

a) Reaffirms the tasks and responsibilities of the churches in the context of the present exposure of humankind to the unprecedented risk of terrible and perhaps irreparable destruction;

b) Emphasizes the need to state more clearly the basis of involvement in the issues of war and peace in the context of the struggle for justice;

c) Emphasizes also the need to articulate the concerns for peace in clear, basic, firm affirmations;

d) Calls upon the churches now to :

1) challenge the military and militaristic policies that lead to disastrous distortions of foreign policy sapping the capacity of the nations of the world to deal with pressing economic and social problems which have become a paramount political issue of our times;

2) counter the trend to characterize those of other nations and ideologies as the "enemy" through the promotion of hatred and prejudice;

3) assist in de-mythologizing current doctrines of national security and elaborate new concepts of security based on justice and the rights of peoples;

4) grapple with the important theological issues posed by new developments related to war and peace and examine the challenges posed to traditional positions;

5) continue, according to the appeal contained in an earlier statement of the Central Committee, "to call attention to the root causes of war, mainly to economic injustice, oppression and exploitation and to the consequences of increasing tension including further restriction of human rights";

e) Commends the many member churches who have made renewed calls to peace-making, started, reactivated or intensified their efforts for peace, disarmament and against militarism and the arms race. This has included such useful initiatives of events like "peace week" or "disarmament week";

f) Calls upon member churches to :

1) intensify further their engagement in efforts for peace and join with others who seek to arouse the conscience of the public regarding the current threats to peace;

2) commit themselves to peace-making as continual witness through preaching, teaching and action;

3) promote bilateral and multilateral discussions among churches with a view to greater understanding among people and the reduction of mutual distrust and fear;

g) Commends the work of a large number of peace and disarmament groups and movements, old and new, around the world, in several of which large numbers of Christians actively participate in obedience to the demands of the Gospel. We call attention to the plea of the Central Committee in Kingston that serious attention be paid to the rights of conscientious objectors;

h) Commends to the churches the forthcoming WCC International Public Hearing on Nuclear Weapons and Disarmament * as an important occasion "to search for ways in which churches, Christian groups and others can help promote a climate of thinking more favourable to nuclear disarmament and for practical ways by which they can most effectively contribute to it";

i) Urges the churches, in the context of the preparations for the Sixth Assembly, whose theme is "Jesus Christ, the Life of the World", to make commitment to peace-making a special concern and to give emphasis to studies on issues related to peace, paying special attention to the under-
   ' lying theological issues."

* The Hearing was held in Amsterdam, Netherlands, 23 - 27 November 1981.

(Adopted by the WCC Central Committee at its meeting in Dresden, GDR, 16 - 26 August 1981)

THE HOLY SEE
ON
DISARMAMENT AND PEACE

The question of Disarmament has been one of major concerns of the supreme Magisterium of the Catholic Church in the whole field of peace. The Pontifical Commission Iustitia et Pax, *in its work of service to the Church, from its beginning, has studied closely the thought and teaching of the Magisterium on this important topic. In response to the real need to make these texts available in a convenient form, the Commission has sought to select the texts of recent Pontiffs and of the Second Vatican Council which can give to the reader the scope of concern and the substance of teaching which mark these last 35 years since the end of the Second World War.*

Before looking at the texts themselves, Catholic and non-Catholic readers alike may not be familiar with the various types and levels of importance of the messages and discourses assembled here. The Pastoral Constitution on the Church in the Modern World, Gaudium et Spes, *has a teaching authority of its own, in the sense that it is an approved declaration of the Catholic bishops gathered under the Pope at the Second Vatican Council. When the Pontiffs themselves speak, they may wish to teach the faithful in a formal way through an encyclical, which is the written presentation of the ordinary Magisterium of the Pontiffs in faith and morals. The Popes may choose to teach in a less solemn but yet in an authoritative way by using special occasions such as Christmas or the World Day of Peace in order that the occasion itself might confer a certain force to the message. The importance of a discourse may also be brought to the fore by the choice of the persons or groups addressed, such as the United Nations Organization, the Sacred College of Cardinals, or the Diplomatic Corps accredited to the Holy See.*

A somewhat different, more "catechetical" approach can be found in the talks the Popes deliver at General Audiences on Wednesday, in the homilies on Sundays or Feastdays, or in the brief remarks which the Popes may choose to make at a Sunday Angelus *when, from the window of the papal apartments, the Pontiffs greet pilgrims and join with them in prayer for some special intention. Finally, there may also be prayers which the Popes offer to God and which express the message inspired by the heart of him who is the universal pastor interceding for everyone before the Almighty.*

In approaching the texts gathered here, one must be aware of the particular nature of these discourses and messages in order to grasp correctly the weight and the importance of the teaching that each one contains. The texts which follow have been chosen according to a double criterion : the importance they have in the development of the subject itself, and the role they play in presenting various aspects of that thought.

As you will quickly see, one deals here with texts that display differences in style and tone. An encyclical, a discourse before the United Nations, a prayer for peace, a telegram to a Head of State will have, each of them, its own character. But with all the differences of tone or accent, there will be found a constant and clear thrust in the will and commitment of the Holy See to contribute to a process that will make of disarmament one of the building blocks of peace.

This concern is expressed "in season and out of season". *It is addressed first and foremost to political leaders and statesmen to help them understand the dimensions of the problem and to urge them to bend all their efforts to enter into a real dialogue that will lead to disarmament with all the necessary guarantees that will ensure a secure and lasting peace, in freedom and mutual respect. But these words are not meant simply for world leaders. The Holy See, in its universal mission as teacher, wants as well to inform and guide Catholics and all men and women of good will so that each one can take up the responsibility which is properly theirs and contribute with intelligence, discernment and sensitivity toward the building of a world which will be marked by peace, freedom and universal brotherhood.*

The texts which follow give clear witness to this commitment and have no need of detailed commentary in order to be understood by the reader. They have been divided into five sections : four of them group the messages of the four successive Popes in this period. The fifth, which has its own proper uniqueness, quotes from the Pastoral Constitution on Church in the Modern World, Gaudium et Spes, *which, as the fruit of the Second Vatican Council, was promulgated during the pontificate of Paul VI.*

PIUS XII (1939 - 1958)

Before turning to the statements of Pius XII after the war, it would be worthwhile to recall that, at the beginning of his pontificate, with the threat of war in the air, Pius XII did not hesitate to appeal "to governments and to peoples... Nothing is lost by peace; eveything is lost by war" *(24 August 1939). Again immediately after the outbreak of hostilities, he spoke to the Sacred College of Cardinals in these terms :* "The fundamental elements for a just and honourable peace are (among others) a disarmament which is mutually agreed upon, organic and progressive in the practical and in the spiritual order." *He then added that* "nations have to be freed from oppressive slavery to arms race" *(24 December 1939).*

After the war, the papal teaching concentrates on the problem of new armaments and their eventual use in some possible new conflict.

Faced by this possibility, the teaching of the Magisterium is starkly clear : a new war would provoke inconceivable destruction; however to avert this danger, it will not be enough to disarm since peace is above all a fruit of man's spiritual dimension : thus for Christians peace must be pursued foremost by prayer and by love that makes it possible to avoid the resort to arms.

So convinced is he of this that Pius XII writes (19 July 1950) an Encyclical Summi Maeroris *inviting all the People of God to pray for peace, conscious that* "technology has introduced and prepared such murderous and unhuman weapons as can destroy... innocent children with their mothers, those who are sick and the help-less aged. Whatever the genius of man has produced that is beautiful and good and holy, all of this can be practically annihilated."

The waste of resources and precious energy which the arms race entails is rejected. However, the use of force to repel an unjust aggressor is not only legitimate : it is in fact, a right and a duty; a duty which is not limitless because one must always apply the criterion of proportionality between the means used and the ends to be achieved, but a duty incumbent on leaders who must protect the life of citizens.

Pius XII was one of the first persons on the world scene to draw attention to the catastrophic effects a misuse of scientific discoveries in the field of atoms might bring about. Several times he spoke of this danger and sought the banishment of atomic, biological and chemical warfare (cf. Easter Radio Message, 18 April 1954).

Equally was he sensitive to the type of constraints that were imposed during "the cold war" *period. He repeated often that it was necessary to move beyond a kind of co-existence through fear in which* "each follows with anxious attention the technical development of the other's armaments and the productive capacity of its economy." *Instead, the question of peace and war ought to be raised to a higher plane of the moral order. Thus he seeks that all take* "the first steps toward an authentic moral order and towards a recognition of the elevated doctrine of the Church regarding just and unjust war and the licitness and illicitness of recourse to arms." *The key to Pius XII lies in* "a return to the fear of God" *and* "to a truly peaceful living-together" *(24 December 1954).*

With great insight Pius XII named the conditions for a true and effective disarmament: "Renunciation of experimentation with atomic weapons, renunciation of the use of such and general control of armaments." *Pius XII saw these as interlinked and that all three were needed together:* "That equal security be established by all" (ibid.).

The Pontiff was hopeful about the role which the United Nations might play in this sphere: "We desire to see strengthened the authority of the United Nations, especially for effecting general disarmament... In fact, only in the ambit of the United Nations can the promise of indiviudal nations to reduce armament... be mutually exchanged under the strict obligation of international law" *(23 December 1956). And finally, on the eve of his last Christmas on earth, he again proclaimed:* "The divine law of harmony in the world strictly imposes on all rulers of nations the obligation to prevent war by means of suitable international organizations, to reduce armaments under a system of effective inspection and to deter whoever should aim at disturbing the nations..." *(22 December 1957).*

JOHN XXIII (1958 - 1963)

In his very first Radio Message, the day after his election, John XXIII made an appeal to governments underlining the fact that their people wanted peace and not war (29 October 1958).

Like his predecessor, he also denounced the arms race and, in his first encyclical Mater et Magistra *insisted that the divine command to dominate nature is for the service of life. He pointed out the necessity of resolving the contradiction that exists between* "the spectre of misery and hunger" *in this world and the use of* "scientific discoveries, technical inventions and economic resources... to provide terrible instruments of ruin and death" *(15 May 1961).*

Twice in that same year, John XXIII raised his voice to make his own the "anxious solicitude" *of his Predecessors and call all people to reflect on* "the modern instruments of war derived from the secrets of nature and capable of unleashing unheard of energy to wreak havoc and destruction" *(10 September 1961), a concern which in December he repeated by saying* "We cannot believe that the terrific energy now under the control of man will be released for the world's destruction... We give voice to a heartfelt appeal that all those who control the economic forces should risk everything but not the peace of the world and the lives of men" *(21 December 1961).*

John XXIII was very sensitive to the tensions that threatened the fragile equilibrium of the international scene in those delicate years. It can be said that he worked incessantly for peace as evidenced by the role he sought to play during the Cuban missile crisis which confronted the world with the danger of warfare between the two super-powers.

This "Pope of Peace", *as he subsequently has been called, gave a legacy to the world on the very eve of his death. Its title announced its aim and its concern, the constant concern of the Pope himself:* Pacem in Terris. *This can honestly be called his spiritual testament for all humanity.*

In this document, he shows concern about "the enormous stocks of armaments" *which leads one country to imitate another in arms production. Instead* "the arms race should cease; the stockpiles which exist in various countries should be reduced equally and simultaneously by the parties concerned; nuclear weapons should be banned and a general agreement should eventually be reached about progressive disarmament and an effective method of control." *He says this realizing that he is dealing with situations that cannot be brought into reality* "unless it proceeds from inner conviction." *Therefore, there is real need* "to banish the fear and anxious expectation of war" *to bring about* "true and solid peace" *no longer founded on* "equality of arms" *but on* "mutual trust alone" *(11 April 1963).*

PAUL VI (1963 - 1978)

One of the first acts of the new Pontiff was to send a message to the President of the United States, the Prime Minister of Great Britain, the head of state of the Soviet Union and the Secretary General of the United Nations on the occasion of the signing of the Limited Test Ban Treaty. Paul VI saw this as "a proof of good will, a pledge of harmony, and a promise of a more serene future" *(5 August 1963).*

In continuity whith his predecessors, Paul VI expressed his concerns for the fact that peace has to be "maintained more by terror of deadly weapons than by mutual harmony and faith among peoples" *(23 December 1963). This means depending on* "the illusory concept that peace can only be based on the terrifying power of homicidal weapons" *(26 August 1964).*

With forcefulness did he propose his vision that disarmament was necessary for development in his message to journalists at Bombay. There he pleaded with each nation to "contribute even a part of its expenditure for arms to a great world fund for the relief of the many problems of nutrition, clothing, shelter and medical care which affect so many peoples" *(4 December 1964).*

The Pope drew a distinction between legitimate defence and a "Militarism... tending rather to build up stockpiles of weapons ever more powerful and destructive... We would like to see a generous minded investigation of how — at least in part and by stages — military expenditure could be diverted to humanitarian ends" *(22 December 1964).*

The first Pope to address the General Assembly of the United Nations, Paul VI used that occasion to appeal in a direct and evangelical manner to the representatives of states gathered there: "If you want to be brothers, let the weapons fall from your hands." *This appeal was not made in an unrealistic or naive way for the Pope acknowledged that* "As long as man remains that weak, changeable and even wicked being he often shows himself to be, defensive armaments will, alas, be necessary" *(4 October 1965).*

Paul VI believed in the dynamism of peace "which cannot be founded on the force of destructive arms" *and which is* "not an apathetic pacifism" *but which is* "the fruit of a united and unflagging practical effort for the construction of a society on the local and universal level, a society which is built on human solidarity in the pursuit of the common good of all" *(4 October 1966).*

Paul VI was convinced that peace had to be built through a profound change of mentalities. "This interiorization of Peace is true humanism, true civilization" *(8 December 1974). It would have to be prepared through patient work seeking to create a communitarian and universal spirit. Because of this he launched a project which was above all pedagogical and open to everyone* "to all the true friends of Peace" *(8 December 1967). This initiative was the World Day of Peace destined to mark the beginning of the New Year, celebrated for the first time on 1 January 1968. Each year the Pope — and Pope John Paul II has chosen to continue this practice — chooses a theme and addresses to the world a Message that develops elements in that theme for the help and instruction of men and women of good will who wish to join efforts in the cause of peace.*

In 1976 Paul VI chose as the theme for that year "The Real Weapons of Peace" *(1 January 1976). In that Message he spoke about the dangers of weapons being stockpiled and of divisive ideologies. What is needed* "above all are moral weapons... arms and wars are, in a word, to be excluded from civilization's programmes. Judicious disarming is another weapon of Peace" *(18 October 1975).*

In the view of Paul VI, nuclear arms constitute one of the grave threats that weigh upon our times. This helps explain the interest he showed in the Nuclear Non-Proliferation Treaty which he considered "an indispensable first step toward further measures in the area of disarmament, until finally we arrive at a total ban on nuclear arms and total, universal disarmament. We look forward to that final goal, and we again urge it in the name of all mankind" *(24 June 1968). This evaluation of the Treaty was at the foundation of the Holy See's decision to sign it on 25 February 1971.*

More and more does Paul VI point to what is at the heart of the crisis of contemporary human life : it is a crisis of hope in the face of a kind of progress that constantly threatens to turn against its very authors : "The use which modern man can make of the murderous forces which he has mastered no longer raises hope on the horizon, but heavy clouds of terror and folly... Thus it happens that anguish takes the place of hope" *(20 December 1968).*

His reflection on the current situation, led Paul VI to discover ever more deeply the reality of an abyss before which humankind stands. Faced with this, he shows us that the search for peace is the only road available to save humanity which is menaced by "the Damoclean sword of an increasingly serious and increasingly possible terror hanging over our heads" *(1 January 1970). The way to advance down this road of peace and hope must always be by the light of prayer and faith that is opposed to ideologies, warfare and violence, that seeks and builds justice, fraternity and peace.*

This ambivalence of the human person and current history reappears often in the thought of the Pontiff. Paul VI was sensitive to both the heights of grandness to which man is called by God and the depth of self-destructiveness toward which his lower nature so often calls him. Realistically, he knew that there was no panacea that would cure human beings of the human condition. He could, however, call the attention of one and all to the reality as he did in his discourse to the Diplomatic Corps (10 January 1972) when he spoke of "a contradiction within the human family, a contradiction between the growing sincere desire for peace on the one hand, and the growing fearsome production of instruments of war on the other." *Knowing this and wishing to encourage the best in man, he reminded the Sacred College of Cardinals (22 December 1972) that the Holy See and the Church would offer its full collaborative effort for* "the limitation and control of arms... the preparation for and progressive putting into practice of a true and general disarmament, the quest for new forms... of forestalling and settling the differences that disturb the peace and security of the peoples."

For Paul VI peace is always possible. He never lost his hope in the ability of peoples and nations to overcome their false divisions and learn to cooperate in the gradual but progressive reduction and control of the instruments of destruction. This was ever present in his words even though he was well aware that a great part of the economy of the world was based on and grew greater through armaments (cf. 1 January 1973). The reason for this hope in the midst of his realist assessment of the situation rests always in his conviction, born of faith, that "Christ, our peace (Eph. 2:14), makes the impossible possible (cf. Lk. 18:27)" *(17 October 1973).*

Buoyed by this faith which gave his words their strength and their profundity, the Pontiff was able to offer sound directives toward helping solve these problems : "It is more necessary than ever that the community of nations should be able to combat effectively the reasons of force... with the force of reason" *(12 January 1974). Man can prevail if he uses his reason and bends his efforts with universal good will. Man can prevail if he sets himself in opposition to possible conflagration and builds a world in which mutual cooperation deepens the possibilities of ever greater mutual trust. One contribution that will help build a world of mutual cooperation was pointed out in Pope Paul's Message to the Special Session on Disarmament (24 May 1978). In it, he called for* "the need for a higher religious awareness" *and said :* "Even those who do not take God into account can and must recognize the fundamental exigencies of the moral law that God has written in the depths of human hearts and that must govern people's mutual relationships on the basis of truth, justice and love."

The force of this reflection which extends throughout his pontificate leads to his rich and penetrating linkage between peace and life when he said : "The formula is : 'If you want Peace, defend Life.' Life is the crown of Peace... The policy of massive armaments is immediately called into question. The ancient saying, which has taught politics and still does so — 'if you want peace, prepare for war' — is not acceptable without radical reservation (cf. Lk. 14:31). With the forthright boldness of our principles, we thus denounce the false and dangerous programme of the 'arms race', of the secret rivalry between peoples for military superiority" *(8 December 1976).*

Instead the proposal of the Pope is a clear and frank one : "Our war against war has not yet been won, and our 'yes' to Peace is rather something wished for than something real" *(8 December 1977), but* "the Birthday of Christ marks, in the name of the Father in heaven, the pathway of peace on earth" *(25 December 1977).*

THE SECOND VATICAN COUNCIL (1962 - 1965)

The Pastoral Constitution Gaudium et Spes *was the last council document approved and was promulgated by Paul VI on 7 December 1965. It set forth both some fundamental principles and some contemporary applications of the role of the Church in the world today. The second part of the pastoral constitution addressed some problems of contemporary urgency including one chapter (pt. II, ch. V.) on* "Fostering of Peace and Promotion of a Community of Nations."

In this chapter attention is first given to the nature of peace saying"peace is not merely the absence of war. Nor can it be reduced solely to the maintenance of a balance of power between enemies. Nor is it brought about by dictatorship... Peace results from the harmony built into human society by its divine Founder and actualized by men as they thrist after ever greater justice" *(78).*

To effect this, the Council Fathers had already stated that "This Council fervently desires to summon Christians to cooperate with all men in making secure among themselves a peace based on justice and love and in setting up agencies of peace. This Christians should do with the help of Christ, the Author of Peace" *(77). This commitment is set forth in clear detail in paragraph 78 pointing out that peace is connected with a concern for the common good, that it demands constant striving by human beings who are marked by sin and have consequently to master their passions. But the Fathers are convinced it can be achieved through respect of other men and peoples and their dignity, and they offer this vision that* "earthly peace which arises from love of neighbour symbolizes and results from the peace of Christ who comes forth from God the Father" *(78).*

Having set forth this Christian hope and commitment to build a world of freedom, dignity and peace, the Fathers acknowledged the reality and the tragedy of a world filled with every kind of weapon and refining the means of war. To this the Council responded by employing the principles of the natural law of nations and by supporting the "various international agreements aimed at making military activity and its consequences less inhuman" *(79).*

The Council re-affirms the traditional teaching of the Church that "governments cannot be denied the right to legitimate defence once every means of peaceful settlement has been exhausted." *This is so because they have* "the duty to protect the welfare of the people entrusted to their care" (ibid.). *In this context the Council speaks approvingly both of those who, for reasons of conscience, refuse to bear arms, asking that they accept some other form of service and also of those who serve their country in the armed services* "as agents of security and freedom on behalf of their people" (ibid.).

Allying themselves with Pius XII and the last encyclical of Pope John, pacem in Terris, *the Fathers made their own the condemnation of total warfare which these two pontiffs had already uttered. What the Fathers were able to add, however, was their reaction, as the College of Bishops, to the type of weaponry that is more and more being developed, to the arms race and the implications that it has for the human family and to the duty to* "work for the time when all war can be completely outlawed by international consent" *(82).*

The multiplication of new and ever more dangerous scientific weapons was a cause of great concern to the Council. The possible results of the use of such weaponry led them to say that we ought to "undertake an evaluation of war with an entirely new attitude" *(80). While the Council does not spell out what are the elements in this new attitude, there is no doubt that the Council Fathers were concerned about the possibility that men can make* "atrocious decisions" *in using such weapons and that these decisions could lead to a chain of events that might affect the entire human race.*

In this context the arms race, especially the amassing of scientific weapons, poses a serious question to everyone. The Council recognized that "the accumulation of arms... also serves, in a way heretofore unknown, as a deterrent to possible enemy attack" *(81). However the Council, like the Popes, is convinced that this is not a safe way to preserve peace because* "the causes of war threaten to grow gradually stronger" (ibid.). *Therefore the Council sees the arms race as* "an utterably treacherous trap for humanity, and one which injures the poor to an intolerable degree" (ibid.).

As a result, the Council comes to the conclusion that no effort be spared to build up the agreements and the international means necessary for obtaining common security. Everyone should take his proper responsibility : world leaders "who work hard to do away with war", *savants whose studies can contribute to solving the problems of war and peace, educators to animate and inspire public opinion, all must do away with their own* "feelings of hostility, contempt and distrust, as well as racial hatred and unbending ideologies (which) continue to divide men and place them in opposing camps" *(82).*

"Hence everyone must labour to put an end at last to the arms race, and to make a true beginning of disarmament, not indeed a unilateral disarmament, but one proceeding at an equal pace according to agreement and backed up by authentic and workable safeguards" (ibid.).

Toward this end the Church never ceases to hope with utmost confidence and to propose that "now is the acceptable time... now is the day of salvation" (ibid.).

JOHN PAUL II (1978 - 1982)

In his first encyclical Redemptor Hominis *(4 March 1979), Pope John Paul II saw modern weapons as often reflecting not legitimate defence* "but rather a form of chauvinism, imperialism and neo-colonialism of one kind or another." *He called for a conversion of funds from armaments into* "investments for food at the service of life" *(*Redemptor Hominis, 16*)*.

In his address to the United Nations, he encouraged those agreements aimed at putting a brake on the arms race and spoke against "the continual preparations for war demonstrated by the production of ever more numerous, powerful and sophisticated weapons in various countries" *leading to the* "risk that sometime, somewhere, somehow, someone can set in motion the terrible mechanism of general destruction" *(2 October 1979).*

A few days later when speaking with President Carter, he expressed the desire that "by reason of its special position, may the United States succeed in influencing the other nations to join in a continuing commitment for disarmament" *(6 October 1979).*

It certainly is the intention of the Pope to make the world conscious of the grave danger nuclear arms represent. In his homily at the World Day of Peace Mass on 1 January 1980, he drew up a picture of "the immediate and terrible consequences of a nuclear war" *and he called for a renewed effort to bring about* "peace to men of good will." *Similarly, when later that same year he travelled to Paris to address the UNESCO, he asked his hearers there* "not to close your eyes to what a nuclear war can represent for the whole of humanity."

When the Holy See Father made his pastoral visit to Japan, he did so as a pilgrim of peace whose voyage included those very places which had been the targets of atomic destruction. Speaking first at the United Nations University, he used that occasion to underline "the anxiety of the scientific world in the face of an irresponsible use of science" *and the consequent role that savants are called to play in building peace. That same day (25 February 1981) in that same city of Hiroshima, the Pope launched an appeal to the whole world :* "To remember the past is to commit oneself to the future. To remember Hiroshima is to abhor nuclear war. To remember Hiroshima is to commit oneself to peace."

A few months later (on 30 August) the Pope made reference to that visit and to the symbolic role that Hiroshima plays by saying, "Unfortunately, since that fatal day nuclear arms have increased in quantity and destructive power."

This Pontiff has not ceased to take advantage of every opportunity given to him to renew his appeal for peace and to encourage every effort that will bring the world further down the road that guarantees peace, security and freedom.

Thus on 29 November 1981, he sent a personal message to the heads of state of the USA and the Soviet Union as an encouragement to them in the opening up of new conversations on arms reductions. "With that wish, I expressed also an encouragement in order that — thanks to common efforts of good will — this opportunity will not pass without results being reached such as to consolidate the hope of a future no longer threatened by the spectre of a possible nuclear conflict." *This hope and this encouragement he then recommended to the prayers of all the faithful.*

The way of step by step negotiation is strongly endorsed by the Pope. He set forth his ideas on the subject first by underlining the right and the duty to defend oneself against unjust aggression. "Peoples have a right and even a duty to protect their existence and freedom by proportionate means against an unjust aggressor." *In this message, he spoke of this right as* "very real in principle" *which ought to* "underline the urgency for world society to equip itself with effective means of negotiation." *And again in his Message for the 1982 World Day of Peace, he focuses his attention on these two factors : the right of self-defence and the urgent need for negotiations.*

One of the means he himself has used in making a contribution to the current debate has been his recent initiative of sending to the four "nuclear capitals", *Washington, Moscow, London and Paris, and to the President of the United Nations General Assembly, delegations from the Pontifical Academy of Sciences who had the task of* "illustrating a scientific document, the fruit of a careful study carried out by the same Academy with the collaboration also of other eminent scholars, on the consequences of the use of these armaments" *(13 December 1981).*

Here one can see a very concrete expression of the concern of the Catholic Church for the good of all humankind. The Pope himself explained this move to the Diplomatic Corps when he received them on 16 January 1982 : "In the perspective of the Holy See, the initiative does not intend to deal with technical details of the negotiations in course or of other possible negotiations; it wants to show clearly, from the human and moral point of view, and appealing to men of science to make their contribution to the great cause of peace, that the only solution possible, in face of the hypothesis of a nuclear war, is to reduce at once, and subsequently to eliminate completely, nuclear armaments by means of specific agreements and effective controls."

William Murphy

The documents presented in this volume are published in their original language in the ACTA APOSTO-LICAE SEDIS (AAS) *of the Vatican Polyglot Press. This is the official publication of the Holy See and each of these texts may be found there in the volume corresponding to the year of publication.*

The Pontifical Commission Iustitia et Pax *has taken the English language translations of these documents from the following periodicals and collections :*
For the Pontificate of Pius XII : The Catholic Mind;
For the Pontificate of John XXIII : The Pope Speaks *and* The Tablet;
For the years 1963-1968 of the Pontificate of Paul VI : The Catholic Mind *and* The Pope Speaks;
For the years 1969-1978 of the Pontificate of Paul VI : The Teachings of Paul VI;
For the Pontificate of John Paul II : L'Osservatore Romano, *weekly English edition;*
Translations done by the Pontifical Commission itself are marked with a note at the bottom of the page.

PIUS XII

ADDRESS TO THE SACRED COLLEGE OF CARDINALS
24 December 1946

... The utter depth of misery into which the horrible war has thrown humanity calls for help and imperiously demands to be healed by means of a peace that is morally noble and irreproachable : such a peace that may teach future generations to outlaw every trace of brutal force and to restore to the idea of right the priority of place from which it was wickedly dislodged.

We justly appreciate the arduous but noble work of those statesmen who, disregarding the insidious voices of revenge and hate, have been toiling and are still toiling without respite for the fulfillment of such a high ideal. But notwithstanding their generous efforts, who could ever say that the discussions and debates of the year that is ending have resulted in a clear plan, drawn up logically in its main outlines, and calculated to reawaken in all nations confidence in a future of tranquillity and justice.

No doubt such a disastrous war, unleashed by an unjust aggression and continued beyond lawful limits when it was clear that it was irreparably lost, could not be terminated simply in a peace which did not include guarantees that similar acts of violence would not be repeated. Nevertheless, all the measures of repression and prevention should keep their character of means and hence remain subordinate to the lofty and ultimate purposes of a true peace which, while providing the necessary guarantees, contemplates the gradual cooperation of conquerors and conquered in the work of reconstruction of the advantage of the entire family of nations and as well of each of its members.

Any balanced observer will be willing to recognize that these indisputable principles have made real progress during the past year in not a few minds and that, too, as a result of the painful repercussion felt by the vital interests of the victorious States themselves. One finds some satisfaction also in noting that competent and authoritative voices in ever-increasing numbers are raised against an unlimited prolongation of the present conditions on the life and economic recovery of the defeated. Immediate contact with the indescribable misery of the post-war period in some zones has awakened in many hearts the consciousness of a common responsibility to lessen effectively, and eventually to overcome, such a great evil. This sentiment is as honorable for one as it is encouraging for the other.

Recently a new factor has arisen to stimulate the desire for peace and the determination to promote it more effectively : the might of new instruments of destruction which modern technique has developed and continues to develop to such an extent that they appear to the terrified eyes of humanity infernal creations. This factor has brought the problem of disarmament into the center of international discussions under completely new aspects, and it provides an incentive that was never felt before; thence springs hope of solving what past generations have longed for in vain.

Notwithstanding these well-founded motives of hope, in which no one can rejoice more than the Church, it seems that, in the present state of affairs, one must expect with great probability that the future peace treaties will only be an "opus imperfectum". Many of those who write them will recognize in them the result of compromises between the policies and claims of differing political powers rather than the expression of their own personal ideas based on the true and just concepts of right and equity, of human feeling and prudence. (II, No. 2).

(The Catholic Mind, Vol. 45, 1947, pp. 69-70)

CHRISTMAS RADIO MESSAGE
24 December 1948

THE COMMUNITY OF PEOPLES

The Catholic doctrine on the State, and civil society has always been based on the principle that, in keeping with the will of God, the nations form together a community with a common aim and common duties. Even when the proclamation of this principle and its practical consequences gave rise to violent reactions, the Church denied her assent to the erroneous concept of an absolutely autonomous sovereignty, divested of all social obligations. The Catholic Christian, persuaded that every man is his neighbour and that every nation is a member, with equal rights, of the family of nations, co-operates wholeheartedly in those generous efforts whose beginnings might be meagre and which frequently encounter strong opposition and obstacles, but which aim at saving individual States from the narrowness of a self-centred mentality. This latter attitude of mind has been largely responsible for the conflicts of the past, and unless finally overcome, or at least held in check, could lead to new conflagrations that might mean death to human civilization.

THE NIGHTMARE OF A NEW WAR

Since the cessation of hostilities, men have never been so obsessed as today by the nightmare of another war and by anxiety for peace. They alternate between two extremes. Some adopt the ancient motto, not completely false, but which is easily misunderstood and has often been misused, '*Si vis pacem, para bellum*' — 'If you desire peace, prepare for war'. Others think to find safety in the formula, 'Peace at any price'. Both parties want peace, while both endanger it; on one side by arousing distrust, on the other by promoting a security which can pave the way for aggression. Thus both, without desiring it, compromise the cause of peace at the very time when the human race, crushed under the weight of arms and in agony at the prospect of fresh and even worse conflicts, shudders at the thought of a future catastrophe. Hence we should like to point out briefly the characteristics of the true Christian will for peace.

THE TRUE CHRISTIAN WILL FOR PEACE

1. IT COMES FROM GOD

The Christian will for peace comes from God. He is the God of Peace. He has created the world to be an abode of peace. He has given His commandment of peace, that tranquillity in order' of which St. Augustine speaks. The Christian will for peace has its weapons, too, but its principal arms are those of prayer and love; constant prayer to the Father in Heaven, Father of us all; brotherly love among all men and all nations, since all are sons of the same Father Who is in Heaven; love which with patience always succeeds in being ready to achieve understanding and agreement with everyone. These two arms have their source in God, and when they are lacking, when people know only how to wield material weapons, there is no real will for peace. For purely material armament necessarily awakens distrust and creates what amounts to a climate of war. Who, then, can fail to see how important it is for the nations to preserve and strengthen the Christian way of life, and how grave is their responsibility in the selection and the supervision of those to whom they entrust the immediate control of armaments?

2. IT IS EASILY IDENTIFIED

The Christian will for peace is easily identified. Obedient to the Divine Precept of Peace, it will never turn a question of national prestige or honour into an argument for war or even for a threat of war. It is very careful to avoid recourse to the force of arms in the defence of rights which, however legitimate, do not offset the risk of kindling a blaze, with all its tremendous spiritual and material consequences...

4. IT MEANS STRENGTH. THE SOLIDARITY OF PEOPLES AGAINST THE SPIRIT OF AGGRESSION

The genuine Christian will for peace means strength, not weakness or weary resignation. It is completely one with the will for peace of the Eternal and Almighty God. Every war of aggression against those goods which the Divine Plan for peace obliges men unconditionally to respect and guarantee, and accordingly to protect and defend, is a sin, a crime, an outrage against the Majesty of God, the Creator and Ordainer of the world. A people threatened with an unjust aggression, or already its victim, may not remain impassively indifferent, if it would think and act as befits Christians. All the more does the solidarity of the family of nations forbid others to behave as mere spectators, in an attitude of apathetic neutrality. Who will ever measure the harm caused in the past by such indifference to wars of aggression, which is quite alien to the Christian instinct? How much more keenly has it brought home to the 'great' and to the 'small' their sense of insecurity? Has it brought any advantage in recompense? On the contrary; it has only reassured and encouraged the authors and fomentors of aggression, while it obliges the several peoples, left to themselves, to increase their armaments indefinitely.

Resting for support on God and on the order He established, the Christian will for peace is thus as strong as steel. Its temper is quite different from mere humanitarian sentiment, too often little more than a matter of pure emotion, which detests war only because of its horror and atrocities, its destruction and its aftermath, but not for the added reason of injustice. Such a sentiment, under a hedonistic and utilitarian disguise, and materialistic in its source, lacks the solid foundation of a strict and unqualified obligation. It creates conditions which encourage the deception resulting from sterile compromise, the attempt to save oneself at the expense of others and the success in every case of the aggressor. This is so true that neither the sole consideration of the sorrow and evils resulting from war, nor the careful weighing of the act against the advantage, avails to determine finally whether it is morally obligatory to repel an aggressor by force of arms.

<hr>

(The Catholic Mind, Vol. 47, 1949, pp. 183-185)

ENCYCLICAL EPISTLE "SUMMI MAERORIS"
19 July 1950

... As the heavens are becoming darkened by heavy clouds, We, who have dearest at heart the liberty, dignity and prosperity of all nations, must needs return to exhorting earnestly all citizens and their governments to a true concord and peace.

Let all of them remember what war brings in its wake, as we know only too well from experience — nothing but ruin, death and every sort of misery. With the progress of time, technology has introduced and prepared such murderous and inhuman weapons as can destroy not only armies and fleets, not only cities, towns and villages, not only the treasures of religion, of art and culture, but also innocent children with their mothers, those who are sick and the helpless aged.

Whatever the genius of man has produced that is beautiful and good and holy, all of this can be practically annihilated. But if a war, especially today, appears to every honest observer as something terrifying and deadly, there is yet reason to hope — through the efforts of all people and particularly of their rulers — that the dark and menacing clouds which presently cause such trepidation may pass away, and that true peace may finally reign among nations.

However, realizing that "every best gift and every perfect gift is from above, coming down from the Father of lights" (James 1:17). We consider it opportune, Venerable Brothers, to call once again for public prayers and supplications to implore concord among peoples...

(The Catholic Mind, Vol. 48, 1950, pp. 628-629)

CHRISTMAS RADIO MESSAGE
23 December 1950

... Unfortunately, in these past weeks the cleavage which in the external world divides the entire international community into opposite camps grows constantly deeper, placing in jeopardy the peace of the world.

Never has the history of mankind known a dissension of greater magnitude; it reaches to the very ends of the earth.

If a regrettable conflict should occur today, weapons would prove so destructive as to make the earth "void and empty", (Genesis 1:2) a desolate chaos, like to a desert over which the sun is not rising, but setting. All nations would be convulsed, and among the citizens of the same country, the conflict would have manifold repercussions; it would place in extreme peril all its civil institutions and spiritual values, seeing that the conflict now embraces all the most difficult problems which normally would be discussed separately.

The grim and threatening danger imperiously demands, by reason of its gravity, that we make the most of every opportune circumstance to bring about the triumph of wisdom and justice under the standard of concord and peace. Let it be used to revive sentiments of goodness and compassion towards all peoples whose one sincere aspiration is to live in peace and tranquillity. Let mutual trust, which presupposes sincere intentions and honest discussions, return to rule over international organizations.

Away with the barriers ! Break down the barbed-wire fences ! Let each people be free to know the life of other peoples; let that segregation of some countries from the rest of the civilized world, so dangerous to the cause of peace, be abolished. (IV) ...

(The Catholic Mind, Vol. 49, 1951, p. 207)

ADDRESS TO THE DELEGATES TO THE FOURTH CONGRESS OF THE UNIVERSAL MOVEMENT FOR WORLD FEDERAL GOVERNMENT

6 April 1951

We are very appreciative of the deference you have displayed by this visit and We take pleasure in addressing you members of the World Movement for World Federal Government. We give you cordial greetings of welcome. Our lively interest in the cause of peace in the midst of a humanity so grievously tormented is well known to you. We have given frequent proofs of this interest. That interest, moreover, is inherent in our mission. The maintenance, or the re-establishment, of peace has always been and always and increasingly will be the object of our constant solicitude. And if, too often, the results have fallen far short of what our efforts and our acts aimed at, lack of success will never discourage us, so long as peace does not reign in the world. Faithful to the spirit of Christ, the Church is striving and working for peace with all her strength; she does this by her precepts and her exhortations, by her incessant activities and by her ceaseless prayers.

The Church is indeed a power for peace, at least wherever are respected and appreciated at their true value the independence and the mission which the Church holds from God, wherever men do not seek to make her the docile servant of a political egoism, wherever she is not treated as an enemy. The Church longs for peace, she strives incessantly for peace, and her heart is ever with those who, like her, desire peace and devote themselves to it. She knows also, and this is her duty, how to distinguish between the true and the false friends of peace.

The Church desires peace, and therefore applies herself to the promotion of everything which, within the framework of the divine order, both natural and supernatural, contributes to the assurance of peace. Your movement dedicates itself to realizing an effective political organization of the world. Nothing is more in conformity with the traditional doctrine of the Church, nor better adapted to her teaching concerning legitimate or illegitimate war, especially in the present circumstances.

It is necessary therefore to arrive at an organization of this kind, if for no other reason than to put a stop to the armament race in which, for decades past, the peoples have been ruining themselves and draining their resources to no effect.

(The Catholic Mind, Vol. 49, 1951, pp. 393-394)

CHRISTMAS RADIO MESSAGE
24 December 1951

... Everyone must be convinced of this spiritual element inherent in the danger of war. To awaken that conviction is in the first place the duty of the Church, and her primary contribution to peace today.

MODERN WEAPONS

We too — and more than anyone else — deplore the monstrous cruelty of modern weapons. We deplore them and do not cease to pray that they may never be employed. But, on the other hand, is it not perhaps a kind of practical materialism and superficial sentimentality to make the existence and threat of these weapons the sole and principal consideration in the question of peace, while no attention is paid to the absence of that Christian order which is the true guarantee of peace ?

Hence, among other reasons, the differences of opinion, and also the inexactitudes, concerning the licitness or illicitness of modern warfare; hence likewise the illusion of statesmen, who count too much on the existence or disappearance of those weapons. The terror they inspire in the long run begins to lose its effect, just like any other cause of terror; or at least it would not suffice, if the occasion should arise, to prevent the outbreak of a war; especially in those countries where the voice of the citizens has not sufficient influence in the decisions of their governments.

DISARMAMENT

On the other hand, disarmament, or rather the simultaneous and reciprocal reduction of armaments, which we have always desired and begged for, is an unstable guarantee of lasting peace, if it is not accompanied by the abolition of the weapons of hate, cupidity and of overweening lust for prestige. In other words, whoever connects too closely the question of material weapons with that of peace is guilty of neglecting the primary and spiritual element in every danger of war. He does not look beyond figures, and besides his calculations are necessarily limited to the moment in which the conflict threatens to break out. A friend of peace, he will always arrive too late to save it.

If the desire to prevent war is to be truly efficacious, above all a remedy must be sought for the spiritual anemia of nations, for the ignorance of individual responsibility before God and man, and for the want of a Christian order which alone is able to guarantee peace. To this goal the resources of the Church are now directed. (III)

(The Catholic Mind, Vol. 50, 1952, pp. 253-254)

ADDRESS TO THE INTERNATIONAL OFFICE OF DOCUMENTATION FOR MILITARY MEDICINE
19 October 1953

... The basic principle of medical ethics commands us not only "to help and cure, not to injure or kill", but also to protect and preserve from harm.

This point is decisive for the position of the doctor in regard to war in general and to modern war in particular. The doctor is the enemy of war and the promoter of peace. As he is ready to heal the wounds of war, once they already exist, so should he do all he can to prevent them.

Mutual good-will always allows states to avoid war as the final means of settling differences between themselves. Several days ago We again expressed Our desire that any war be punished at the international level which is not absolutely necessary for the self-defence of a community very seriously threatened by an injustice that cannot be prevented in any other way. Even such a war, however, must be waged at the risk of giving a free hand in international affairs to brute violence and lack of conscience. It is not enough, therefore, to have to defend oneself against just any injustice in order to justify resorting to the violent means of war. When the damages caused by war are not comparable to those of "tolerated injustice", one may have a duty to "suffer the injustice".

What We have just discussed applies especially to ABC warfare — atomic, biological and chemical. As to the question of knowing whether it (ABC warfare) can become clearly necessary in *self-defence* against ABC warfare, let it suffice for Us to have posed it here. The answer can be deduced from the same principles which are today decisive for permitting war in general. In any case, another question arises first : is it not possible through international understandings to proscribe and avert ABC warfare ?

After the horrors of two world conflicts We do not have to remind you that any apotheosis of war is to be condemned as an aberration of mind and heart. Certainly spiritual strength and bravery, even to the point of giving one's life when duty demands it, are great virtues; but to want to start a war because it is the school of great virtues and the occasion for practising them must be characterized as a crime and madness.

What We have said shows the direction in which one will find the answer to that other question : may the doctor put his knowledge and activity at the service of ABC warfare ? "Injustice" he can never support, even in the service of his own country, and when that type of war constitutes an injustice, the doctor may not take part in it... (I)

(The Catholic Mind, Vol. 52, 1954, pp. 49-50)

EASTER RADIO MESSAGE
18 April 1954

... How greatly We would wish that the joy of the Christian feast of Easter should be poured forth upon all men, so that the Church might be able to proclaim in the fullness of its extension : *"In resurrectione tua, Christe, coeli et terra laetentur"* (Brev. Rom. Dom. in Albis, ad Laudes). "In thy resurrection, O Christ, the heavens and the earth rejoice !"

But if in the heavens all is peace and joy, on earth the reality is quite otherwise. Here, in place of the serene joy whose secret was revealed by Christ Himself, there is year by year a mounting anxiety and, one might say, trepidation on the part of the peoples of the world by reason of their fear of a third world conflict and of a dreadful future, placed at the mercy of new destructive arms of unprecedented violence.

These means of destruction — as We had already occasion to state and to fear as far back as February, 1943 — are capable of bringing about "a dangerous catastrophe for our entire planet" (*Acta Apostolicae Sedis* 1943, page 75), of causing the total extermination of all animal and vegetable life and of all the works of man over vaster regions : and they are now capable, with artificially radioactive isotopes of extended average life, of polluting in a lasting manner the atmosphere, the land and also the oceans, even where these areas are very distant from the zones directly stricken and contaminated by the nuclear explosions.

Thus, before the eyes of a terrified world there is presented a preview of gigantic destruction, of extensive territories rendered uninhabitable and unfit for human use over and above the biological consequence that can result, either by the changes brought about by germs and micro-organisms, or through the uncertain effect which a prolonged radioactive stimulus can have upon greater organisms, including man, and upon their future offspring.

In this connection We do not wish to omit a reference to the danger that could result for future generations from mutagenic intervention, obtainable or perhaps already obtained by new means, for the purpose of deviating the patrimony of man's hereditary factors from their natural development; and this also for the reason that among such deviations there probably are not lacking, or would not be lacking, those pathogenic mutations which are the causes of transmittable diseases and monstrosities.

For Our part, We will tirelessly endeavour to bring about, by means of international agreements — always in subordination to the principle of legitimate self-defence (cf., however, *Acta Apostolicae Sedis,* 1953 pp. 748-49) — the effective proscription and banishment of atomic, biological and chemical warfare (*ibid.*, p. 749).

At the same time, We ask : For how long will men insist on turning their backs on the salutary light of the Resurrection, seeking security instead in the deadly blasts of new weapons of war ? For how long will they oppose their designs of hatred and of death to the Divine Saviour's precepts of love and His promises of life ? When will the rulers of nations realize that peace cannot consist in an exasperating and costly relationship of reciprocal terror, but in the Christian rule of universal charity, and particularly in justice voluntarily applied rather than extorted, and in confidence that is inspired rather than exacted ?

When will it come about that the learned ones of the world will turn the wonderful discovery of the profound forces of matter exclusively to purposes of peace : to enable man's activity to produce energy at a low cost which would alleviate the scarcity and correct the unequal geographical distribution of the sources of wealth and work, as also to offer new arms to medicine and agriculture, and to peoples new fountains of prosperity and well-being ?...

(The Catholic Mind, Vol. 52, 1954, pp. 438-439)

ADDRESS TO THE EIGHTH CONGRESS OF
THE WORLD MEDICAL ASSOCIATION
30 September 1954

WAR AND PEACE

... Has not the doctor also a role to play in producing, perfecting and increasing the methods of modern warfare, in particular the methods of ABC warfare? One cannot answer this question without having first resolved this other one : is modern "total war", especially ABC warfare, permissible in principle ? There can be no doubt, particularly in view of the horrors and immense sufferings caused by modern warfare, that to unleash it without a just cause (that is to say, without its being forced upon one by an obvious, extremely serious and otherwise unavoidable injustice) constitutes a "crime" worthy of the most severe national and international sanctions.

One cannot even in principle pose the question of the lawfulness of atomic, bacteriological and chemical warfare except in the case where it must be judged as indispensable in order to defend oneself under the circumstances pointed out above. Even then, however, one must strive to avoid it by all possible means through international understandings or to impose limits on its use that are so clear and rigorous that its effects remain restricted to the strict demands of defence. When, moreover, putting this method to use involves such an extension of the evil that it entirely escapes from the control of man, its use must be rejected as immoral. Here there would no longer be a question of "defence" against injustice or a necessary "safeguarding" of legitimate possessions, but the pure and simple annihilation of all human life within the radius of action. This is not permitted for any reason whatsoever.

Let us return to the doctor. If ever, within the compass of the limits already indicated, a modern (ABC) war can be justified, the question of the morally lawful collaboration of the doctor can then be raised. But you will be in agreement with Us : one prefers not to see the doctor occupied with a task of this sort. It is in too great a contrast to his basic duty : to give aid and cure, not to do injury or kill...

(The Catholic Mind, Vol. 53, 1955, pp. 243-244)

CHRISTMAS RADIO MESSAGE
24 December 1954

I. CO-EXISTENCE IN FEAR

It is a common impression, derived from the simple observation of facts, that the principal foundation on which the present state of relative calm rests is fear. Each of the groups into which the human family is divided tolerates the existence of the other, because it does not wish itself to perish. By thus avoiding a fatal risk, the two groups do not live together; they co-exist. It is not a state of war, but neither is it peace : it is a cold calm. Each of the two groups smarts under the fear of the other's military and economic power. In both of them there is a grave apprehension of the catastrophic effect of the latest weapons.

Each follows with anxious attention the technical development of the other's armaments and the productive capacity of its economy, while it entrusts to its own propaganda the task of turning the other's fear to its advantage by strengthening its meaning. It seems that in the field of concrete politics reliance is no longer placed on either rational or moral principles, for these, after so many delusions, have been swept away by an extreme collapse into skepticism.

The most obvious absurdity of the situation resultant from such a wretched state of affairs is this : current political practice, while dreading war as the greatest of catastrophes, at the same time puts all its trust in war, as if it were the only expedient for subsistence and the only means of regulating international relations. This is, in a certain sense, placing trust in that which is loathed above all other things.

On the other hand, the above-mentioned political practice has led many, even of those responsible for government, to revise the entire problem of peace and war, and has induced them to ask themselves sincerely if deliverance from war and the ensuing of peace ought not to be sought on higher and more humane levels than on that dominated exclusively by terror. Thus it is that there has been an increase in the numbers of those who rebel against the idea of having to be satisfied with mere co-existence, of renouncing relationships of a more vital nature with the other group, and against being forced to live all the days of their lives in an atmosphere of enervating fear. Hence they have come back to consider the problem of peace and war as a fact involving a higher and Christian responsibility before God and the moral law.

Undoubtedly in this changed manner of approach to the problem there is an element of "fear" as a restraint against war and a stimulus to peace; but here the fear is that salutary fear of God — Guarantor and Vindicator of the moral law — and, therefore, as the Psalmist teaches (Ps. 110:10), it is the beginning of wisdom.

Once the problem is elevated to this higher plane, which alone is worthy of rational creatures, there again clearly appears the absurdity of that doctrine which held sway in the political schools of the last few decades : namely, that war is one of many admissible forms of political action, the necessary, and as it were the natural, outcome of irreconcilable disputes between two countries; and that war, therefore, is a fact bearing no relation to any kind of moral responsibility. It is likewise apparent how absurd and inadmissible is the principle — also so long accepted — according to which a ruler who declares war would only be guilty of having made a political error should the war be lost. But he could in no case be accused of moral guilt and of crime for not having preserved peace, when he was able to do so.

It was precisely this absurd and immoral concept of war which rendered vain, in the fatal weeks of 1939, Our efforts to uphold in both parties the will to continue negotiations. War was then thought of as a die, to be cast with greater or less caution and skill, and not as a moral fact involving obligation in conscience and higher responsibilities. It required tombs and ruins without number to reveal the true nature of war : namely, that it was not a luckier or less lucky gamble between conflicting interests but a tragedy, spiritual more than material, for millions of men; that it was not a risking of some possessions, but a loss of all : a fact of enormous gravity.

How is it possible — many at that time asked with the simplicity and truth of common sense — that, while every individual feels within himself an urgent sense of moral responsibility for his own most ordinary acts, the dreadful fact of war, which is also the fruit of the free act of somebody's will, can evade the dominion of conscience, and that there be no judge to whom its innocent victims may have recourse ? In the atmosphere of that time, when people were beginning to return to common sense, widespread approval was given Our cry, "war against war", with which in 1944 We declared Our opposition to the pure formalism of political action and to doctrines of war which take no account of God or of His commandments. That salutary return to common sense, instead of being weakened, became more profound and more widespread in the years of the cold war, perhaps because prolonged experience made more clearly evident the absurdity of a life lived under the incubus of fear. Thus the cold peace, with all its incoherences and uneasiness, shows signs of taking the first steps toward an authentic moral order and towards a recognition of the elevated doctrine of the Church regarding just and unjust war, and the licitness and illicitness of recourse to arms.

This goal will assuredly be attained if, on one side and the other, men will once again sincerely, almost religiously, come to consider war as an object of the moral order, whose violation constitutes in fact a culpability which will not go unpunished. In the concrete this goal will be attained if statesmen, before weighing the advantages and risks of their decisions, will recognize that they are personally subject to eternal moral laws, and will treat the problem of war as a question of conscience before God.

In the conditions of our times, there is no other way to liberate the world from its agonizing incubus except by a return to the fear of God, which in no way debases the man who willingly submits to it; rather, it saves him from the infamy of that awful crime — unnecessary war. And who can express astonishment if peace and war thus prove to be closely connected with religious truth ? Everything that is, is of God : the root of all evil consists precisely in separating things from their beginning and their end.

Hence also it becomes clear that pacifist efforts or propaganda originating from those who deny all belief in God — if indeed not undertaken as an artful expedient to obtain the tactical effect of creating excitement and confusion — is always very dubious and incapable of lessening or of eliminating the anguished sense of fear.

The present co-existence in fear has thus only two possible prospects before it : either it will raise itself to a co-existence in fear of God, and thence to a truly peaceful living-together, inspired and protected by the Divine moral order : or else it will shrivel more and more into a frozen paralysis of international life, the grave dangers of which are even now foreseeable.

In fact, prolonged restraint of the natural expansion of the life of peoples can ultimately lead them to that same desperate outlet that it is desired to avoid : war. No people, furthermore, could support indefinitely a race of armaments without disastrous repercussions being felt in its normal economnic development. The very agreements directed to imposing a limitation on armaments would be in vain. Without the moral foundation of fear of God, they would become, if ever reached, a source of renewed mutual distrust.

There remains, therefore, the auspicious and lightsome other way which, based upon the fear of God and aided by Him, leads to true peace, which is sincerity, warmth and life, and is thus worthy of Him Who has been given to us that men might have life in Him and have it more abundantly (John 10:10).

(The Catholic Mind, Vol. 53, 1955, pp. 180-182)

CHRISTMAS RADIO MESSAGE
24 December 1955

... Man, face to face with opinions and systems opposed to the true religion, is, of course, always bound by the limits established by God in the natural and supernatural order. In obedience to this principle, our peace programme cannot approve of an indiscriminate co-existence at all costs with everybody; certainly not at the cost of truth and justice. These irremovable boundary marks, in effect, demand complete observance. Where this is so, including today in the question of peace, religion is in a sure manner protected against abuse from the political quarter; whereas when it has been restricted to purely interior life, religion itself is more exposed to that danger.

NUCLEAR ARMS AND ARMAMENT CONTROL

This thought of its own accord leads Us on to the ever acute question of peace which constitutes an object of solicitude always present to Our heart and at this moment one of its partial problems begs for special consideration. We propose to direct Our attention to a recent proposal which aims at suspending experiments in nuclear weapons by means of an international agreement. There has been talk also of taking further steps toward conventions through which use of those weapons would be renounced and all states subjected to effective arms control. Thus there would be a question of three measures : renunciation of experimentation with atomic weapons, renunciation of the use of such, and general control of armaments.

The supreme importance of these proposals is tragically illustrated if one stops to consider what science thinks it can predict about such actions, and which We think is useful to sum up briefly here.

As for *experiments* of atomic explosions, the opinion of those who fear the effects produced if they are multiplied would seem to be finding greater acceptance. Too many such explosions would in time cause an increased density of radioactive products in the atmosphere, whose diffusion depends on elements not under man's control; thus would be generated conditions very dangerous for many living beings.

Concerning the *use* : in a nuclear explosion an enormous amount of energy equivalent to several thousand million kilowatts is developed in an exceedingly short time; this energy is composed of electromagnetic radiations of very great density distributed within a vast gamut of wave lengths even to the most penetrating, and of tiny bodies produced by nuclear disintegration which are hurled at nearly the speed of light. This energy is transferred to the atmosphere and within thousandths of a second increases the temperature of surrounding air masses by hundreds of degrees; their displacement is violent, propagated at the speed of sound. On the earth's surface, in an area of many square kilometres, reactions of unimaginable violence take place, materials are volatilized and utterly destroyed by direct radiation, by heat, by mechanical action, while an enormous amount of radioactive materials of varying life-span completes and continues the destruction through their activity.

This is the spectacle offered to the terrified gaze as the result of such use : entire cities, even the largest and richest in art and history, wiped out; a pall of death over pulverised ruins, covering countless victims with limbs burnt, twisted and scattered while others groan in their death agony. Meanwhile the spectre of a radioactive cloud hinders survivors from giving any help and inexorably advances to snuff out any remaining life. There will be no song of victory, only the inconsolable weeping of humanity, which in desolation will gaze upon a catastrophe brought on by its own folly.

Concerning *control* : inspection by properly equipped planes has been suggested for the purpose of watching over any atomic activities in large territories. Others might perhaps think of the possibility of a worldwide network of observation posts, each one staffed by experts of different countries and protected by solemn international pacts. Such centres would have to be equipped with delicate and precise meteorological and seismic instruments, with equipment for chemical analysis, with spectographs and such like; they would render possible the real control of many, unfortunately not all, of the activities which antecedently would be outlawed in the field of atomic experimentation.

We do not hesitate to declare, as We have in previous allocutions, that the sum total of those three measures as an object of international agreement is an obligation in conscience of nations and of their leaders. We said sum total of those measures, because the reason they are morally binding is also that equal security be established for all. If, however, only the first point, concerning experimentation, were put into effect, the result would be that the conviction would not be verified, the more so that there would be given sufficient reason to doubt the sincere desire to put into effect the other two conventions. We speak so frankly because the danger of insufficient proposals concerning peace depends in large part on the mutual suspicions that often trouble the dealings of powers concerned, each accusing the other in varying degrees of mere tactics, even of lack of sincerity in a matter basic to the fate of the whole human race... (III)

(The Catholic Mind, Vol. 54, 1956, pp. 170-172)

CHRISTMAS RADIO MESSAGE
23 December 1956

MILITARY SERVICE, ARMS AND WAR

Present-day conditions, which find no counterparts in the past, should be clear to everyone. There is no longer room for doubt concerning aims and methods which rely on tanks, when these latter noisily crash over borders and sow death in order to force civilian people into a pattern of life they explicitly detest, when, destroying as it were the stages of possible negotiation and mediation, the threat is made of using atomic weapons to gain certain demands, be they justified or not. It is clear that in the present circumstances there can be verified in a nation the situation wherein, every effort to avoid war being expended in vain, war — for effective defence and with the hope of a favourable outcome against unjust attack — could not be considered unlawful.

If, therefore, a body representative of the people and a goverment — both having been chosen by free elections — in a moment of extreme danger decides, by legitimate instruments of internal and external policy, on defensive precautions, and carries out the plans which they consider necessary, it does not act immorally. Therefore, a Catholic citizen cannot invoke his own conscience in order to refuse to serve and fulfil those duties the law imposes. On this matter we feel that We are in perfect harmony with Our predecessors, Leo XIII and Benedict XV, who never denied that obligation, but lamented the headlong armaments race and the moral dangers accompanying barracks life, and urged, as We do likewise, general disarmament as an effective remedy (see Acts of Leo XIII, volume 14, Rome, 1895, p. 210; Archives of Extraordinary Ecclesiastical Affairs, Notes of Cardinal Gasparri, Secretary of State of Benedict XV, to Prime Minister of United Kingdom of Great Britain and Ireland, September 28, 1917)...

UNITED NATIONS AUTHORITY

No one expects or demands the impossible, not even from the United Nations. But one should have a right to expect that their authority should have had its weight, at least through observers, in the places in which the essential values of man are in extreme danger.

Although the United Nations' condemnation of the grave violations of the rights of men and entire nations is worthy of recognition, one can nevertheless wish that, in similar cases, the exercise of their rights, as members of this organization, be denied to states which refuse even the admission of observers — thus showing that their concept of state sovereignty threatens the very foundations of the United Nations. This organization ought also to have the right and the power of forestalling all military intervention of one state in another, whatever the pretext under which it is effected, and also the right and power of assuming, by means of a sufficient police force, the safeguarding of order in the state which is threatened.

GENERAL DISARMAMENT AND NEW METHODS OF CONTROL

If We allude to these defects, it is because We desire to see strengthened the authority of the United Nations, especially for effecting general disarmament which We have so much at heart and on which We have already spoken in other discourses. In fact, only in the ambit of an institution like the United Nations can the promise of individual nations to reduce armament, especially to abandon the production and use of certain arms, be mutually exchanged under the strict obligation of international law. Likewise, only the United Nations is at present in a position to exact the observance of this obligation by assuming effective control of the armaments of all nations without exception. Its exercise of aerial observation will assure certain and effective knowledge of production and military preparedness for war with relative ease, while avoiding the disadvantages which the presence of foreign troops in a country can give rise to.

It indeed almost approaches the miraculous what technical science has been able to attain in this field. In fact, by the use of an adequate wide-angle lens and sufficient light, it is possible now to photograph, from a height of several kilometres and in sufficiently great detail, objects which are on the earth's surface. Scientific progress, modern techniques both mechanical and photographical, have succeeded in constructing cameras which have reached extraordinary perfection in all aspects. Film of high sensitivity with very fine grain makes it possible to enlarge pictures to hundreds of times their original size. Such cameras, mounted on airplanes which go at a speed very close to that of sound, are able automatically to take thousands of pictures, so that hundreds of thousands of square kilometres can be explored in a relatively short time.

The experiments conducted in this field have given exceptionally important results, permitting one to produce concrete evidence of machines, individual persons and objects existing on the ground and even, at least indirectly, in subterranean places. Researches thus far made have shown how very difficult it would be to camouflage the movement of troops or artillery, vast stores of arms or industrial centres important for war production. If these surveys could be permanent and systematic, it would be possible to bring out the minutest details and thus give a solid guarantee against eventual surprises.

The acceptance of control : this is the point crucial for victory, where every nation will show its sincere desire for peace.

THE WILL FOR PEACE

The desire for peace : free man's most valuable possession, this life's inestimable treasure, peace, is the fruit of men's effort, but also a precious gift of God. The Christian knows it since he has understood it at the cradle of the newborn Son of God. On His truth and on His commandments, the supreme absolute values, all order is founded and by them guarded and rendered fruitful in works of progress and civilization. (3)

(The Catholic Mind, Vol. 55, 1957, pp. 178-181)

CHRISTMAS RADIO MESSAGE
22 December 1957

ORDER AND HARMONY, THE BASIS OF ACTION OF ALL MEN OF GOOD WILL

For the sake of the common good, the chief basis of action, not only of Christians but of all men of good will, should be order and divine harmony in the world. Their preservation and development should be the supreme law which ought to govern the important meetings among men. If humanity today should fail to agree on the supremacy of this law, that is, on absolute respect for universal order and harmony in the world, it would be difficult to foresee what would be the proximate destiny of nations. The need for this agreement has been felt in practice when, lately, some specialists in the modern sciences have expressed doubts and internal disquiet at the development of atomic energy. Whatever may be, at present, the result of their deductions and resolutions, it is certain that the doubts of these men of the highest standing were directed at the problem of existence, the very foundations of order and harmony in the world.

At the present time, one must be convinced that every resolution concerning the development or abandonment of any achievement within the scope of man's ability ought to be made with due consideration for the preservation of order and harmony in the world. Nowadays an apparently blind fascination for progress leads nations to overlook evident dangers and to neglect to take quite considerable losses into account. Everyone is aware of how the development and application of any invention to a military purpose almost everywhere brings harm out of proportion, even in the political sphere, to the advantages which are derived from them and which could be secured by other paths at less cost and danger, or be quite simply postponed to a more convenient time.

Who can give an accurate calculation of the economic damage from a progress which is not inspired by wisdom ? Such quantities of material, such sums of money derived from saving and the result of restrictions and toil and such expenditure of human labour taken away from urgent needs are consumed to prepare these new arms that even the wealthiest nations must foresee the times in which they will regret the dangerously weakened harmony of the national economy, or are in fact already regretting it, though they endeavour to conceal the fact.

INTERNATIONAL COMPETITION IN THE DEVELOPMENT OF ARMAMENTS

To a person pondering and forming a judgment on the actual state of affairs — and always allowing for the right of self-defence — the present-day competition between nations in demonstrating their individual progress in war equipment assuredly offers new "signs in the skies". But even more it offers signs of pride, of that pride which produces on earth wide differences between souls, nourishes hatreds and prepares the way for conflict. Let those who observe today's competition, therefore, know how to reduce the facts to their true proportions. While not rejecting approaches aiming at peace agreements which are always desirable, let them not permit themselves to be misled by records which are often of very short duration. Let them not be too much influenced by fears skillfully evoked to win the interest and support of others who may be glad to be connected with a class of men among whom the "*homo faber*" takes precedence over the "*homo sapiens*". May the advantage then go to the Christian man who, making use of the liberty of spirit which is derived from a truly broad understanding of things, recovers in the objective consideration of events that peace and stability of soul which has its source in the Divine Spirit who, by His constant presence, holds the world in His care.

THE PROBLEM OF PEACE

But finally, the supporters of divine harmony in the world have been invited to direct their best efforts to the problem of peace. To all of you who know Our thoughts, it will be enough for Us on this occasion — if only to satisfy Our own mind, which is untiringly devoted to the cause of peace — to recall the immediate ends which the nations ought to aim at and bring to realization. We do this with a father's heart, as interpreting the tender cries of the Divine Infant of Bethlehem, source and pledge of all peace on earth and in the heavens.

The divine law of harmony in the world strictly imposes on all rulers of nations the obligation to prevent war by means of suitable international organizations, to reduce armaments under a system of effective inspection and to deter whoever should aim at disturbing the nations which sincerely desire it. We are sure that, at the first sign of danger, the tightening of that bond to a greater degree would not be wanting, as has been clearly attested and revealed on several occasions, even recently.

But at the moment, it is a question not so much of hastening to the defence as of preventing the overthrow of order and of giving a deserved breathing space to the world, which has already experienced too much suffering. We have endeavoured more than once in times of crisis, with warnings and counsel, to strengthen that mutual dependence. We regard it as a special task imposed by God on Our Pontificate to forge between nations the bonds of true brotherhood. We renew Our appeal so that among the true friends of peace all possible rivalry may come to an end and so that every reason for lack of trust may be removed. Peace is a good so precious, so productive, so desirable and so desired that every effort on its behalf, even with reciprocal sacrifices of legitimate individual ambitions, is well spent. We are sure that the peoples of the world are wholeheartedly in agreement with Us, and that they expect a like sentiment from their rulers.

May "the Prince of Peace" from the Crib of Bethlehem arouse, preserve and strengthen these aims. In the common unity of all men of good will, may He be pleased to fill up what is particularly wanting today in the realization of the order and harmony desired in the world by its Creator. (III)

(The Catholic Mind, Vol. 56, 1958, pp. 177-179)

JOHN XXIII

FIRST RADIO MESSAGE AFTER HIS ELECTION
29 October 1958

... Now, however, We would like to address the rulers of all nations, men into whose hands have been placed the lot, fortune, and hopes of their people. Why do they not settle their differences and disputes at last on an impartial basis ? Why are the powers of human ingenuity and material resources so often directed to the production of weapons — grim instruments of death and destruction — rather than to the advance of prosperity among the various classes of citizens, especially among those who live in want ?

We know that great and complex difficulties stand in the way of realizing this worthy objective and settling these disagreements, but they must be surmounted and overcome, for this is a most serious matter and a serious goal, intimately involved with the happiness of the whole human race.

Take action, then, boldly and with confidence. Heavenly light will shine upon you; God's help will be granted you. Look at the people who are entrusted to you ! Listen to them ! What do they want ? What do they ask you for ? Not for the new weapons our age has begotten for fratricide and general slaughter ! But for *peace*, in which the human family may live, thrive, and prosper freely...

(Pope John XXIII, TPS Press, Washington, D.C., 1964, pp. 13-14)

CHRISTMAS RADIO MESSAGE
23 December 1959

... Peace is a gift of God beyond compare. Likewise, it is the object of man's highest desire. It is, moreover, indivisible. None of the lineaments which make up its unmistakable appearance can be ignored or excluded.

In addition, since the men of our time have not completely carried into effect the conditions of peace, the result has been that God's paths toward peace have no meeting point with those of man. Hence there is the abnormal situation of this postwar period which has created, as it were, two blocs, with all their uneasiness. There is not a state of war, but neither is there peace, the thing which nations ardently desire.

At all times, because true peace is indivisible in its various aspects, it will not succeed in establishing itself on the social and international planes unless it is also, and in the first place, an interior fact. This requires then before all else — it is necessary to repeat — "men of good will". It is precisely to them that the angels of Bethlehem announced peace : "Peace among men of good will" (Luke 2:14). Indeed they alone can give reality to the conditions contained in the definition of peace given by St. Thomas, "the orderly harmony of citizens" (Contra Gentiles 3, c. 146), and therefore order and harmony.

But how will true peace be able to put forth the twofold blossom of order and harmony if the persons who hold positions of public responsibility, before pondering the advantages and risks of their decisions, fail to recognize themselves as persons subject to the eternal moral laws ?

It will be necessary again and again to remove the obstacles erected by the malice of man. And the presence of these obstacles is noted in the propaganda of immorality, in social injustice, in involuntary unemployment, in poverty contrasted with the luxury of those who can indulge in dissipation, in the dreadful lack of proportion between the technical and moral progress of nations, and in the unchecked armaments race, where there has yet to be a glimpse of a serious possibility of solving the problem of disarmament...

(Pope John XXIII, TPS Press, Washington, D.C., 1964, pp. 205-206)

ENCYCLICAL LETTER "MATER ET MAGISTRA"
15 May 1961

IN THE SERVICE OF LIFE

Genesis relates how God imposed on the first human beings two commands : that of transmitting life : "Increase and multiply" (Gen. I:28) and that of dominating nature : "Fill the earth and subdue it" (Ibid.), commands which complement each other.

Certainly the divine command to dominate nature is not aimed at destructive purposes; instead it is for the service of life.

We point out with sadness one of the most disturbing contradictions by which our epoch is tormented and by which it is being consumed, namely that, while on the one hand are brought out in strong relief situations of want, and the spectre of misery and hunger haunts us; on the other hand scientific discoveries, technical inventions and economic resources are being used, often extensively, to provide terrible instruments of ruin and death...

MUTUAL DISTRUST

One can thus understand how in the minds of individual human beings and among different peoples the conviction of the urgent necessity of mutual understanding and cooperation is becoming ever more widespread. But at the same time, it seems that men, especially those entrusted with greater responsibility, show themselves unable to understand one another. The root of such inability is not to be sought in scientific, technical or economic reasons but in the absence of mutual trust. Men, and consequently States, fear each other. Each fears that the other harbours plans of conquest, and is waiting for the favourable moment to put these plans into effect. Hence, each organizes its own defences and arms itself not for attacking, so it is said, but to deter the potential aggressor against any effective invasion.

As a consequence, vast human energies and gigantic resources are employed in non-constructive purposes; meanwhile, in the minds of individual human beings and among peoples, a sense of uneasiness and reluctance which lessens the spirit of initiative for works on a broad scale arises and grows. (Part III)

(Typis Polyglottis Vaticanis, 1961, pp. 43-45)

RADIO MESSAGE FOR PEACE
10 September 1961

Venerable brethren, beloved sons !

The Apostle Peter in his speech to those who were come together in the house of the Roman centurion Cornelius declared that all the nations of the earth without distinction were henceforth invited to pay heed to the universal Fatherhood of God. And he summed up this heavenly doctrine in words of peace : *annuntians pacem per Iesum Christum* (Acts. 10:36).

This same message is the very beat of Our Heart, the heart of a father and of a bishop of the Holy Church. It comes more anxiously to Our lips whenever clouds seem to be gathering darkly on the horizon.

We have before Us the memory of the popes who most closely preceded Us and their outspoken manifestations of solicitude and anxious appeals, which have become part of history.

From the exhortation of Pius X a few days before his saintly death (cf. AAS6 (1914) 373), when the first European conglagration was imminent, to the encyclical of Benedict XV, "*Pacem, Dei Munus Pulcherrimum*" (AAS12 (1920) 209 ff.), "Peace, the Most Beautiful Gift of God"; from the warning call of Pius XI, which looked to true peace "*non tam tabulis inscriptam, quam in animis consignatam*" (cf. the papal bull. "Infinita Dei", May 29, 1924; AAS16 (1924) 213), to that fervent last appeal of Pius XII on August 24, 1939 : "It is by the power of sound reason, not by force of arms, that justice makes its way" (Pius XII, Discorsi e Radiomessaggi, I (1939) 306), — we have a whole series of pleas, sometimes deeply sorrowful and moving, always paternal, calling upon the whole world to guard against the danger while there is yet time, and assuring the nations that whereas everything is lost, and lost to everyone, through war, nothing will be lost through peace.

We make this appeal Our own, extending it once more to those who bear on their consciences the gravest weight of public, recognized responsibility. The Church by her very nature cannot remain indifferent to human suffering, even were it no more than anxiety and worry. And this is why We call upon the rulers of nations to face squarely the tremendous responsibilities they bear before the tribunal of history, and, what is more, before the judgment seat of God; this is why We entreat them not to fall victims to false, deceptive pressures.

It is indeed upon wise men that the issue depends : that force shall not prevail, but right, through free and sincere negotiations; that truth and justice shall be affirmed through the safeguarding of the essential liberties and invincible values of every nation and every human person.

Without exaggerating the importance of what has so far had only the appearance — though We must say the very irresponsible and tragically deplorable appearance — of a threat of war, as reported in the sources of daily public information, it is quite natural that We should make Our own the anxious solicitude of Our predecessors and express it through a sacred warning to all Our children, as We feel it Our right and duty to name them, believers in God and in His Christ, and unbelievers as well, for all men belong to God and to Christ by right of origin and of redemption...

Anyone who remembers the history of the not too distant past, a past recorded in books as an epoch of misfortune, and who still has a vivid recollection of the bloodstained half century between 1914 and the present, and who remembers the sufferings of our peoples and our lands — although there were peaceful interludes between one tribulation and the next — trembles at the thought of what can happen to each one of us and to the whole world. Every war brings upheaval and destruction to individuals, to peoples, to entire regions. What could happen today — considering the frightful effects of new weapons of destruction and ruin which human ingenuity continues to multiply, to everyone's loss ?

In Our youth We were always deeply moved by the ancient cry of despair of Desiderius, the King of the Lombards, which he uttered when the army of Charlemagne first appeared on the Alps : he tore his hair and cried out, "*O ferrum, heu ferrum*" (Monachi San Gallensis Gesta Karoli, Lib. II, par. 17. — Monumenta Germaniae Historica, Scriptores, t. 2, Hannoverae 1829, p. 760, line 3.). What then should be said of the modern instruments of war derived from the secrets of nature and capable of unleashing unheard-of energy to wreak havoc and destruction ?

Thanks be to God, We are persuaded that up to now there is no serious threat of war, immediate or remote. In making this reference of Our own to a subject that the press of all nations is discussing, We mean nothing more than to seize yet another opportunity of appealing with confidence to the calm, sure wisdom of the statesmen and men of government in every country who preside over the direction of public affairs...

(The Pope Speaks, Vol. 7, pp. 251-254)

CHRISTMAS RADIO MESSAGE
21 December 1961

... And finally all humanity must be good. These words which resound through the ages and are now repeated with modern accents, recall the duty incumbent on all men to be good, that means, to be just, upright, generous, disinterested, willing to understand and to forgive, ready to grant pardon with magnanimity. As an invitation to the exercise of this duty, We turn to the appeal, which with all trust We started out to make in this radio braodcast — to desire peace and to eliminate all obstacles in its way.

We cannot believe that the terrific energy now under the control of man will be released for the world's destruction. For side by side with elements of fear and apprehension, there are positive signs of goodwill that is constructive and productive of good. While We give thanks to the Lord, the source of goodness, We also give voice to a heartfelt appeal that all those who control the economic forces should risk everything but not the peace of the world and the lives of men — to seek every means that modern progress has put at their disposal to increase the welfare suspicion. And again, to use the words of Our encyclical *Mater et Magistra*, "We point out with sadness... that, while on the one hand are brought out in strong relief situations of want, and the spectre of misery and hunger haunts us; on the other hand scientific discoveries, technical inventions and economic resources are being used, often extensively, to provide terrible instruments of ruin and death." (A.A.S. LIII (1961) p. 448) ...

(The Tablet, Vol. 216, 1962, p. 8)

148

RADIO MESSAGE FOR PEACE
25 October 1962

"I beseech Thee, O Lord, let thy ear be attentive to the prayer of thy servant, and to the prayer of thy servants who desire to fear thy name." (Ne. 1:11).

This ancient biblical prayer rises to Our trembling lips today from the depths of a heart that is greatly moved and afflicted.

While the Second Vatican Ecumenical Council has just been opened amidst the joy and hopes of all men of good will, threatening clouds now come to darken once again the international horizon and to sow fear in millions of families.

As We stressed when welcoming the 86 extraordinary missions present at the opening of the Council (cf. TPS, VIII, 268-71), the Church has nothing nearer to her heart than peace and brotherhood among all men, and she strives tirelessly to achieve this.

We recalled in this regard the grave duties of those who bear the responsibility of power, and We added : "In all conscience let them give ear to the anguished cry of 'peace ! peace !' which rises up to heaven from every part of the world, from innocent children and those grown old, from individuals and from communities." (Ibid., 270)

THE VALUE OF NEGOTIATING

Today We repeat that solemn warning. We beseech all rulers not to remain deaf to the cry of mankind. Let them do everything in their power to save peace. By so doing, they will spare the world the horrors of a war that would have disastrous consequences such as no one can foresee.

Let them continue to negotiate, because their sincere and open attitude is of great value as a witness for the conscience of each one and in the face of history. To promote, favour and accept negotiations, at all levels and at all times, is a rule of wisdom and prudence which calls down the blessing of heaven and earth.

A WORLDWIDE PRAYER FOR PEACE

May all Our children, may all those who have been marked with the seal of Baptism and nourished by Christian hope, may all those, finally, who are united to Us by faith in God, join their prayers to Ours to obtain from heaven the gift of peace : a peace which will be true and lasting only if it is based on justice and equity.

And upon all those who contribute to this peace, upon all those who work with a sincere heart for the true welfare of men, may there descend the special blessing which We lovingly bestow in the name of Him who wished to be called the "Prince of Peace". (Is. 9:6)

(Pope John XXIII, TPS Press, Washington, D.C., 1964, pp. 222-223)

ENCYCLICAL LETTER "PACEM IN TERRIS"
11 May 1963

DISARMAMENT

On the other hand, it is with deep sorrow that We note the enormous stocks of armaments that have been and still are being made in more economically developed countries, with a vast outlay of intellectual and economic resources. And so it happens that, while the people of these countries are loaded with heavy burdens, other countries as a result are deprived of the collaboration they need in order to make economic and social progress.

The production of arms is allegedly justified on the grounds that in present-day conditions peace cannot be preserved without an equal balance of armaments. And so, if one country increases its armaments, others feel the need to do the same; and if one country is equipped with nuclear weapons, other countries must produce their own, equally destructive.

Consequently, people live in constant fear lest the storm that every moment threatens should break upon them with dreadful violence. And with good reason, for the arms of war are ready at hand. Even though it is difficult to believe that anyone would deliberately take the responsibility for the appalling destruction and sorrow that war would bring in its train, it cannot be denied that the conflagration may be set off by some incontrollable and unexpected chance. And one must bear in mind that, even though the monstrous power of modern weapons acts as a deterrent, it is to be feared that the mere continuance of nuclear tests, undertaken with war in mind, will have fatal consequences for life on the earth.

Justice, then, right reason and humanity urgently demand that the arms race should cease; that the stockpiles which exist in various countries should be reduced equally and simultaneously by the parties concerned; that nuclear weapons should be banned; and that a general agreement should eventually be reached about progressive disarmament and an effective method of control. In the words of Pius XII, Our Predecessor of happy memory : *The calamity of a world war, with the economic and social ruin and the moral excesses and dissolution that accompany it, must not be permitted to envelop the human race for a third time.* (AAS 34 (1942) p. 17).

All must realize that there is no hope of putting an end to the building up of armaments, nor of reducing the present stocks, nor, still less, of abolishing them altogether, unless the process is complete and thorough and unless it proceeds from inner conviction : unless, that is, everyone sincerely cooperates to banish the fear and anxious expectation of war with which men are oppressed. If this is to come about, the fundamental principle on which our present peace depends must be replaced by another, which declares that the true and solid peace of nations consists not in equality of arms but in mutual trust alone. We believe that this can be brought to pass, and We consider that it is something which reason requires, that it is eminently desirable in itself and that it will prove to be the source of many benefits.

In the first place, it is an objective demanded by reason. There can be, or at least there should be, no doubt that relations between states, as between individuals, should be regulated not by the force of arms but by the light of reason, by the rule, that is, of truth, of justice and of active and sincere co-operation.

Secondly, We say that it is an objective earnestly to be desired in itself. Is there anyone who does not ardently yearn to see war banished, to see peace preserved and daily more firmly established ?

And finally, it is an objective which will be a fruitful source of many benefits, for its advantages will be felt everywhere, by individuals, by families, by nations, by the whole human family. The warning of Pius XII still rings in our ears : *Nothing is lost by peace; everything may be lost by war.* (AAS 31 (1939) p. 334).

Since this is so, We, the Vicar on earth of Jesus Christ, Saviour of the World and Author of Peace, and as interpreter of the very profound longing of the entire human family, following the impulse of Our heart, seized by anxiety for the good of all, We feel it Our duty to beseech men, especially those who have the responsibility of public affairs, to spare no labour in order to ensure that world events follow a reasonable and human course.

In the highest and most authoritative assemblies, let men give serious thought to the problem of a peaceful adjustment of relations between political Communities on a world level : an adjustment founded on mutual trust, on sincerity in negotiations, on faithful fulfilment of obligations assumed. Let them study the problem until they find that point of agreement from which it will be possible to commence to go forward towards accords that will be sincere, lasting and fruitful.

We, for Our part, will not cease to pray God to bless these labours so that they may lead to fruitful results. (Part III)

(Typis Polyglottis Vaticanis, 1963, pp. 28-30)

PAUL VI

TELEGRAMME TO THE SIGNATORIES OF THE TREATY BANNING NUCLEAR EXPERIMENTS
5 August 1963

The 7 August edition of *L'Osservatore Romano* published the message which Pope VI addressed on 5 August to the President of the United States, the Prime Minister of Great Britain and the Head of the Goverment of the Soviet Union, who had just signed the Treaty of Moscow about the prohibition of nuclear tests. The same message was also sent to the General Secretary of the United Nations Organization.

"The signing of the Treaty banning nuclear experiments has also touched very intimately Our heart, because We see therein a proof of good will, a pledge of harmony, and a promise of a more serene future.

Welcoming in Our soul, always solicitous for the welfare of humanity, the echo of satisfaction and hope which rises from every corner of the world, We express Our felicitations on the conclusion of an act so comforting and so significant, and We pray God that He prepare the way for a new and true peace in the world."

(Acta Apostolicae Sedis, Vol. LV, 1963, p. 760)

CHRISTMAS RADIO MESSAGE
23 December 1963

PEACE, SUPREME GOOD IN TRANQUILLITY AND SECURITY

While We view the entire panorama of nations, We can not but mention again another pressing need of mankind — peace.

This is suggested by Christmas itself since, as we all know, this feast is presented to us as a message of peace bestowed from Heaven upon all men of goodwill.

This is treated in the greatest encyclical of Our venerated predecessor, John XXIII, who addressed himself to the fundamental question of peace in our modern world. The developments and controversies of our time force us continually to consider the nature of peace, its forms and weaknesses, its needs and progress.

This encyclical (*pacem in Terris*) has shown us, if We may so put it, the new problems of peace and the dynamism of the elements from which peace must result.

St. Augustine's classic definition of peace as the "tranquillity of order" seems to be applicable today, in the sense that the tranquillity and security of peace are the product of the well-ordered movement of component parts, rather than being something static and fixed. Peace lies in well-balanced motion.

There are other reasons for mentioning peace in Our Christmas message. First, it is necessary to heed the yearning of the new generation. Youth desires peace. Secondly, we see that peace is still weak, fragile, threatened, and that in not a few, fortunately limited, regions of the earth, peace is violated.

We observe with some apprehension other obvious facts. Peace in the present time is based more on fear than on friendship. It is maintained more by terror of deadly weapons than by mutual harmony and faith among peoples. And if tomorrow peace were to be broken — which God forbid — all humanity could be destroyed.

How can we celebrate Christmas with serenity when such a threat hangs over the world? Therefore, We urgently beseech all men of good will, yes, all men who hold responsible positions in the field of culture and politics, to consider as fundamental the problem of peace.

True peace is not that hypocritical propaganda aimed at lulling the adversary to sleep and concealing one's own preparation for war. Peace does not consist in pacifist rhetoric that refuses the indispensable, patient and tiresome negotiations which are the only efficacious means of achieving peace.

Peace is not based merely on the precarious balance of opposing economic interests, nor on the dream of proud supremacy. But true peace is based on the abolition, or at least on the mitigation, of the causes that endanger its security, as nationalistic or ideological pride, the arms race, lack of confidence in the methods or in the organizations that have been constituted to render the relations among nations orderly and friendly.

Peace in truth, in justice, in freedom, in love — this is the peace we pray for...

(The Catholic Mind, Vol. 62, 1964, pp. 50-51)

ADDRESS AT THE GENERAL AUDIENCE
26 August 1964

APPEAL FOR PEACE

... Peace is a supreme good for humanity living not in eternity but in time. But it is a fragile good, arising from mobile and complex factors, in which man's free and responsible will is in continual play. Therefore peace is never completely stable and secure; it must at every moment be rethought and reconstituted; rapidly it weakens and degenerates, if it is not incessantly brought back to those true principles which alone can generate and preserve it.

CRUMBLING OF BASIC PRINCIPLES AND REBIRTH OF PERILOUS CRITERIA

We are now witnessing this frightening phenomenon : the crumbling of some of those basic principles on which peace must be founded, and the firm possession of which was thought achieved after the tragic experiences of the two World Wars. At the same time, we see the rebirth of several perilous criteria, which are once again serving to guide a short-sighted quest for equilibrium, or rather of an unstable truce in relations of nations and of the ideologies of peoples with one another.

Yet again there is obscured the concept of the sacred and inviolable character of human life, and once more men are being calculated in function of their numbers, their possible efficiency in war, and not by reason of their dignity, their needs, their common brotherhood.

New symptoms are noted of a regrowth of divisions and oppositions between peoples, between the various races and different cultures. This spirit of division is guided by nationalistic pride, by prestige, politics, the armaments race, social and economical antagonisms.

There returns the illusory concept that peace can only be based on the terrifying power of homicidal weapons; and, while on the one hand noble but weak discussion and efforts are made to limit and abolish armaments, on the other the destructive capacity of military apparatus is being continually developed and perfected.

Once again the terror and execration of war grows less, war as a vain means of resolving international questions by force; and in various parts of the world episodes of war explode in fearful sparks, exhausting the mediating capacity of the organizations instituted to maintain peace in security, and to ensure to the method of free and honorable diplomatic negotiation the exclusive prerogative of conclusive procedure.

Thus arise political and ideological egoism as the direct expression of the life of peoples. Attempts are made upon the tranquillity of entire naions, by the organization from outside of subversive propaganda and revolutionary disorders. Even pacifist declamation is misused to promote social and political contrasts.

Thus arise egoism, exclusivist interests, passionate tensions, hate between peoples. And thus falls the esteem of loyalty, of brotherhood and of solidarity. Thus dies love !

If the security of peoples still rests on the hypothesis of a lawful and collective use of armed force, we must recall that security reposes still more on an effort at mutual understanding, on the generosity of loyal mutual trust, on the spirit of collaboration for common advantage and for aid, particularly to developing countries.

In a word, it rests upon love !...

(The Catholic Mind, Vol. 62, 1964, pp. 57-58)

MESSAGE TO THE WORLD
ON THE OCCASION OF THE VISIT
TO THE INTERNATIONAL EUCHARISTIC CONGRESS
OF BOMBAY
4 December 1964

Gentlemen of the Press,

Although Our pilgrimage to Bombay is brief and filled with appointments, We have desired to dedicate a short period to a meeting with you. We thank you for your intense work in regard to Our visit, reminding you that the Press which you represent can be a most potent instrument for great good. Always be faithful to the truth, remembering your responsibility to the public and eventually to history.

We entrust to you Our special message to the world. Would that the nations could cease the armaments race, and devote their resources and energies instead to the fraternal assistance of the developing countries ! Would that every nation, thinking "thoughts of peace and not of affliction" and war, would contribute even a part of its expenditure for arms to a great world fund for the relief of the many problems of nutrition, clothing, shelter and medical care which affect so many peoples !

From the peaceful altar of the Eucharistic Congress, may this Our anguished cry go forth to all the governments of the world, and may God inspire them to undertake this peaceful battle against the sufferings of their less fortunate brothers !

(L'Osservatore Romano, 5.12.1964, p. 1)

CHRISTMAS RADIO MESSAGE
22 December 1964

... So too, we cannot help being alarmed at a militarism no longer focused on the legitimate defence of the countries concerned or on the maintenance of world peace, but tending rather to build up stockpiles of weapons ever more powerful and destructive — a process which consumes enormous quantities of money and manpower, feeds popular sentiment with thoughts of power and war, and induces men to make mutual fear the treacherous and inhuman basis of world peace.

In this context, we have no hesitation in expressing our hopes that the rulers of nations will find a way to promote, prudently and magnanimously, the process of disarmament. We would like to see a generous minded investigation of how — at least in part and by stages — military expenditure could be diverted to humanitarian ends; and this, not only to the advantage of the particular countries concerned, but also of others in the course of development or in a state of need...

(The Catholic Mind, Vol. 63, 1965, p. 62)

ADDRESS TO THE SACRED COLLEGE OF CARDINALS
24 June 1965

SAVE, DIFFUSE, CONSOLIDATE PEACE BETWEEN PEOPLES

Then there is another major question that has to do with Our apostolic ministry and involves it, even if indirectly : We mean peace in the world.

We have raised Our anguished voice many times in recent months in the face of the doleful conflicts which are causing grief and bloodshed for innocent people, and which are threatening to spread further, to upset the peace even more profoundly.

By the infinite goodness of the Most High, nothing has happened that is irreparable, but the threat is far from past. Instead it has been aggravated, and new fires of discord have been enkindled in other parts of the world.

And so, let no one take it amiss if We appeal once again on behalf of peace, for it is still in danger. We would like to say to the men in positions of responsibility : this has to stop while there is still time. The spark that is not put out can cause a fire whose proportions frighten the imagination. Mankind can still clearly recall the disasters that go with a world war; it still bears the scars of such a war in its flesh. And so it looks with trepidation upon these events and wants to be spared new and bitter trials.

We cannot hide Our uneasiness. Our mind and the minds of all men who are worthy of the name, are horrified at the prospect of a war in which the terrible instruments of destruction which science and technology have discovered, would be employed. It would be a tragic, irreversible, fatal eventuality; it would be the end, not of difficulties, but of civilization.

Let anyone who wants to prolong, or who is helping to prolong, a conflict which cannot have sufficient justification, keep in mind the lessons of history : events can escape from the hands of the men who think they can control them.

War — and the experience of the last one proves it — doesn't solve problems; instead it creates new and more complicated ones. Safety is to be found in frank, honest, sincere negotiation.

And so We want to express Our pleasure and satisfaction with those government leaders who show that they want a sincere and honorable peace; who also undertake positive initiatives, which may at times be genuinely bold and unusual, to bring the contending parties closer together and to induce them to replace armed conflicts with negotiations which will result in new forms of equilibrium, mutual respect, observance of treaties, and fraternal collaboration among free peoples. May Our encouragement lend support to these noble efforts, and may Our prayers make Our wishes effective and helpful to everyone.

PATERNAL WISHES FOR THE PEOPLES OF VIETNAM, CONGO, SANTO DOMINGO AND ALGERIA

And so an expression of Our thanks goes to all those who have re-echoed the proposal We made during Our trip to Bombay last December — to take at least a part of the savings which individual states could realize by adopting plans for effective disarmament, and divert it to aiding the needy and hungry peoples of the world and the developing nations. Our suggestion for the institution of an international fund with these means and with this purpose has, for the most part, met with a warm reception among the competent authorities — to such an extent as to raise the hope that the undertaking may be realized in the not too distant future, in a practical way which will be extremely beneficial and exemplary...

(The Pope Speaks, Vol. 10, pp. 218-219)

ADDRESS TO THE GENERAL ASSEMBLY
OF THE UNITED NATIONS ORGANIZATION
4 October 1965

... 5. And now We come to the most important point of Our message, which is, at first, a negative point. You are expecting Us to utter this sentence, and We are well aware of its gravity and solemnity : *not some peoples against others*, never again, never more ! It was principally for this purpose that the Organization of the United Nations arose : against war, in favour of peace! Listen to the lucid words of a great man, the late John Kennedy who proclaimed four years ago : "Mankind must put an end to war, or war will put an end to mankind." Many words are not needed to proclaim this loftiest aim of your institution. It suffices to remember that the blood of millions of men, that numberless and unheard of sufferings, useless slaughter and frightful ruin, are the sanction of the past which unites you with an oath which must change the future history of the world : No more war, war never again ! Peace, it is peace which must guide the destinies of peoples and of all mankind.

Gratitude and high praise are due to you, who for twenty years have laboured for peace; gratitude and praise for the conflicts which you have prevented or have brought to an end. The results of your efforts in recent days in favour of peace, even if not yet proved decisive, are such as to deserve that We, presuming to interpret the sentiments of the whole world, express to you both praise and thanks.

Gentlemen, you have performed and you continue to perform a great work : the education of mankind in the ways of peace. The U.N. is the great school where that education is imparted, and we are today in the assembly hall of that school. Everyone who takes his place here becomes a pupil and also a teacher in the art of building peace. When you leave this hall, the world looks upon you as the architects and constructors of peace.

Peace, as you know, is not built up only by means of politics or the balance of forces and of interests. It is constructed with the mind, with ideas, with works of peace. You are already working in this direction. But your work is still at the initial stages. Will the world ever succeed in changing that selfish and contentious mentality from which so much of its history has been woven? It is not easy to foresee. On the other hand, it is easy to affirm that we must resolutely march towards a new future, a future of truly human peace, that peace which God has promised to men of good will. The paths that lead to such a peace have already been marked out : the first is that of disarmament.

If you offensive to be brothers, let the weapons fall from your hands. You cannot love with weapons in your hands. Long before they mete out death and destruction, those terrible arms supplied by modern science foment bad feelings and cause nightmares, distrust, and dark designs. They call for enormous expenditures and hold up projects of human solidarity and of great usefulness. They lead astray the mentality of peoples. As long as man remains that weak, changeable and even wicked being he often shows himself to be, defensive armaments will, alas, be necessary. But you, gentlemen, men of courage and outstanding merit, are seeking means to guarantee the stability of international relations without the need of recourse to arms. This is a goal worthy of your efforts; this is what the peoples of the world expect from you. This is what must be achieved! For that unchallenged confidence in this Organization must increase; its authority must be strengthened. Then your aim, it may be hoped; will be accomplished. You will thus win the gratitude of all peoples, relieved of an overburdening expenditure on armaments, and freed from the nightmare of ever imminent war.

We are happy to know that many of you have given favourable consideration to the appeal We addressed last December at Bombay to all nations, when We invited them in the interests of peace to apply for the benefit of developing nations a portion at least of the savings that would result from a reduction in armaments. We here renew that invitation, confident of your feelings of humanity and generosity...

(Typis Polyglottis Vaticanis, 1965, pp. 13-17)

MESSAGE TO THE GENERAL SECRETARY
OF THE UNITED NATIONS ORGANIZATION
24 January 1966

Mr. Secretary General,

You know with what attention We follow the peace efforts of the United Nations Organization.

At a time when the "Committee of Eighteen for Disarmament" is about to resume its activities in Geneva and inspired by the desire to see the work of this Committee achieve a positive and concrete result, We should like to address this urgent appeal to you, with the hope that these deliberations will mark a new stage towards the realization of disarmament as is unanimously expected and hoped for.

In doing so, We feel encouraged by the recent position taken by more than 2,000 Catholic Bishops meeting in Rome as an Ecumenical Council. We likewise feel encouraged by the echo Our Bombay appeal has found with the Commission on Disarmament and by the favourable reception of Our discourse to the United Nations on the part of world opinion.

In raising Our voice in favour of the great cause of disarmament, We are conscious of faithfully following the path of Our predecessors. To mention one of the most recent ones, we all know with what clarity Pius XII faced the problem on the occasion of the first Christmas of the war during his pontificate. In expressing his wish for the establishment of a right order, which would follow the war, he said : "So that the order thus established may have the tranquillity and duration which are the foundations of a true peace, nations must be freed from the heavy servitude of an arms race and from the danger that material force, instead of being used to guarantee the right, rather becomes a tyrannical instrument of violation. Peace resolutions which do not give a basic importance to an organic, progressive and mutually agreed upon disarmament, both in the practical and spiritual order, and which cannot be applied to honestly achieving disarmament, will sooner or later reveal their weakness and precariousness." (Discorsi e Radiomessaggi, 1,441)

In his memorable encyclical "Pacem in terris", John XXIII proclaimed : "Justice, right reason and humanity urgently demand that the arms race should cease; ... that a general agreement should eventually be reached about progressive disarmament and an effective method of control."

As We, in turn, intervene in this field, We do not claim to disregard the complexity of the problem, nor to ignore the enormous difficulties which qualified organizations of the United Nations, ever since their founding, are facing with constancy and a competence that are rightfully to be commended.

But no one can deny the fact that every passing day shows ever more clearly that no stable peace can be established among men as long as there is no effective, general and controled reduction of armaments. Also, every passing day shows ever more painfully and tragically the contrast between the huge sums swallowed up in the manufacture of arms and the immense and growing material distress of more than half of humanity who still wait for the satisfaction of their most elementary needs.

Mr. Secretary General, We trust that you will receive this intervention on Our part as an expression of Our esteem for the authority of the United Nations Organization and the great capabilities of the members of the "Committee of Eighteen".

We hope that you may discern in it an echo of the fervent hope of the people of our time, for whom, in the name of the Ecumenical Council recently held in Rome, We thought that we could and should be their interpreter to you.

It is with this sense of awareness that We express Our best wishes for the complete success of the coming Geneva deliberations and that We invoke upon them and upon all who take part in them the blessings of God Almighty.

Pope Paul VI

(Acta Apostolicae Sedis, Vol. LVIII, 1966, pp. 135-136; Translation by Pontifical Commission "Iustitia et Pax")

HOMILY ON THE DAY OF PRAYER FOR PEACE
4 October 1966

My dear brothers, sisters and all who have accepted Our invitation to pray for peace. Let us meditate together for a moment on the reasons that prompt Us to take such a spiritual action. They were presented in Our encyclical letter *"Christi Matri"*, but it is useful to briefly recall them here, in order to give greater consciousness and vigour to the religious act that we are celebrating together.

Again, We are dealing with peace. We have no fear that the repetition of this theme will lead Us into mere rhetorics or superfluous discourses. The theme of peace is a matter for inexhaustible reflection, because it relates to a human reality of supreme importance and is constantly exposed to the most serious and unexpected changes. It is a theme that We should never tire of contemplating and discussing, since it deals with the bustle of events in which the fate of humanity is played out.

One year ago, on this very day, We had the priviledge of addressing a word about peace to the most authoritative and best qualified world institution for promoting and safeguarding peace in the world : the United Nations Organization which has its headquarters in New York.

Still today, We are grateful for that invitation which gave Us an opportunity of bringing Our fraternal message to the representatives gathered there from many nations. Still today, We think with joy and amazement at the wonderful correspondence, enhanced by an evidence and a solemnity as never before, which exists between the highest aim of this Supreme Assembly and the humble, joyful and eternal voice of Our Gospel. They both agree in a remarkable and mysterious way on the one identical word : peace.

We also recall the memory of that historical and moving moment in order to renew the wish — then the wish of all — while the world listened, reflected and applauded : may peace reign in the world; no more war, never ! No more rivalries, conflicts, violent dominations and selfishness, but universal brotherhood in justice and freedom.

Yes, today We renew Our wish, or better said Our cry for peace, because we all know how great is the need for it, how fervent the desire for it, how arduous its realization. However, We repeat it with sorrow : the conditions for peace have not improved in the world since last year. This was said by a witness, very highly qualified because of his important responsibility as Secretary General of the United Nations, who states in the introduction of his annual report : "The international political situation has not improved". Rather, we all know how delicate it is, and how unfortunately justified is the fear of a new and heightened tension.

Nevertheless, We add that we should not give in to disappointment. We should not be surprised if the human ascent to the peaks of civilization includes times of uncertainty, fatigue and difficulties. We know what complex problems arise from the life of men in society. We know man's weakness. And the fact that man, at a certain point on his difficult way, is tempted to stop and turn back; to go on in word but to move back in action, is a cause for sadness not for astonishment.

Man is like that : not only weak but also inconsistent; more confident in his own empiric calculation than assured by the goodness of great, human, true and progressive ideas. Even if man so moves on in his march towards peace, in an oscillating and intermittent way, we should not lose our faith in the validity of the cause of peace, or the courage to continue defending and promoting it, or the confidence that it will ultimately be achieved. We should always maintain that peace is possible. We must make all efforts to make it possible.

What then are some of the thoughts that come into our minds at this moment devoted to their highest expressions ?

The first thought, the first proposition is perseverance in the search for peace. Mankind must remain faithful to the great idea conceived after the widespread tragedy of the war : that we must all of us, and at all times, look for peace, universal peace.

And if at the outset of this formidable resolution there was the agonizing experience of war, if there was fear, if there was the terror to see it repeated in increased and apocalyptic proportions, today it is love that should sustain such a resolution, love for all men; We say, love of peace rather than fear of war. Love is fruitful in the principles and ideas that breed true peace, namely brotherhood, justice, freedom, cooperation and generosity.

This suggests to us another consideration, another proposition : all of us must form and educate ourselves for peace, we must nourish our spirit with "thoughts of peace" (Jer. 28:11). Those ideas which, before creating peace in the political world and in external equilibrium, establish it in the depth of conscience, in the mentality of modern man and in the behaviour of a civilized people.

In this respect we should note that despite everything, the idea of peace is growing in the consciousness, if not always in the activity, of our contemporary world. We observe that less and less attention is being paid to equivocal propaganda aimed at exploiting peace for aims other than an order based on the respect for the rights of the human person and of the free peoples.

We see an inner conviction growing that true and lasting peace cannot be based on the power of deadly weapons or on the static tension of opposing ideologies. The political concept of peace is in the process of being formed. Peace is neither an apathetic pacifism, nor a greedy selfishness, or indifference or lack of interest for the needs of others, but the fruit of a united and unflagging practical effort for the construction of a society on the local and universal level, a society which is built on human solidarity in the pursuit of the common good of all.

If we look at the great needs of mankind and the great dangers jeopardizing its serenity today, the name for peace, as We have said, is development : development of peoples still in need of so many basic things for their life and who still represent a large part of mankind.

If this is so, then another thought comes to mind, another proposition makes its way into our hearts. Peace is difficult ! But peace is something great, something necessary, something sought after and fostered by many. It is something difficult, extremely difficult. Yet, as We have said, it is certainly not impossible. Why is it not impossible ? Are human forces sufficient to achieve and maintain it ? At this moment, We prefer not to give an exhaustive answer to this agonizing question which queries the most arduous theses of thinking and history; We simply wish to close with the words of Christ regarding the solution of this great problem : "For men this is impossible, but with God all things are possible" (Matthew 19:26).

These words justify the act we are performing at this moment : a prayer for peace. This act has its logical foundation in faith, in the faith that man is not left to his own forces alone, but rather that a paternal and mightier force can intervene in the development of the decisive events related to him. This force is the help of Divine Providence; it is love coming from Heaven; it is the victorious love of the Father for the salvation of man.

(Insegnamenti di Paolo VI, Vol. IV, 1966, pp. 457-461; Translation by Pontifical Commission "Iustitia et Pax")

ENCYCLICAL LETTER "POPULORUM PROGRESSIO"
26 March 1967

... WORLD FUND...

51. But it is necessary to go still further. At Bombay We called for the establishment of a great World Fund, to be made up of part of the money spent on arms, to relieve the most destitute of this world. (Message to the World, given to Journalists on 4 Dec. 1964, AAS 57 (1965), p. 135.) What is true of the immediate struggle against want, holds good also when there is a question of development. Only worldwide collaboration, of which a common fund would be both means and symbol, will succeed in overcoming vain rivalries and in establishing a fruitful and peaceful exchange between peoples.

... ITS URGENCE

53. Besides, who does not see that such a fund would make it easier to take measures to prevent certain wasteful expenditures, the result of fear or pride ? When so many people are hungry, when so many families suffer from destitution, when so many remain steeped in ignorance, when so many schools, hospitals and homes worthy of the name remain to be built, all public or private squandering of wealth, all expenditure prompted by motives of national or personal ostentation, every exhausting armaments race, becomes an intolerable scandal. We are conscious of Our duty to denounce it. Would that those in authority listened to Our words before it is too late !

(Typis Polyglottis Vaticanis, 1967, pp. 37-38)

ANGELUS MESSAGE
27 August 1967

In this spiritual moment, let us recall the positive fact of the week : the presentation of the text of the nuclear non-proliferation treaty.

This fact seems to Us to be a positive one, because it shows that the responsible leaders are aware of the dreadful and incalculable danger represented by nuclear arms, and because it marks the first step — not yet decisive, of course, but initial — to conjure up this danger which is weighing on the whole of humanity.

It seems to be positive also because it institutes an episode of international concord and collaboration, without which it is impossible to hope for security and peace in the world.

This is why, apart from any political innuendo, We too express Our satisfaction for this act which seems to take on a moral and human value worth being underlined and encouraged.

In order to see this result followed by others, more thorough and reassuring for the good, peace and concord among all peoples, We now offer our humble prayer.

(Insegnamenti di Paolo VI, Vol. V, 1967, pp. 891-892; Translation by Pontifical Commission "Iustitia et Pax")

MESSAGE FOR THE WORLD DAY OF PEACE, 1968
8 December 1967

... The proposal to dedicate the first day of the new year to Peace is not intended, therefore, as exclusively ours, religious, that is, Catholic. It would hope to have the adherence of all the true friends of Peace, as if it were their own initiative, to be expressed in a free manner, congenial to the particular character of those who are aware of how beautiful and how important is the harmony of all voices in the world for the exaltation of this primary good, which is peace, in the varied concert of modern humanity.

The Catholic Church, with the intention of service and of example, simply wishes to "launch the idea", in the hope that it may not only receive the widest consent of the civilized world, but that such an idea may find everywhere numerous promoters, able and capable of impressing on the "Day of Peace", to be celebrated on the first day of every new year, that sincere and strong character of conscious humanity, redeemed from its sad and fatal bellicose conflicts, which will give to the history of the world a more happy, ordered and civilized development.

The Catholic Church will call the attention of its children to the duty of observing "the Day of Peace" with the religious and moral expressions of the Christian faith. But it considers it its duty to remind all those who agree on the opportuneness of such a "Day" of some points which ought to characterize it. First among these is : the necessity of defending Peace in the face of dangers which always threaten it; the danger of the survival of selfishness in the relations among nations; the danger of violence into which some populations can allow themselves to be drawn by desperation at not having their right to life and human dignity recognized and respected; the danger, today tremendously increased, of recourse to frightful weapons of extermination, which some nations possess, spending enormous financial means, the expenditure of which is reason for painful reflection in the presence of the grave needs which hinder the develop- ment of so many other peoples; the danger of believing that international controversies cannot be resolved by the ways of reason, that is, by negotiations founded on law, justice, and equity, but only by means of deterrent and murderous forces...

(Insegnamenti di Paolo VI, Vol. V, 1967; Translation Typis Polyglottis Vaticanis, 1967, pp. 41-43)

ADDRESS TO THE PONTIFICAL ACADEMY OF SCIENCES
27 April 1968

... This time, however, We should like to focus Our attention on another aspect of science, one to which your present meetings bear eloquent testimony. Let Us put it in the form of a question : To what practical use should science — or better yet, men of science and their brilliant pupils, the technicians — put their discoveries ? Only one answer is possible : everything must be employed to serve the welfare of humanity.

Surely We need not remind you, of all people, that the spectre of horrendous destructiveness, capable of reducing the whole inhabited earth to ashes, has taken on shape and substance in the most up-to-date laboratories of the physical sciences. How could We pass over this spectre in silence ? For although the responsibility of political leaders in this area is very grave, this does not diminish the responsibility of scientists. That is why We shall continue to take advantage of such opportunities as this to plead with men of science.

God grant that men will have the courage to say "no", when it must be said ! God grant that every step will be taken to proscribe the development and use of nuclear weapons, of bacteriological warfare, and of all the other means which would derive from modern science the diabolical power to inflict awesome devastation on whole nations, even on nations that are not party to the would-be conflict itself. God grant that mankind will come to its sense ! God grant that its leaders and rulers will find the strength and wisdom to reject the evil use of the science of destruction ! God grant that humanity will ask science to teach it the secret of its own well-being...

(The Pope Speaks, Vol. 13, pp. 111-112)

ADDRESS TO THE SACRED COLLEGE OF CARDINALS
24 June 1968

... While all these bloody conflicts continue to rage, and while even in Europe recourse to violence and subversion becomes more frequent, a hopeful and comforting sign appeared on the international horizon a few days ago.

After long work by a special commission and much debate in its chambers, the United Nations approved the text of an international agreement, designed to end the proliferation of atomic weapons and to halt the nuclear arms race. The effectiveness of the agreement, of course, will depend on the number of nations which choose to sign and ratify it — particularly those nations most able to procure such weapons.

We know that the agreement, in the opinion of many, contains numerous limitations that may keep some governments from giving it their unconditional support. But it is an indispensable first step toward further measures in the area of disarmament, until finally we arrive at a total ban on nuclear arms and total, universal disarmament. We look forward to that final goal, and We again urge it in the name of all mankind.

A HOPEFUL SIGN AT THE INTERNATIONAL HORIZON

While this agreement was being worked out and submitted for approval, We did not fail to express Our encouragement. Our pastoral duty could not let Us do otherwise. And We promptly expressed Our satisfaction and hope over the conclusion of the negotiations and the ready attainment of the agreement's aims. Among these aims We should like to stress : the pledge made by the nuclear powers — three of them at least — to work toward a gradual reduction of their atomic stockpile; the pledge by non-nuclear nations not to manufacture these weapons or to procure them for themselves; the pledge to develop forms of international cooperation for the peaceful use of nuclear energy, so that it may benefit the developing nations.

May these aims, which relate to the peace and progress of the whole family of man, be accepted earnestly and followed faithfully. May they eventually result in total disarmament, the prelude to the creation of a climate of trust and mutual respect among all nations...

(The Pope Speaks, Vol. 13, pp. 216-217)

CHRISTMAS RADIO MESSAGE
20 December 1968

... BEYOND THE MOST SERIOUS AND GRIEVOUS CRISIS OF HOPE

We live in the era of hope. It is, however, a hope in the kingdom of this earth, a hope in human self-sufficiency. And it is precisely in our day that this hope is undergoing a most serious crisis.

Before the terrified gaze of contemporary man, a grandiose and complex phenomenon emerges. First of all, prosperity itself, built up by intelligent and painful human efforts, easily becomes a source of new needs, and often of even greater evils. Progress itself, in some fields, creates enormous and terrible dangers for all humanity. The use which modern man can make of the murderous forces which he has mastered no longer raises hope on the horizon, but heavy clouds of terror and folly. The peace of peoples — or, to be more exact, the existence of man upon the face of the earth — is placed in peril. Modern man's destructive power is incalculable. And the fatal probability of such power devastating the City of Man depends upon causes which are tragically free, which neither science nor technology can of themselves dominate. Thus it happens that anguish takes the place of hope...

(The Pope Speaks, Vol. 13, p. 358)

ADDRESS TO THE DIPLOMATIC CORPS
ACCREDITED TO THE HOLY SEE
11 January 1969

... In the presence of these mixed sentiments of hope and fear aroused by this brief recall of the menaces weighing upon the peace of the world, We pose the question that We have taken for the theme of this address : you and We — you, the nations, and We, the Holy See — what are we able to do together in this area ? Or more precisely, because the question has two aspects : how are you able to help Us, and how are We able to help you ?

You are able to help Us by following closely, as you have done, the activity of the Holy See in favour of peace, in being attentive witnesses to whatever the duty of Our responsibility inspires Us to say and do on this subject, in contributing to making this known in your countries, and in promoting its application. Who does not see, for example, how much the cause of peace would gain by putting into effect on a greater scale the suggestions of the encyclical *Populorum Progressio* ? Or of a less timid response to Our appeals for a progressive and reciprocal reduction of armaments ? To the constitution of a world fund for development ? It seems to us that on these points and others, you, as diplomats with the authority which is attached to your title and your function, you are able to be to Us a precious help by seconding Our action...

(The Teachings of Pope Paul VI, Vol. 2, 1969, pp. 11-12)

HOMILY ON THE WORLD DAY OF PEACE
1 January 1970

... Before being a policy, Peace is a spirit. Before being expressed, victorious or vanquisher, in historical happenings and social relationships, it is expressed, formed and asserted in our consciences, in that philosophy of life which everyone must acquire as a light for his footsteps along the pathways of the world and in the experiences of daily life.

That means, beloved Brothers and Sons, that Peace demands an education. We affirm it here at the altar of Christ, while celebrating the Holy Hass which recalls His Word and renews in an unbloody and sacramental form His sacrifice which made peace between heaven and earth : here, as disciples, as pupils, ever needing to listen, to learn, to begin anew the apprenticeship of our "metanoia", that is, of the transformation of our instinctive and, regrettably, traditional mentality.

We must shake the foundations of ingrained prejudices : the idea that force and revenge are the ruling criterion of human relationships; that an injury received calls for another injury, often graver, in return — "an eye for an eye, a tooth for a tooth" (Mt. 5:38); — that self-interest must prevail over the interests of others, without regard for their needs or for common right. We must place at the foundation of our social psychology hunger and thirst for justice, together with that seeking for peace which merits for us the title of children of God (cf. Mt. 5: 6-9).

It is no Utopia; it is progress today more than ever before, it is demanded by the evolution of civilization and by the Damoclean sword of an increasingly serious and increasingly possible terror hanging over our heads. Civilization has succeded in banishing, at least in principle, slavery, illiteracy, epidemics, social classes, etc., evils, that is, which were long established and which were tolerated as if they were unavoidable and were inherent in the sad tragic social life of mankind : civilization must also succeed in banishing war. Mankind's "good manners" demand it. The terrible increasing danger of a world conflagration prescribes it.

Have we, individual weak mortals, no means of averting the possibility of catastrophic disasters of universal proportions ? Yes, we do. We have recourse to public opinion, which in this emergency becomes the expression of mankind's moral conscience; and we all know how great can be its power for good. We have our individual personal duty to be good. That does not mean to be weak. It means to be capable of breaking the sad logical chain of evil by patience and forgiveness. It means to love, that is, to be Christians...

PEACE DAY PRAYER

Lord, our hands are still bloodstained from the last World Wars, so that not all our peoples have yet been able to take each other's hands in friendship.

Lord, we are today more heavily armed than ever we were in centuries past, and we are so provided with instruments of death that we could in a single instant set the world ablaze and perhaps even destroy mankind.

Lord, we have based the development and prosperity of many of our giant industries on the diabolical capacity to produce arms of every size and shape, all designed to slaughter and exterminate men who are our brothers. Thus we have cruelly established the economic stability of so many powerful nations upon the trading of arms to poor nations lacking plows, schools and hospitals.

Lord, we have allowed to reappear among us the ideologies that make men enemies of one another : revolutionary fanaticism, class hatred, nationalistic pride, racial exclusiveness, tribal rivalry, commercial selfishness, self-satisfied individualism that is indifferent to the needs of others.

Lord, sorrowful and powerless, we are listening daily to the news of three wars still raging in the world.

Lord, it is true ! We are not in the right path !

Lord, look nonetheless at our inadequate but sincere efforts for peace in the world. There are wonderful international organizations; there are proposals for disarmament and for peace talks.

Lord, there are above all so many graves that tear our hearts; families broken up by wars, conflicts and death-inflicting repression; women in tears; children dying; refugees and prisoners crushed by the weight of solitude and suffering; and there are many young people rebelling that justice may be advanced and that concord may be the law of coming generations.

Lord, you know that there are upright souls doing good in silence, courageously and unselfishly, and praying with penitent and with innocent hearts. There are

Christians in the world — and how many they are, Lord — who want to follow Your gospel and who practice self-sacrifice and love.

Lord, Lamb of God, who takes away the sins of the world, grant us peace.

(The Teachings of Pope Paul VI, Vol. 3, 1970, pp. 8-10); Prayer : The Catholic Mind, Vol. 68, 1970, p. 64)

ADDRESS AT THE GENERAL AUDIENCE
25 March 1970

... THE CROSS : "SPES UNICA"

How can we remain indifferent to what is happening in the world today ? There are so many reasons for grief that We will not even try to give a complete and orderly list of them. We will only say that We are especially affected by the armed conflicts which are going on in the Middle East and in the Far East : instead of tending towards peace those conflicts are growing fiercer and longer. Increasing armaments strike Us as irrational phenomena and disconsoling portents for the future. In some cases they are a considerable part of trade between big industrial countries and weaker nations which have need of quite different supplies...

(The Teachings of Pope Paul VI, Vol. 3, 1970, p. 97)

MESSAGE TO THE GENERAL SECRETARY
OF THE UNITED NATIONS
FOR THE XXVth ANNIVERSARY OF THE ORGANIZATION
4 October 1970

... As the Second Development Decade dawns, who better than the United Nations Organization and its specialized agencies will be able to take up the challenge presented to all mankind ? It is a question of ensuring that the nations, while preserving their identity and original way of life, shall agree at least on the means to be taken to support their common will to live, and, in the case of some of them, to assure their survival. Let us recognize this fact : the common good of the nations, be they large or small, demands that states should rise above their merely nationalistic interests, so that the most brilliant schemes may not remain a dead letter and that well-ordered dialogue structures may not be dislocated by plans capable of putting all mankind in peril. Is it not surrendering mankind to an uncertain and perhaps catastrophic future to continue to throw away on war budgets the most astonishing opportunities for progress that mankind has ever known ? Has not the hour struck for reason to take stock of that terrifying future which so much wasted energy risks preparing for the world ? "They will hammer their swords into ploughshares, their spears into sickles" (Is. 2:4). May your untiring perseverance, placed at the service of all plans for reciprocal and controlled disarmament, ensure in our industrial age the realization of those words of this ancient prophet of the agricultural era. May it ensure that the resources thus made available are employed for scientific progress, for the harnessing of the immense resources of land and sea and for the sustenance of the ever growing numbers of the members of the human race. May the work of the living never be used against life; on the contrary, let it be used to feed that life and to make it truly human. With imagination, courage and perseverance, you will thus enable all peoples peacefully to take their rightful place in the concord of nations...

(The Teachings of Pope Paul VI, Vol. 3, 1970, pp. 346-347)

INSTRUMENT OF ACCESSION OF THE HOLY SEE TO THE TREATY ON THE NON-PROLIFERATION OF NUCLEAR WEAPONS
25 February 1971

The undersigned Cardinal Secretary of State and Prefect of the Council for the Public Affairs of the Church has the honour to certify hereby that the Holy See accedes to the Treaty on the Non-Proliferation of Nuclear Weapons which was opened for signature on 1 July 1968 and which entered into force on 5 March 1970.

By this act, which the Holy See has decided on in the belief that the aims of disarmament and easing of international tension by which the Treaty is inspired correspond with its own mission of peace, the Holy See intends to give its support and moral encouragement to the dispositions of the Treaty, considering that it constitutes an important step forward towards the desired creation of a system of general and complete disarmament under effective international control with a view to guaranteeing security and strengthening trust in relations between States, and to promoting on a just and stable basis peace and co-operation between peoples.

In witness whereof the undersigned Cardinal Secretary of State has signed this document and has affixed thereto his seal.

From the Vatican, 25 February 1971.

J. Card. Villot

(Translation by Pontifical Commission "Iustitia et Pax")

DECLARATION ANNEXED TO THE INSTRUMENT OF ACCESSION

1. This accession by the Holy See to the Treaty on the Non-Proliferation of Nuclear Weapons is inspired by its constant desire, illuminated by the teaching of universal brotherhood and of justice and peace between men and peoples contained in the Gospel message, to make its contribution to undertakings which, through disarmament as well as by other means, promote security, mutual trust and peaceful co-operation in relations between peoples.

In that perspective, the Holy See judges — as is said in the official document of accession — that the aims of disarmament and easing of international tension by which the Treaty is inspired correspond with its own mission of peace, and that the Treaty, although it has its intrinsic limitations, constitutes a noteworthy step forward on the road to disarmament. In fact, in so far as the Treaty proposes to stop the dissemination of nuclear weapons — while awaiting the achievement of the cessation of the nuclear arms race and the undertaking of effective measures in the direction of complete nuclear disarmament — it has the aim of lessening the danger of terrible and total devastation which threatens all mankind, and it wishes to constitute a premise for wider agreements in the future for the promotion of a system of general and complete disarmament under effective international control.

2. In the first place, therefore, the Holy See appreciates and shares the following considerations and intentions which the States Party to the Treaty have expressed or declared in the Preamble of the Treaty:

1) The awareness of the devastation "that would be visited upon all mankind by a nuclear war and the consequent need to make every effort to avert the danger of such a war and to take measures to safeguard the security of peoples";

2) The reaffirmation of the principle that "in accordance with the Charter of the United Nations, States must refrain in their international relations from the threat or use of force against the territorial integrity or political independence of any State, or in any other manner inconsistent with the Purposes of the United Nations, and that the establishment and maintenance of international peace and security are to be promoted";

3) The intention "to achieve at the earliest possible date the cessation of the nuclear arms race and to undertake effective measures in the direction of nuclear disarmament";

4) The intention "to further the easing of international tension and the strengthening of trust between States in order to facilitate the cessation of the manufacture of nuclear weapons, the liquidation of all their existing stockpiles, and the elimination from national arsenals of nuclear weapons and the means of their delivery pursuant to a Treaty on general and complete disarmament under strict and effective international control".

3. The Holy See is furthermore convinced that the Treaty on the Non-Proliferation of Nuclear Weapons will be able to attain in full the noble objectives

of security and peace which constitute the reasons for contracting it and justify the limitations to which the States Party to the Treaty submit only if it is fully executed in every clause and with all its implications.

In the Holy See's view, that actuation concerns not only the obligations to be applied immediately but also those which envisage a process of ulterior commitments. Among the latter, the Holy See considers it suitable to point out the following :

a) The adoption of appropriate measures to ensure, on a basis of equality, that all non-nuclear-weapon States Party to the Treaty will have available to them the benefits deriving from peaceful applications of nuclear technology, in the spirit of paragraphs 4, 5, 6 and 7 of the Preamble, and in conformity with articles IV and V of the Treaty;

b) The pursuit of negotiations in good faith "on effective measures relating to cessation of the nuclear arms race at an early date and to nuclear disarmament, and on a treaty on general and complete disarmament under strict and effective international control", in accordance with the commitment foreseen in article VI.

The Holy See, therefore, expresses the sincere wish that these undertakings will be executed by all the Parties. In particular it declares its special interest and expresses its earnest desire :

1) That the current talks between the United States of America and the Union of Soviet Socialist Republics on the limitation of strategic armaments may soon lead to a satisfactory agreement which will make possible the cessation in an effective and lasting manner of the preoccupying arms race in that costly and murderous sector of warlike preparations, both offensive and defensive;

2) That the proposals and drafts of agreements which have been put forward for some time past by various sources, especially within the Conference of the United Nations Committee for Disarmament, and which concern complete nuclear disarmament, the prohibition of bacteriological and chemical weapons and the limitation and control of conventional armaments, as well as the draft treaty on general and complete disarmament under strict and effective international control, may attain speedy and concrete results, in conformity with the repeated resolutions of the United Nations Organization and in fulfilment of the justified and anxious expectations of men and peoples of every continent.

4. In the spirit of the considerations expressed above, which gave rise to and which accompany this accession to the Treaty, the Holy See is convinced that the attainment of the Treaty's aims of security and peace will be all the more complete and effective according as the extent of its application is the wider and more universal.

From the Vatican, 25 February 1971.

(L'Osservatore Romano, English edition, No. 10, 1971, pp. 4-8; Translation by Pontifical Commission "Iustitia et Pax")

ADDRESS TO THE CONFERENCE OF EX-SERVICE MEN AND WAR VICTIMS OF EUROPEAN COUNTRIES
20 November 1971

... Peace ! Who would not desire it sincerely ? Who would dare today not to plead eloquently for it ? But what unconsciousness sometimes still exists at the very heart of certain manifestations that set themselves up as peaceful ! And what lies or dominating manoeuvres are concealed behind certain claims of peace ! Your testimony is of far greater moral weight. You cherish for your homelands an attachment that you have sealed with your commitment, with your sufferings, often at the risk of your very lives; and at the same time you preach the ways of reconciliation, negotiation, active cooperation, respect for other frontiers and other countries. Your solemn appeal, made to your European brothers, and particularly to the leaders of the peoples, must be heard.

The aims you put forward, as conditions of safety and peace, coincide to a great extent, we are glad to point out, with those inspired in us by our evangelical concern with justice and peace, and our desire to serve mankind with the very love of Our Lord Jesus Christ : the right of persons and of peoples to be considered in their dignity, their originality, their sovereignty, and consequently the elimination of recourse to offensive force, the renunciation of the ruinous race for more and more deadly armaments, the rejection of hatred and of discriminations of all kinds. We, too, think that these are the ways that must be taken to save mankind, and Europe in the first place, the horrors it has known...

(L'Osservatore Romano, English edition, No. 48, 1971, p. 2)

ADDRESS TO THE DIPLOMATIC CORPS
ACCREDITED TO THE HOLY SEE
10 January 1972

... In this regard, gentlemen, may We draw your attention for a few moments to what is perhaps the most disconcerting phenomenon of our time : the arms race. It is an epidemic; no people seems now able to escape its contagion.

The result is that the current world expenditure on armaments already adds up to astronomical figures and *every* country shares in it : the great powers, the medium ones, even the weak nations or those of the so-called "Third World".

What is most troubling is that this is occurring at a time when men have become more aware of their own dignity and have a livelier sense of being members of the same human family; when individuals and peoples are more keenly aspiring to peace in justice, and when protests against the arms race among the younger generation — for many of whom the human family is already a living unity — are continuing to spread.

What is the explanation for so deep-rooted and distressing a contradiction within the human family, a contradiction between the growing sincere desire for peace on the one hand and the growing fearsome production of instruments of war on the other ?

There are some who see armaments, at least for the great and medium powers, as a necessity of the economic system which is based on their production, if economic imbalances and mass unemployment are to be avoided. But such motivation is radically opposed to the spirit of civilization and still more to that of Christianity. How can it be conceded that there is no way of finding work for hundreds of thousands of workers other than by setting them to making instruments of death ?

This is all the more true because we live in an era when there is an urgent need in many fields for quite different constructive and beneficial works on a continental and world scale, in order to eliminate the scourges of hunger, ignorance and disease. In these matters not all that the tragic situation of so many of our brothers demands has yet, alas, been done, in spite of the generosity of so many people. There is likewise a need to safeguard the good things indispensable to life, for example, by protecting the environment from the various pollutants.

It must further be observed that there continues to be a widespread conviction that a policy of armaments, while not justifiable in itself, can be accounted for by the fact that, if peace is possible today it can only be one based on a balance of armed forces.

"Whatever may be the fact about this method of deterrence", declares the Constitution on the Church in the World of Today, "men should be convinced that the arms race in which an already considerable number of countries are engaged is not a safe way to preserve a steady peace, nor is the so-called balance resulting from this race a sure and authentic peace." (Pastoral Constitution on the Church in the World of Today, No. 81).

For this reason the realization of peace in justice demands — and attempts are already being made through courageous and wise initiatives — that the opposite road, progressive disarmament, be followed. For its part, the Church, the People of God, cannot but enliven its commitment to teach man to have confidence in man; that is, to see others not as probable aggressors but as possible future collaborators, made capable of doing good for the building of a more human world.

(The Pope Speaks, Vol. 16, pp. 309-311)

EASTER MESSAGE
2 April 1972

... Our greeting of peace goes even further : it wishes to reach where there is still conflict of war, hatred, bloodshed, destruction, and ever more numerous and murderous weaponry : peace, peace ! Men today have the ability and the means to give the modern world wonderful displays of progress and organization, and will they not have the wisdom and strength to defend and restore peace where it is injured, where mankind fails not only itself but also the transcendental law of the God of peace ? Our wish of peace therefore rings out with greater strength and love, and, under the protecting mantle of Christ, who rose again and conquered for all, it rings out with greater confidence...

(The Teachings of Pope Paul VI, Vol. 5, 1972, p. 237)

ADDRESS TO THE SACRED COLLEGE OF CARDINALS
22 December 1972

.... This unity and peace according to the supreme desire of Christ though directly and principally directed towards the transcendant world of the spirit, must equally be a blessing and an achievement of the members of the human family in their earthly existence as brothers and sisters, as sons and daughters of the same Father who is in heaven, as sharers in the same natural and supernatural vocations, and as pilgrims, with equal rights and duties of mutual help, towards their common Father's house.

The Church's mission and indeed ardent desire for peace thus overflows its bounds and in an almost spontaneous and necessary movement spreads to civil societies, in the individual nations and in their relationships one with another.

An ardent desire for peace, we said; it is an ardent desire above all, in the deepest sense of the word, in those places where peace, longed for by the peoples, is wounded and endangered — sometimes by objectively serious situations of conflict and sometimes, in part at least, by a lack of sufficient commitment (God grant that it is not through lack of sincere good will) on the part of those who have responsibility for peace.

Those who remember the conflagrations of not long ago, conflagrations that even today mark the flesh of the nations with the scars of still painful wounds, and remember too the consequence of these conflagrations, will consider it a very valuable result that humanity or whole continents have been preserved for a considerable number of years from the repetition of similar terrible tragedies.

Certainly this is a consideration of no little importance. But who does not realize that this peace, largely based upon a true or presumed balance of powers, has too fragile and dangerous a foundation ? And who does not shudder at the thought that the conquering sway of passion or a wrong calculation could unforeseeably place at the disposal of aggression the fearsome arsenal that it is now considered necessary to acquire for the sake of defence ?

We have spoken on another occasion about this fear in our recent message for the next World Day of Peace. This was a message that in its basic inspiration of positive optimism could not but reflect the complexity of a problem-filled reality containing too many uncertainties, too many dramatic and bloodstained manifestations.

If, in spite of this, we have wished to remind the world that peace is nevertheless always possible, we did so not simply in order to illumine with a glimmer of hope present sufferings or growing forebodings; we did so in order at the same time to call all to a sense of their own responsibilities, so that no one should be tempted to seek in alleged historical inevitability a moral alibi that would excuse him from searching willingly and untiringly for the roads — difficult, but not closed — to peace.

And in this regard it is our pleasure and indeed our duty to give renewed recognition here to all those in positions of leadership in the various States and in the great International Organizations who are devoting their efforts to the service of the great cause of peace. These efforts are often very hard; they are not always duly recognized, not always drowned with the success one would hope for.

To these men we express our heartfelt gratitude and offer our encouragement. We pray for them, that the Lord may grant them sufficient wisdom and firmness for their noble and arduous enterprise.

The limitation and control of arms, and especially of those means of warfare which are most dangerous and repugnant to that sense of humanity that should not be lacking even in the most bitter conflicts; the preparation for and progressive putting into practice of a true and general disarmament; the quest for new forms, on a worldwide or regional scale, of forestalling and settling the differences that disturb the peace and security of the peoples : all these efforts cannot but receive the applause, the support, and (in the measure permitted by their nature and their mission) the collaboration of the Apostolic See and the Church.

Nor do we consider it right to give in to the sense of distrust that ever and again pervades mankind when, after the blossoming of hope for a stable peace — as happens after the conclusion of every great conflict — it sees the gradual increase of fresh rivalries and tensions, the forerunners of even more menacing dangers.

On the contrary, it is the duty of all those who have the responsibility and means, in however small measure, to make every effort to ensure that situations of conflict that occur one after another may find a fair and rapid solution, while they are still confined to a small area — a solution that takes into account the considerations and respect of mutual rights and legitimate interests, but one which at the same time takes account of the common and higher interest of peace...

(The Teachings of Pope Paul VI, Vol. 5, 1972, pp. 333-335)

ANGELUS MESSAGE ON THE OCCASION OF
THE WORLD DAY OF PEACE
1 January 1973

... We would like to remind you of two things : first, that peace is possible : it must be possible ! We must desire it above all else. It is part of the indispensable values of humanity and civilization. As it is possible to conquer epidemics, illiteracy, poverty and hunger, so must it also be possible to eliminate those fractures, threats and dangers which compromise the peaceful existence of humanity on earth.

It is not easy, especially when so much of the world's economy and organization are founded on armaments and on criteria which seek domination over others. It is necesary for peace to become a necessity in men's consciences. Then only will it become a reality.

The second affirmation is based on the first : peace will only become possible if the Lord — who in his sovereign and mysterious mercy guides the hearts of men and the destiny of the world — will help us to desire and work for peace. Peace, in fact, implies and demands that we be courageous, tenacious, wise and good. Therefore, it can be obtained only with the powerful and fatherly help of God...

(L'Osservatore Romano, English edition, No. 1, 1973, p. 11)

ADDRESS AT THE GENERAL AUDIENCE
17 October 1973

... And what shall we say about social reconciliation? Oh! what a chapter with its thousand pages! We will just say that reconciliation, that is, peace, becomes more and more every day an urgent necessity, an increasing necessity. Did we not all hope, after the last world war, that at last peace would be achieved for ever? Has not the world made really grandiose efforts to give peace a constitutional place in the development of civilization? To make peoples safe for themselves, brothers for others? But the atrocious and dreadful experience of these years recalls us to a sad reality: war is still possible! The production and sale of armaments show us, rather, that it is easier and more disastrous than before. Even today we are experiencing a painful event of war, and not the only one. We are humiliated and frightened.

Is it possible that this is an incurable disease of mankind? We should also point out here the congenital disproportion in mankind between its capacity of idealization and its moral aptitude to remain consistent and faithful to its programmes of civil progress. Thus one is tempted to say: it is impossible for the world to remain at peace. We answer: no; Christ, our peace (Eph. 2:14), makes the impossible possible (cf. Lk. 18:27). If we follow his Gospel, the union of justice and peace can be realized; certainly not to be crystalized in the immobility of a history that is, on the contrary, in continual development: but it is possible! It can be reborn!...

(The Teachings of Pope Paul VI, Vol. 6, 1973, p. 144)

MESSAGE FOR THE WORLD DAY OF PEACE, 1974
8 December 1973

... But this does not mean that Peace should be regarded as a utopia. The certainty of Peace is based not only on being but also on becoming. Like man's life, Peace is dynamic. Its realm extends more and principally into the field of moral obligation, that is, into the sphere of duties. Peace must not only be maintained; it must be produced. Therefore Peace is, and must always be, in a process of continuous and progressive realization. We shall go further and say : Peace is possible only if it is considered a duty. It is not even enough that it be based on the conviction, in general perfectly justified, that it is advantageous. Peace must take hold of the consciences of men as a supreme ethical objective, as a moral necessity, an *ἀνάγκη*, deriving from the innate demands of human co-existence.

This discovery, for this is what it is in the positive process of our reasoning, teaches us certain principles from which we ought never again to depart. And in the first place it enlightens us about the original nature of Peace : that Peace is above all an idea. It is an inner axiom and a treasure of the spirit. Peace must grow out of a fundamentally spiritual concept of humanity : humanity must be at Peace, that is, united and consistent in itself, closely bound together in the depth of its being. The absence of this basic concept has been, and still is, the root cause of the calamities which have devasted history. To regard struggle among men as a structural need of society is not only an error of philosophy and vision but also a potential and permanent crime against humanity. Civilization must finally redeem itself from the ancient fallacy, still existing and active : *homo homini lupus*. This fallacy has been at work from the time of Cain. Modern man must have the moral and prophetic courage to liberate himself from this inborn ferocity and to arrive at the conclusion which is precisely the idea of Peace as something essentially natural, necessary, obligatory and therefore possible. We must henceforth consider humanity, history, work, politics, culture and progress in terms of their relationship to Peace.

But what is the use of this spiritual, subjective, interior and personal idea ? What is the use of such an idea, so defenceless, so remote from the actually lived, effective and frightening happenings of our present time ? While the tragic experience of the last World War recedes into history, we unfortunately have to record the reapperance of a spirit of rivalry between the Nations as well as in the political dialectic of society. Today the potential of war and struggle is far greater — not less — than that which was at mankind's disposal before the World Wars. Can you not see — any observer could object — that the world is moving towards conflicts even more terrible and horrible than those of yesterday? Can you not see the lack of effectiveness of propaganda for peace and the insufficient influence of the international institutions that were set up while the bloodied and weakened world was recovering from the World Wars? Where is the world going? Are not ever more catastrophic and abhorrent conflicts being prepared? Alas, we should hold our peace in the face of such pressing and implacable reasoning, as in the face of a desperate fate.

But no. Are we blind too? Are we ingenuous? No, brethren, we are certain that our cause, the cause of Peace, must prevail. In the first place : because in spite of the folly of a contrary policy, the idea of Peace is already victorious in the thought of all men in posts of responsibility. We have confidence in their up-to-date wisdom, their energy and ability. No head of a nation can today wish for war; every one yearns for the general Peace of the world. It is something great! We dare to exhort leaders never again to deny their programme, indeed the common programme, of Peace...

_____

(The Teachings of Pope Paul VI, Vol. 6, 1973, pp. 337-339)

HOMILY ON THE WORLD DAY OF PEACE
1 January 1974

... Will peace endure? Shall we really be able to guarantee our children and the generations to come tranquillity, safety, peaceful existence or, on the contrary, shall we have to live always in the shadow of this nightmare, this fear of the imminence of a dreadful tragedy that might break out in the world overnight?

The civilization we have promoted is a marvellous civilization. One is really spellbound on seeing what man is, and has been able to do, how he can organize things, dominate the elements, and now traverse space. But we see that the instruments in men's hands, as they become more perfect, advanced and powerful, become a tremendous danger for men's very lives. Men are really able to force matter, the laws of nature, into their service, but they are also capable of turning them against life itself. The potential of armaments is, unfortunately, enormous.

The world has become apparently balanced, it is true, but this balance is nothing but a tug-of-war, one fear against another fear. And this fear is growing. Again there is talk of atomic arms as if it were a natural thing. My God! Just think of what happened in Japan to end the war ! And we are making it an almost normal pattern, something possible — though we hope it will never take place — not impossible...

(L'Osservatore Romano, English edition, No. 2, 1974, p. 3)

ADDRESS TO THE DIPLOMATIC CORPS
ACCREDITED TO THE HOLY SEE
12 January 1974

... Nowadays, in fact, the development of the relations of forces and interests has the effect that the weal or woe of one part of the international community cannot be considered the good or ill of another part of it; and happily the world finds itself almost obliged to seek the common advantage together, if it wishes to avoid common injury or even common catastrophe.

It is true that even among those most responsible for the lives of peoples, not all succeed in grasping or keeping in mind, as they should, this fundamental truth. And that is why it is not uncommon, particularly among those who are or think they are the strongest, for one or other to succumb to the temptation of solving situations of tension or conflicts in his favour, by force or violence.

But it is no less true that reality takes vengeance for these miscalculations. Unfortunately, those who pay the price are as often as not innocent victims, among whom there may sometimes figure those very persons who had endeavoured to dissuade the protagonists.

It is, therefore, more necessary than ever that the community of nations should be able to combat effectively the reasons of force — which are frequently unjust and which, today more than in the past, prove powerless to ensure the general advantage or even the advantage of those who have resorted to it — with the force of reason, justice and fair and generous understanding of the rights and interests of all.

The effort in question is such a vast one, such a noble one — such a difficult one, too — that it is impossible to stress its importance enough and to pass over in silence the serious commitment it calls for : an effort in which diplomacy worthy of the name is called to play a very important part...

(The Teachings of Pope Paul VI, Vol. 7, 1974, p. 180)

MESSAGE FOR THE WORLD DAY OF PEACE, 1975
8 December 1974

... This interiorization of Peace is true humanism, true civilization. Fortunately it has already begun. It is maturing as the world develops. It finds its persuasive strength in the universal dimensions of the relations of every kind which men are establishing among themeselves. It is a slow and complicated work, but one which, to a great extent, is happening spontaneously; the world is progressing towards its unity. Nevertheless we cannot delude ourselves, and while peaceful concord among men is spreading, through the progressive discovery of the complementary and interdependence of countries, through commercial exchanges, through the diffusion of an identical vision of man, always however respectful of the original and specific nature of the various civilizations, through the ease of travel and social communications, and so on, we must take note that today new forms of jealous nationalism are being affirmed, enclosed in manifestations of touchy rivalries based on race, language and traditions; there remain sad situations of poverty and hunger. Powerful economic multinational expressions are arising, full of selfish antagonisms. Exclusive and arrogant ideologies are being organized into social systems. Territorial conflicts break out with frightening ease. And above all, there is an increase in the number and the power of murderous weapons for possible catastrophic destruction, such as to stamp terror with the name of Peace. Yes, the world is progressing towards its unity, but even as it does so there increase the terrifying hypotheses which envisage more possible, more easy and more terrible fatal clashes — clashes which are considered, in certain circumstamces, inevitable and necessary, and called for, as it were, by justice. Will justice be one day the sister no longer of peace but of wars ? (cf. St. Augustine, De Cit. Dei, VII; PL 41, 634).

We are not playing at utopias, either optimistic ones or pessimistic. We want to remain in the realms of reality — a reality which, with its phenomenology of illusory hope and deplorable desperation, warns us once more that there is something not functioning properly in the monumental machine of our civilization. This machine could explode in an indescriptible conflagration because of a defect in its construction. We say a defect, not a lack. The defect, that is, of the spiritual element, though we admit that this element is already present and at work in the general process of the peaceful development of contemporary history, and worthy of every favourable recognition and encouragement. Have we not awarded to UNESCO our prize named after Pope John XXIII, the author of the Encyclical *Pacem in Terris* ?

But we dare to say that more must be done. We have to make use of and apply the spiritual element in order to make it capable not only of impeding conflicts among men and predisposing them to peaceful and civilized sentiments, but also of producing reconciliation among those same men, that is, of generating Peace. It is not enough to contain wars, to suspend conflicts, to impose truces and armistices, to define boundaries and relationships, to create sources of common interest; it is not enough to paralyze the possibility of radical strife through the terror of unheard destruction and suffering. An imposed Peace, a utilitarian and provisional Peace is not enough. Progress must be made towards a Peace which is loved, free and brotherly, founded, that is, on a reconciliation of hearts...

(The Teachings of Pope Paul VI, Vol. 7, 1974, pp. 375-377)

ADDRESS TO THE DIPLOMATIC CORPS
ACCREDITED TO THE HOLY SEE
11 January 1975

... The message of reconciliation that the Catholic Church extends to mankind in this Holy Year seems to us indeed to have a very special importance precisely for the international community, no less than for the peoples that live together in the different national communities and for the groups into which they are divided.

We shall not conceal from you that our gaze cannot fall today without growing preoccupation upon the developments of a world situation that — as it seems to us and to not a few others — appears to be gradually deteriorating, to the extent that it causes some to speak of a transition, already begun, from a "postwar" to a "pre-war" phase.

This is a prospect — should it in fact come to correspond to reality — whose fearful, indeed terrifying import we would not need to underline to you who are the experts in such problems.

Has there not perhaps been in fact hitherto a sort of convergence of judgments — and of fears — concerning what could be the meaning for the world of the outbreak of a conflict that — should it prove impossible to keep it in proportion, always very painful for the victims thereof, but at least territorially limited — would almost inevitably become atomic, because of its seriousness and extension ?

This "terror", of which laborious efforts are being made to ensure a kind of "balance", has been, indeed, and is currently considered to be the main, if not perhaps the only, guarantee against happenings that would appear for that very reason too dangerous for the very people who would have felt sufficiently strong to be able to win by surviving the other contenders.

As you know, the Holy See has never shown itself enthusiastic for the formula of the "balance of terror" as a means of safeguarding peace. Without ignoring the practical, even if in cause negative, advantages that such a formula can temporarily present, it has always seemed to this Apostolic See to be too detached from the moral basis upon which alone peace can prosper. It has likewise seemed too extravagant, through continual competition in equalling and surpassing one another in terms of power and arms, too extravagant, we say, of means and energies that ought on the contrary to be devoted to quite other ends — to the well-being and progress of all peoples. It has seemed destructive of thoughts of harmony and mutual understanding; it has seemed, finally, too fragile a shield against the onslaught of temptations to predominance and oppression which are at the root of so many situations of tension and conflict, also because of the justified reasons of defence that they evoke or, sometimes, because of the danger of an erroneous calculation in preventing the feared manifestations resulting to one's own disadvantage.

This fragility is confirmed, unfortunately, by the present situation, to which we have referred...

(The Teachings of Pope Paul VI, Vol. 8, 1975, pp. 169-170)

MESSAGE FOR THE WORLD DAY OF PEACE, 1976
18 October 1975

"THE REAL WEAPONS OF PEACE"

To you, Statesmen !

To you, Representatives and Promoters of the great international Institutions!

To you Politicians ! To you, Students of the problems of life in international society, Publicists, Workers, Sociologists, and Economists concerned with the relationship between Peoples.

To you, Citizens of the world, whether you are fascinated by the ideal of a universal brotherhood or disappointed and sceptical regarding the possibility of establishing relationships of equilibrium, justice and collaboration between Peoples !

And finally to you, the followers of Religions which promote friendship between people : to you, Christians, to you, Catholics : who make peace in the world the principle of your faith and the goal of your worldwide love !

*　*　*

In this year 1976, as in previous years, we once more presume respectfully to come before you with our message of Peace.

We preface our message with an invitation : that you should listen to it; that you should be attentive and patient. The great cause of Peace deserves a hearing; it deserves your reflection, even though it may seem that our voice is repeating itself on this recurrent theme at the dawn of the new year; and even though, erudite as you are by reason of your studies and perhaps even more by your experiences, you may think that you already know everything about Peace in the world.

And yet, perhaps it may be of some interest to you to know the nature of our spontaneous feelings concerning this implacable theme of Peace — feelings that derive from immediate experiences of the historical situation in which we are all immersed.

Our first feelings in this regard are twofold, and they are at variance one with the other. First and foremost, we see with pleasure and hope that progress is being made by the *idea* of Peace. This idea is gaining importance and attention in men's minds; and it is accompanied by the development of the structures of the organization of Peace; there is an increase of official and academic manifestations in its favour. Activities are developing in the direction indicated by Peace : journeys, congresses, assemblies, tradelinks, studies, friendships, collaboration, aid, and so forth. Peace is gaining ground. The Helsinki Conference of July-August 1975 is an event which gives reason for hope in this regard.

But unfortunately, at the same time we see the manifestation of phenomena contrary to the content and purpose of Peace; and these phenomena too are making progress, even though they are often restricted to a latent state, yet with unmistakable symptoms of incipient or future conflagrations. For example, accompanying the sense of national identity which is a legitimate and commendable expression of the many-sided oneness of a People, there is a rebirth of nationalism, which exaggerates national expression to the point of collective egoism and exclusivist antagonism. In the collective consciousness it brings about the rebirth of dangerous and even frightening seeds of rivalry and of very probable contentions.

There is a disproportionate growth — and the example causes shivers of fear — of the possession of arms of every kind, in every individual Nation. We have the justified suspicion that the arms trade often reaches the highest levels in international markets, with this obsessive sophism : defence, even if it is planned as something purely hypothetical and potential, demands a growing competition in armaments, which can ensure Peace only through their opposed balance.

This is not the complete list of the negative factors eating away at the stability of Peace. Can we give the name *peaceful* to a world that is radically divided by irreconcilable ideologies — ideologies that are powerfully and fiercely organized, ideologies that divide Peoples from one another, and, when they are allowed free rein, subdivide those Peoples within themselves, into factions and parties that find their reason for existence and activity in poisoning their ranks with irreconcilable hatred and systematic struggle within the very fabric of society itself ? The apparent normality of such political situations does not conceal the tension of a corresponding iron hand, ready to crush the adversary as soon as he should betray a sign of fatal weakness. Is this Peace ? Is it civilization ? Can we give the name *people* to a mass of citizens who are opposed one to another to the bitter end ?

And where is Peace in the festering centres of armed conflicts, or of conflicts that are barely contained by the impossibility of more violent explosions ? We follow with admiration the efforts being made to calm these centres of warfare and guerilla activity which for years have been devastating the face of the earth, and which every minute are threatening to break out into gigantic struggles involving continents, races, religions and social ideologies. But we cannot conceal the precariousness of a Peace which is merely a truce of already clearly defined future conflicts, that is, the hypocrisy of a tranquillity which is called peaceful only with cold words of simulated reciprocal respect.

We recognized that Peace, in historical reality, is a work of continual therapy. Its health is by its very nature frail, consisting as it does in the establishment of relationships between overbearing and fickle men. Peace demands a wise and unceasing effort on the part of that higher creative imagination which we call diplomacy, international order or the dynamic of negotiations. Poor Peace !

What then are your weapons ? Fear of unheard-of and fatal conflagrations, which could decimate, indeed almost annihilate humanity ? Resignation to a certain state of endured oppression, such as colonialism, imperialism or revolution which begins as violence and inexorably becomes static and terribly self-perpetuating ? Preventive and secret weapons ? A capitalist, that is, egoistical organization of the economic world, which is obliged by hunger to remain subdued and quiet ? The self-absorbed bewitchment of an historical culture, presumptuous and convinced of its own perennial triumphant destinies ? Or the magnificent organizational structures intent on rationalizing and organizing international life?

Is it sufficient, is it sure, is it fruitful, is it happy — a Peace sustained only by such foundations?

More is needed. This is our message. It is necessary before all else to provide Peace with other weapons — weapons different from those destined to kill and exterminate mankind. What is needed above all are moral weapons, those which give strength and prestige to international law — the weapon, in the first place, of the observance of pacts. *Pacta sunt servanda* is the still valid axiom for the consistency of effective relations between States, for the stability of justice between Nations, for the upright conscience of Peoples. Peace makes this axiom its shield. And where pacts do not reflect justice? Here is the justification for the new international Institutions, the mediators for consultations, studies and deliberations, which must absolutely exclude the ways of the so-called *fait accompli*, that is to say, the contention of blind and uncontrolled forces, which always involve human victims and incalculable and unimputable ruin, rarely attaining the pure object of effectively vindicating a truly just cause. Arms and wars are, in a word, to be excluded from civilization's programmes. Judicious disarming is another weapon of Peace. As the prophet Isaiah said : "He will wield authority over the nations and adjudicate between many peoples; these will hammer their swords into ploughshares, their spears into sickles" (Is. 2:4). And then let us listen to the words of Christ : "Put your sword back, for all who draw the sword will die by the sword" (Mt. 26:52). Is this utopia ? For how much longer?

Here we enter into the speculative world of ideal humanity of the new man-kind still to be born, still to be educated — mankind stripped of its grievous weight of murderous military weaponry, and rather clothed and strengthened by moral principles which are natural to it. These are principles which already exist, but still in a theoretical and in practice immature, weak and tender state, only at the beginning of their penetration into the profound and operative conscious-ness of Peoples. Their weakness, which seems incurable to the diagnosticians, the so-called realists of historical and anthropological studies, comes especially from the fact that military disarmament, if it is not to constitute an unforgivable error of impossible optimism, of blind ingenuousness, of a tempting opportunity for others' oppression, should be common and general. Disarmament, is either for everyone, or it is a crime of neglect to defend oneself. Does not the sword, in the concert of historical and concrete life in society, have its own *raison d'être*, for justice and for peace ? (cf. Rom. 13:4). Yes, we must admit it. But has there not come into the world a transforming dynamism, a hope which is no longer unlikely, a new and effective progress, a future and longed-for history which can make itself present and real, ever since the Master, the Prophet of the New Testament, proclaimed the decline of the archaic, primitive and instinctive tradition, and, with a Word having in itself power not only to denounce and to announce but also to generate, under certain conditions, a new mankind, declared : "Do not imagine that I have come to abolish the Law or the Prophets. I have come not to abolish but to complete them... You have learnt how it was said to our ancestors : 'You must not kill'; and if anyone does kill he must answer for it before the court. But I say this to you : Anyone who is angry with his brother will answer for it before the court" (Mt. 5:17, 21-22).

It is no longer a simple, ingenuous and dangerous utopia. It is the new Law of mankind which goes forward, and which arms Peace with a formidable principle : "You are all brethren" (Mt. 23:8). If the consciousness of universal brotherhood truly penetrates into the hearts of men, will they still need to arm themselves to the point of becoming blind and fanatic killers of their brethren who in themselves are innocent, and of perpetrating, as a contribution to Peace, butchery of untold magnitude, as at Hiroshima on 6 August 1945 ? And in fact has not our own time had an example of what can be done by a weak man, Gandhi — armed only with the principle of non-violence — to vindicate for a Nation of hundreds of millions of human beings the freedom and dignity of a new People ?

*　　*　　*

Civilization walks in the footsteps of Peace armed only with an olive branch. Civilization is followed by the Doctors with the weighty volumes on the Law which will lead moves in this ordered procession, now no longer proud and cruel but completely intent on defending the weak, punishing the violent and ensuring an order which is extremely difficult to achieve but which alone is worthy of that divine name : order in freedom and conscious duty.

Let us rejoice : this procession, though interrupted by hostile attacks and by unexpected accidents, continues along its way before our eyes in this tragic time of ours. Its step is perhaps a little slow, but it is nonetheless sure and beneficial for the whole world. It is a procession intent on using the real weapons of peace.

*　　*　　*

This message too must have its appendix for those properly called followers and servants of the Gospel — an appendix which recalls how explicit and demanding Christ our Lord is in regard to this theme of peace stripped of every weapon and armed only with goodness and love.

The Lord makes statements, as we know, which appear paradoxical. Let it not be distasteful to us to rediscover in the Gospel the rules for a Peace which we could describe as self-abnegating ! Let us recall, for example : "If a man takes you to law and would have your tunic, let him have your cloak as well" (Mt. 5:40). And then that prohibition of revenge — does it not undermine Peace ? Indeed, does it not aggravate, rather than defend, the position of the injured party ? "If anyone hits you on the right cheek, offer him the other as well" (Mt. 5:40). So there are to be no reprisals, no vendettas (and these are all the more wrong if they are committed to prevent injuries not yet received !). How many times in the Gospel is forgiveness recommended to us, not as an act of cowardly weakness, nor as a surrender in the face of injustice, but as a sign of fraternal love, which is laid down as a condition for us to obtain God's forgiveness, which we need and which is a far more generous forgiveness ! (cf. Mt. 18:23 ff., 5:44; Mk. 11:25; Lk. 6:37; Rom. 12:14, etc.).

Let us remember the pledge we give to be forgiving and to pardon when we invoke God's forgiveness in the "Our Father". We ourselves lay down the condition and the extent of the mercy we ask for when we say : "And forgive us our debts, as we have forgiven those who are in debt to us" (Mt. 6:12).

For us also therefore, who are disciples of the school of Christ, this is a lesson to be meditated on still more and to be applied with confident courage.

Peace expresses itself only in peace, a peace which is not separate from the demands of justice but which is fostered by personal sacrifice, clemency, mercy and love.

(The Teachings of Pope Paul VI, Vol. 8, 1975, pp. 385-391)

ADDRESS TO THE SACRED COLLEGE OF CARDINALS
22 December 1975

... God grant that the peoples will set out more and more generously and wisely along this path, abandoning, on the contrary, the dangerous and morally deprecable one of the production and commerce (also in the form of "gifts", but how onerous)! of destructive arms! And may He grant also that the negotiations for disarmament, both general and qualified, such as the SALT (Strategic Arms Limitation Talks) ones, will not stop or continue to mark time because of the obstacles they meet on their way : serious obstacles, without any doubt, but which goodwill and the tenacity and political wisdom of the responsible statesmen must find a way to overcome...

(The Teachings of Pope Paul VI, Vol. 8, 1975, pp. 453-454)

MESSAGE FOR THE WORLD DAY OF PEACE, 1977
8 December 1976

... Peace and Life. They are supreme values in the civil order. They are also values that are interdependent.

Do we want Peace ? Then let us defend Life !

The phrase "Peace and Life" may seem almost tautological, a rhetorical slogan. It is not so. The combination of the two terms in the phrase represents a hard-won conquest in the onward march of human progress — a march still short of its final goal. How many times in the drama of human history the phrase "Peace and Life" has involved a fierce struggle of the two terms, not a fraternal embrace. Peace is sought and won through conflict, like a sad doom necessary for self-defence.

The close relationship between Peace and Life seems to spring from the nature of things, but not always, not yet from the logic of people's thought and conduct. This close relationship is the paradoxical novelty that we must proclaim for this year of grace 1977 and henceforth for ever, if we are to understand the dynamics of progress. To succeed in doing so is no easy and simple task : we shall meet the opposition of too many formidable objections, which are stored in the immense arsenal of pseudo-convictions, empirical and utilitarian prejudices, so-called reasons of State, and habits drawn from history and tradition. Even today, these objections seem to constitute insurmountable obstacles. The tragic conclusion is that if, in defiance of logic, Peace and Life can in practice be dissociated, there looms on the horizon of the future a catastrophe that in our days could be immeasurable and irreparable both for Peace and Life. Hiroshima is a terribly eloquent proof and a frighteningly prophetic example of this. In the reprehensible hypothesis that Peace were thought of in unnatural separation from its relationship with Life, Peace could be imposed as the sad triumph of death. The words of Tacitus come to mind : "They make a desert and call it Peace" (*ubi solitudinem faciunt, pacem appellant : Agricola,* 30). Again, in the same hypothesis, the privileged Life of some can be exalted, can be selfishly and almost idolatrously preferred, at the expense of the oppression or suppression of others. Is that Peace ?

This conflict is thus seen to be not merely theoretical and moral but tragically real. Even today it continues to desecrate and stain with blood many a page of human society. The key of truth in the matter can be found only by recognizing the primacy of Life as a value and as a condition for Peace. The formula is : "If you want Peace, defend Life". Life is the crown of Peace. If we base the logic of our activity on the sacredness of Life, war is virtually disqualified as a normal and habitual means of asserting rights and so of ensuring Peace. Peace is but the incontestable ascendancy of right and, in the final analysis, the joyful celebration of Life.

Here the number of examples is endless, as is the case-history of the adventures, or rather the misadventures, in which life is put at peril in the face of Peace. We make our own the classification which, in this regard, has been presented according to "three essential imperatives". According to these imperatives, in order to have authentic and happy Peace, it is necessary "to defend life, to heal life, to promote life".

The policy of massive armaments is immediately called into question. The ancient saying, which has taught politics and still does so — "if you want peace, prepare for war" (*si vis pacem, para bellum*) — is not acceptable without radical reservation (cf. Lk. 14:31). With the forthright boldness of our principles, we thus denounce the false and dangerous programme of the "arms race", of the secret rivalry between peoples for military superiority. Even if through a surviving remnant of happy wisdom, or through a silent yet tremendous contest in the balance of hostile deadly powers, war (and what a war it would be !) does not break out, how can we fail to lament the incalculable outpouring of economic resources and human energies expended in order to preserve for each individual State its shield of ever more costly, ever more efficient weapons, and this to the detriment of resources for schools, culture, agriculture, health and civic welfare. Peace and Life support enormous and incalculable burdens in order to maintain a Peace founded on a perpetual threat to Life, as also to defend Life by means of a constant threat to Peace. People will say : it is inevitable. This can be true within a concept of civilization that is still so imperfect. But let us at least recognize that this constitutional challenge which the arms race sets up between Life and Peace is a formula that is fallacious in itself and which must be corrected and superseded. We therefore praise the effort already begun to reduce and finally to eliminate this senseless cold war resulting from the progressive increase of the military potential of the various Nations, as if these Nations should necessarily be enemies of each other, and as if they were incapable of realizing that such a concept of international relations must one day be resolved in the ruination of Peace and of countless human lives...

(The Teachings of Pope Paul VI, Vol. 9, 1976, pp. 379-381)

ADDRESS TO THE FIRST SECRETARY OF PUWP
(POLAND UNIFIED WORKERS PARTY), Mr. GIEREK
1 December 1977

... A prosperous and serene Poland is also in the interest of tranquillity and good collaboration among the peoples of Europe.

We gratefully appreciate what you said about the work carried out by the Holy See and by us personally in the service of peace, in Europe and in the world. As it corresponds to the deep conviction of a duty imposed upon us by our very mission, a duty distinct but not separated from the one incumbent upon us in the service of the Catholic Church, religious interests and the human rights of individuals and peoples, we will not tire of exerting ourself, now and always, to the best of our abilities, in order that conflicts among nations may be prevented or solved justly and in order that there may be ensured and improved the indispensable foundations for peaceful coexistence among countries and continents : not least of all, a more just world economic order; the abandonment of the race for more and more dangerous armaments, also in the nuclear sector, as preparation for a gradual and balanced disarmament; the development of better economic, cultural and human relations among peoples, individuals and associated groups...

(L'Osservatore Romano, English edition, No. 50, 1977, p. 4)

MESSAGE FOR THE WORLD DAY OF PEACE, 1978
8 December 1977

... In this Message of Peace we are speaking about violence as the antagonistic term of Peace, and we have not spoken about war. War still deserves our condemnation, even though today it is being rejected ever more widely : against it a praiseworthy and ever more authoritative effort is being made, both socially and politically. Another reason is that war is being kept in check by the terrible nature of its own arms, which it would immediately have at its disposal in the extremely tragic eventuality that it should break out. Fear, which is common to all Peoples, and to the strongest ones especially, holds in check the eventuality that war might turn into a cosmic conflagration. And fear, which is more an imagined restraint than a real one, is accompanied, as we have said, by a lofty and rational effort being made at the highest political levels — an effort which must tend not so much towards balancing the forces of the possible contenders as towards showing the supreme irrationality of war, and the same time towards establishing relationships between Peoples, which are ever more interdependent, with ultimate solidarity, and ever more friendly and human. God grant that it be so.

But we cannot shut our eyes to the sad reality of partial war, both because it is still raging in certain regions, and because psychologically it is not at all excluded in the uncertain possibility of contemporary history. Our war against war has not yet been won, and our "yes" to Peace is rather something wished for than something real; for in many geographical and political situations which have not yet been settled in just and peaceful solutions the possibility of future conflicts remains endemic. Our love for Peace must remain on guard; other prospects too, besides that of a new world war, oblige us to consider and exalt Peace even outside the trenches...

(The Teachings of Pope Paul VI, Vol. 10, 1977, pp. 526-527)

CHRISTMAS MESSAGE
25 December 1977

... Let us therefore on this radiant day welcome the invitation of the angels, the invitation of the Gospel. Let us repeat it as if to stir up within us a more convinced and secure adherence to it : where God is honoured, man is also honoured; the glory of God is the foundation of man's dignity. The Birthday of Christ marks, in the name of the Father in heaven, the pathway of peace on earth. "The Birthday of the Lord is the birthday of peace" (Saint Leo, *Sermo XXVI,* 5).

The modern world, as all can witness, needs peace. For many situations of history in the course of actuation one would say that the earth has exhausted its provisions of peace, which had been enriched with formidable promises by the tragic experience of the two world wars that stained with blood the first half of the century now drawing to a close. Human beings are still each other's adversaries. Injustice, hunger and misery still awaken instincts of struggle and delinquency. The sacred pacts of concord and collaboration between peoples still seem incapable of bearing the weight of the commitments undertaken towards a renouncement of violence. The fear of terrible armaments, whose frightful spectres can be more easily stirred up today by an inhuman science, still takes sleep from the rulers of peoples, who cannot foresee any peace without the defence of ever more potent means of war and death. Peace seems to give free play to new unimaginable possibilities of the furies of war.

No, let it not be so ! The loyal promises of friendship and collaboration, like the evident questions which divide nations, must renew their fidelity to Peace.

(The Teachings of Pope Paul VI, Vol. 10, 1977, p. 554)

LETTER TO HIS HOLINESS PIMEN,
PATRIARCH OF MOSCOW AND THE WHOLE OF RUSSIA
22 May 1978

We entrust our venerable brother Ramon Torrella Cascante, titular bishop of Minervino Murge and Vice-President of our Secretariat for Christian Unity, with the task of bringing to your Holiness, together with our fraternal greetings, the assurance that we have given serious attention to your letter of 22 December last, in which you make known to us the appeal addressed by the leaders and representatives of religious confessions and associations in the USSR to religious leaders and believers of the whole world about the neutron bomb.

United with Your Holiness and with the other signatories of the appeal, in the awareness of our common responsibility to defend the sacred gift of life and to promote the cause of peace among peoples, we did not fail to consider this serious problem in its moral and human implications.

As in the past, so also in the future we shall not desist to take all the necessary steps, within our possibilities, to make sure that concrete means and efficient ways are urgently sought by all concerned to protect humanity — starting with Europe, which is particularly exposed — against the tremendous hecatombs that a possible recourse to atomic weapons, in any of their present or potential forms, would bring about.

To this end, we shall continue to insist with those in charge of nations, that they undertake negotiations without delay, and pursue them tenaciously and in good faith, so that they may all stop manufacturing this kind of arms — as well as other means of massive destruction — and start dismantling the existing stock-piles until they are totally non-existant.

We hope that the now imminent special session of the United Nations Assembly, dedicated to the problem of disarmament, may result in a good opportunity to launch a generous and determined action in that sense.

As to us Christians, together with all those who believe in God the Father and Lord of Life, we shall accompany with our prayers the efforts of the statesmen engaged in this enterprise, which is as just and necessary as it is difficult, so that they may not lack courage, wisdom, and goodwill.

May our message and example, with God's help, diffuse more and more in the hearts of men feelings of brotherhood and resolutions for peace !

We renew to Your Holiness the expression of our fraternal charity in the love of the Lord.

From the Vatican, 22 May 1978.

(La Documentation Catholique, No. 22, 1978, p. 1061; Translation by Pontifical Commission "Iustitia et Pax")

MESSAGE TO THE UNITED NATIONS' GENERAL ASSEMBLY AT A SPECIAL SESSION ON DISARMAMENT
24 May 1978

On the occasion of the Special Session which the General Assembly of the United Nations has decided to devote to the problem of disarmament, there exists a widespread expectation, and its echo has reached us. Does not the Holy See have something to say on a subject of such burning relevance and such vital importance for the future of the world ?

Without being a member of your Organization, the Holy See follows its many activities with the greatest attention and with a profound understanding, sharing its preoccupations and its generous intentions. We cannot remain insensitive to an expectation such as this.

We therefore very willingly accept the opportunity that has been given to us to address once again a message to the General Assembly of the United Nations, as we had the honour to do, in person, in that already distant October of 1965. The present circumstance is in effect absolutely exceptional in the life of your Organization and for the whole of humanity.

1. We come to you once again today, in the spirit and with the sentiments of our first meeting, the remembrance of which is always vivid and dear to our heart. Please accept our respectful and cordial greeting.

We come to you as the representative of a Church that is made up of hundreds of millions of people spread throughout all the continents. But at the same time we have the consciousness of giving a voice to the aspirations and hopes of other hundreds of millions of people, Christians and non-Christians, believers and non-believers : we would like to gather them together, as in an immense choir ascending towards God and towards those who have received from God the responsibility for the destiny of the nations.

2. Our message is meant to be, first of all, a message of congratulations for your having resolved to confront decisively, in this lofty forum, the problem of disarmament. Yours is an act of courage, and wisdom. It is the response to an extremely grave and urgent need.

Our message is also a message of understanding. We know the exceptional difficulties that you must face, and we fully realize the weight of your responsibilities, but we have confidence in the seriousness and sincerity of your commitment.

Our message is meant to be above all — if you permit us to say so — a message of encouragement.

3. The peoples are manifesting such interest in the theme of your discussion because they believe that to disarm is, first of all, to deprive war of its means : peace is their dream, their deepest aspiration.

The desire for peace is also the noble and profound motive that has brought you to this Assembly. But, in the eyes of statesmen, the problem of disarmament presents itself under a much more articulated and much more complex form.

Faced with the situation as it is, the statesman asks himself, not without reason, if it is just and if it is possible not to recognize the right of the members of the International Community to make their own provisions for their legitimate defence, and hence to procure the means necessary for such a goal.

And the temptation is strong to ask oneself if the best possible protection for peace does not in fact continue to be ensured, basically, by the old system of the balance of forces between the different States or groups of States. A disarmed peace is always exposed to danger; its very weakness is an incentive to attack it.

Against this background one can and must — it is said — develop, in a parallel way, efforts aimed on the one hand at perfecting the methods and bodies for preventing and resolving peacefully conflicts and confrontations; and on the other hand to render less inhuman those wars that are not successfully avoided. At the same time, one can and must endeavour to reduce the arsenals of war, in a way that does not destroy the existing balances, but lessens the temptation to have recourse to weapons and lightens the enormous military budgets.

Such seems to be the path of political realism. It claims justification in reason and experience. To go further seems to many people a useless or indeed dangerous effort.

4. Let us say at once that all substantial progress towards improving the mechanism of preventing conflicts, towards eliminating particularly dangerous and inhumane weapons, and towards lowering the level of armaments and military expenditure, will be hailed by us as an extremely valuable and beneficial result.

But this is still not enough. The question of war and peace, in fact, presents itself today in new terms.

It is not that the principles have changed. Aggression by one State against another was illicit yesterday just as it is today. Even in the past, an "act of war directed to the indiscriminate destruction of whole cities or vast regions with their inhabitants" was "a crime against God and humanity itself" (*Gaudium et Spes*, 80). And war — although one must honour the heroism of those who sacrifice their very lives to the service of their native land or of some other noble cause — has always been, in itself, a supremely irrational and morally unacceptable means of regulating the relationships between States, though without prejudice to the right of legitimate defence.

But today, war has at its disposal means which have "immeasurably magnified its horrors and wickedness" (*ibid.*).

The logic underlying the request for the balances of power impels each of the adversaries to seek to ensure a certain margin of superiority, for fear of being left at a disadvantage. This logic, in conjunction with the amazing progress of humanity in the spheres of sciences and technology, has led to the discovery of ever more sophisticated and powerful instruments of destruction. These instruments have accumulated, and, by virtue of an almost autonomous process, they tend to self-perpetuate unendingly, in a continual escalation both in quantity and quality, with an immense expenditure of men and means, to the point of reaching today a potential amply capable of wiping out all life on the planet.

Developments in nuclear armament make up a special chapter, and certainly the most typical and striking one, of this quest for security through the balance of power and fear. But can one forget the "progress" that has also been made and that, alas, might still be made in the sphere of other arms of mass destruction or with the capacity to produce particularly damaging effects — arms that are considered to have, for that very reason, a special power of "dissuasion" ?

But even though the "balance of terror" has been able to avoid the worst and may do so for some time more, to think that the arms race can thus go on indefinitely, without causing a catastrophe, would be a tragic illusion.

Certainly, the subject above all concerns, at least directly, the Great Powers and the countries forming their blocs, but it would be very hard for the other countries not to feel concerned.

Humanity therefore finds itself forced to turn back on itself and ask itself where it is going, or rather, what it is plunging into. It is forced above all to ask whether the point of departure is not mistaken and should therefore be radically altered.

The reasons for a change of this kind — whether moral reasons, or reasons of security or of particular and general interest — are certainly not lacking.

But, is it possible to find a substitute for the security — however uncertain and costly it may be — that each is trying to ensure by acquiring the means of his own defence ?

5. Few problems appear today so inevitable and difficult as the problem of disarmament. Few problems respond so much to the needs and expectations of the peoples, and at the same time so readily provoke mistrust, scepticism and discouragement. Few problems demand, on the part of those who must face them, such great resources of idealism and such an acute sense of reality. It seems to be a problem situated at the level of a prophetic vision open to the hopes of the future. And yet one cannot really face this problem without remaining solidly based upon the hard and concrete reality of the present.

Disarmament therefore calls for an extraordinary effort of intelligence and political will on the part of all the members of the great family of nations, in order to reconcile demands that seem to contradict one another and cancel one another out.

The problem of disarmament is substantially a problem of mutual trust. It would therefore be largely useless to seek possible solutions of the technical aspects of disarmament if one were to fail to cure at its source the situation that serves as fertile soil for the proliferation of armaments.

Even the terror of new weapons runs the risk of being ineffective, to the extent that other guarantees are not found for the security of States and for the solution of the problems capable of bringing those States into confrontation on points vital to them.

If one wishes — as one must — to make substantial progress along the road to disarmament, it is therefore essential to find the means of replacing "the balance of terror" by "the balance of trust".

But, in practice, is this possible ? And to what extent ?

Certainly, a first step consists in trying to improve with good faith and good-will the atmosphere and the reality of international relations, especially between the Great Powers and the blocs of States. In this way the fears and suspicions that today divide them can lessen, and it will be easier for them to believe in the real desire for mutual peace. It involves a long and complicated effort, but one that we would like to encourage with all our power.

Détente in the real sense, that is to say, founded upon a proven willingness to exercise mutual respect, is a condition for setting in motion a true process of disarmament. In turn, balanced and properly supervised disarmament measures assist détente to progress and grow stronger.

However, the international situation is too exposed to the ever possible changes and caprices of tragically free wills. Solid international trust therefore also presupposes structures that are objectively suitable for guaranteeing, by peaceful means, security and respect for or recognition of everyone's rights, against always possible bad will. In other words, such trust presupposes an international order capable of giving everyone what each is today seeking to ensure for himself by the possession and threat of arms, if not by their use.

But is there not a risk of thus slipping into utopianism ?

We think that we can and must resolutely answer no. It is true that the task in question is extremely arduous, but it is not beyond the tenacity and wisdom of people who are aware of their own responsibilities before humanity and history — above all before God. This means the need for a higher religious awareness.

Even those who do not take God into account can and must recognize the fundamental exigencies of the moral law that God has written in the depths of human hearts and that must govern people's mutual relationships on the basis of truth, justice and love.

At a time when humanity's horizons are widening far beyond the confines of our planet, we refuse to believe that man, animated by such an awareness, is not capable of exorcising the demon of war which threatens to destroy him, even if this demands of him immense efforts and a reasonable renunciation of old-fashioned concepts that continue to set peoples and nations at odds.

6. In making our own, and expressing to you anew, the hope and anguish of humanity aspiring to the peace it needs, we are aware that the path which must lead to the coming of a new international order capable of eliminating wars and the causes of wars and thus making arms superfluous cannot in any case be as short as we would like it to be.

It will therefore be indispensable in the meantime to plan and promote a strategy of peace and disarmament — a step-by-step strategy but one that is at the same time almost impatient, a strategy that is balanced yet courageous — always keeping our eyes and our wills fixed on the final goal of general and complete disarmament.

We do not have the competence or authority to indicate to you the methods and mechanisms for such a strategy, which in any case presupposes the setting up of reliable and effective international controls systems. We believe however that there is common agreement with you on the need to lay down some priorities in the effort aimed at halting the arms race and reducing the amount of existing arms.

a) Nuclear weapons certainly have first place : they are the most fearsome menace with which mankind is burdened. We appreciate very much the initiatives that have already been taken in this area, but we must encourage all countries, particularly those which have the chief responsibility for it, to continue and to develop these initiatives, with the final goal of completely eliminating the atomic arsenal. At the same time means must be found for giving all peoples access to the immense resources of nuclear energy for their peaceful use.

b) Next comes already existing or possible weapons of mass destruction, such as chemical, radiological and all other such weapons, and those that strike indiscriminately or, to use an expression that is itself rather cruel, weapons with excessively and needlessly cruel effects.

c) Mention must also be made of trade in conventional weapons, which are, so to speak, the principal fuel for local or limited wars. In comparison with the immensity of the catastrophe that a war resorting to the whole arsenal of strategic and other weapons would mean for the world or for whole continents, such conflicts may seem of minor importance, if not negligible.

But the destruction and suffering that they cause to the peoples that are their victims are no less than those that would be brought about on quite a different scale by a general conflict. Furthermore, the increase in arms budgets can stifle the economy of countries that are often still at the developing stage. Besides, account must be taken of the danger that in a world which has grown small and in which different interests interfere and clash a local conflict could gradually provoke much wider conflagrations.

7. The arms race is a matter of scandal; the prospect of disarmament is a great hope. The scandal concerns the crying disproportion between the resources in money and intelligence devoted to the service of death and the resources devoted to the service of life. The hope is that, by cutting down on military expenditure, a substantial part of the immense resources that it now absorbs can be employed in a vast world development project.

We feel the scandal. We make the hope our own.

In this same hall where you are gathered today we renewed on 4 October 1965 the appeal we made to all States on the occasion of our journey to Bombay the previous December "to devote to the benefit of developing nations at least a part of the money that could be saved through a reduction of armaments".

We now repeat this appeal with still more force and insistence, calling on all countries to study and put into operation an organic plan within the framework of the programmes for the fight against inequality, underdevelopment, hunger, disease and illiteracy. Justice demands it; the general interest recommends it. For progress by each of the members of the great human family will be to the advantage of progress by all and will serve to give a more solid foundation to peace.

8. Disarmament, a new world order, and development are three obligations that are inseparably bound together and that by their essence presuppose a renewal of public outlook.

212

We know and understand the difficulties presented by these obligations. But it is our will and our duty to remind you strongly, as people who are conscious of responsibility for the destiny of mankind, of the very serious reasons that make it necessary to find means of overcoming these difficulties. Do not depart without having laid the foundations and given the indispensable impulse to the solution of the problem that has brought you here together. Tomorrow may be too late.

But, you will ask, what contribution can and will the Holy See make to this immense common effort for disarmament and peace ?

It is a question you have a right to ask. It places us in our turn face to face with our responsibilities, with respect to which our means are much inferior to our will.

The Holy See is not a World Power, nor has it political power. It has declared in a solemn treaty that "it wishes to remain and will remain extraneous to all temporal disputes between States and to international congresses held for such objects, unless the contending parties make concordant appeal to its mission of peace; at the same time reserving the right to exercise its moral and spiritual power" (Lateran Treaty, Article 24).

Sharing your problems, conscious of your difficulties, and strong by our very weakness, we accordingly say to you with great simplicity : If you ever think that the Holy See can help overcome the obstacles blocking the way to peace, it will not shelter behind the argument of its "non-temporal" character nor shy away from the responsibilities that could be involved in interventions that have been desired and asked for. For the Holy See greatly esteems peace and greatly loves it.

In any case, we shall continue to proclaim aloud, untiringly and without losing courage, the duty of peace, the principles that govern its dynamism, and the means of gaining and defending it through renouncing by common accord the weapons that threaten to kill it while claiming to serve it.

We know the strength of public opinion when it is upheld by solid ideals, convictions firmly rooted in consciences. We shall therefore continue to co-operate in order to educate dynamically for peace the new humanity. We shall continue to recall that there will be no disarmament of weapons if there is no disarmament of hearts.

We shall continue to pray for peace.

Peace is the fruit of the good will of men and women, but it remains continually exposed to perils that good will does not always succeed in controlling. That is why peace has always appeared to mankind as above all else a gift from God. We shall ask him for it. Grant us peace. And we shall ask him to guide your work, in order that its results, both immediate and future, will not disappoint the hope of the peoples.

(The Teachings of Pope Paul VI, Vol. 11, 1978, pp. 199-207)

VATICAN COUNCIL II

PASTORAL CONSTITUTION "GAUDIUM ET SPES"
7 December 1965

Chapter V
FOSTERING OF PEACE AND ESTABLISHMENT
OF A COMMUNITY OF NATIONS

INTRODUCTION

77. In our generation, which has been marked by the persistent and acute hardships and anxiety resulting from the ravages of war and the threat of war, the whole human race faces a moment of supreme crisis in its advance towards maturity. Mankind has gradually come closer together and is everywhere more conscious of its own unity; but it will not succeed in accomplishing the task awaiting it, that is, the establishment of a truly human world for all men over the entire earth, unless everyone devotes himself to the cause of true peace with renewed vigour. Thus the message of the Gospel, which epitomizes the highest ideals and aspirations of mankind, shines anew in our times when it proclaims that the advocates of peace are blessed "for they shall be called sons of God" (Mt. 5:9).

Accordingly, the Council proposes to outline the true and noble nature of peace, to condemn the savagery of war, and earnestly to exhort Christians to co-operate with all in securing a peace based on justice and charity and in promoting the means necessary to attain it, under the help of Christ, author of peace.

NATURE OF PEACE

78. Peace is more than the absence of war : it cannot be reduced to the maintenance of a balance of power between opposing forces nor does it arise out of despotic dominion, but it is appropriately called "the effect of righteousness" (Is. 32:17). It is the fruit of that right ordering of things with which the divine founder has invested human society and which must be actualized by man thirsting after an ever more perfect reign of justice. But while the common good of mankind ultimately derives from the eternal law, it depends in the concrete upon circumstances which change as time goes on; consequently, peace will never be achieved once and for all, but must be built up continually. Since, moreover, human nature is weak and wounded by sin, the achievement of peace requires a constant effort to control the passions and unceasing vigilance by lawful authority.

But this is not enough. Peace cannot be obtained on earth unless the welfare of man is safeguarded and people freely and trustingly share with one another the riches of their minds and their talents. A firm determination to respect the dignity of other men and other peoples along with the deliberate practice of fraternal love are absolutely necessary for the achievement of peace. Accordingly, peace is also the fruit of love, for love goes beyond what justice can ensure.

Peace on earth, which flows from love of one's neighbour, symbolizes and derives from the peace of Christ who proceeds from God the Father. Christ, the Word made flesh, the prince of peace, reconciled all men to God by the cross, and, restoring the unity of all in one people and one body, he abolished hatred in his own flesh, 1 having been lifted up through his resurrection he poured forth the Spirit of love into the hearts of men. Therefore, all Christians are earnestly to speak the truth in love (cf. Eph. 4:15) and join with all peace-loving men in pleading for peace and trying to bring it about. In the same spirit we cannot but express our admiration for all who forgo the use of violence to vindicate their rights and resort to those other means of defence which are available to weaker parties, provided it can be done without harm to the rights and duties of others and of the community.

Insofar as men are sinners, the threat of war hangs over them and will so continue until the coming of Christ; but insofar as they can vanquish sin by coming together in charity, violence itself will be vanquished and they will make these words come true : "They shall beat their swords into ploughshares, and

---

1. Cf. Eph. 2:16; Col. 1:20-22.

their spears into pruning hooks; nation shall not lift up sword against nation, neither shall they learn war any more" (Is. 2:4).

SECTION 1 : AVOIDANCE OF WAR

CURBING THE SAVAGERY OF WAR

79. Even though recent wars have wrought immense material and moral havoc on the world, the devastation of battle still rages in some parts of the world. Indeed, now that every kind of weapon produced by modern science is used in war, the savagery of war threatens to lead the combatants to barbarities far surpassing those of former ages. Moreover, the complexity of the modern world and the intricacy of international relations cause incipient wars to develop into full-scale conflict by new methods of infiltration and subversion. In many cases terrorist methods are regarded as new strategies of war.

Faced by this deplorable state of humanity the Council wishes to remind men that the natural law of peoples and its universal principles still retain their binding force. The conscience of mankind firmly and ever more emphatically proclaims these principles. Any action which deliberately violates these principles and any order which commands such actions is criminal and blind obedience cannot excuse those who carry them out. The most infamous among these actions are those designed for the reasoned and methodical extermination of an entire race, nation, or ethnic minority. These must be condemned as frightful crimes; and we cannot commend too highly the courage of the men who openly and fearlessly resist those who issue orders of this kind.

On the question of warfare, there are various international conventions, signed by many countries, aimed at rendering military action and its consequences less inhuman; they deal with the treatment of wounded and interned prisoners of war and with various kindred questions. These agreements must be honoured; indeed public authorities and specialists in these matters must do all in their power to improve these conventions and thus bring about a better and more effective curbing of the savagery of war. Moreover, it seems just that laws should make humane provision for the case of conscientious objectors who refuse to carry arms, provided they accept some other form of community service.

War, of course, has not ceased to be part of the human scene. As long as the danger of war persists and there is no international authority with the necessary competence and power, governments cannot be denied the right of lawful self-defence, once all peace efforts have failed. State leaders and all who share the burdens of public administration have the duty to defend the interests of their people and to conduct such grave matters with a deep sense of responsibility. However, it is one thing to wage a war of self-defence; it is quite another to seek to impose domination on another nation. The possession of war potential does not justify the use of force for political or military objectives. Nor does the mere fact that war has unfortunately broken out mean that all is fair between the warring parties.

All those who enter the military service in loyalty to their country should look upon themselves as the custodians of the security and freedom of their fellow - countrymen; and when they carry out their duty properly, they are contributing to the maintenance of peace.

TOTAL WARFARE

80. The development of armaments by modern science has immeasurably magnified the horrors and wickedness of war. Warfare conducted with these weapons can inflict immense and indiscriminate havoc which goes far beyond the bounds of legitimate defence. Indeed if the kind of weapons now stocked in the arsenals of the great powers were to be employed to the fullest, the result would be the almost complete reciprocal slaughter of one side by the other, not to speak of the widespread devastation that would follow in the world and the deadly after-effects resulting from the use of such arms.

All these factors force us to undertake a completely fresh reappraisal of war. 2 Men of this generation should realize that they will have to render an account of their warlike behaviour; the destiny of generations to come depends largely on the decisions they make today.

With these considerations in mind the Council, endorsing the condemnations of total warfare issued by recent popes, 3 declares : Every act of war

---

2. Cf. John XXIII, Litt. Encycl. *Pacem in Terris : AAS 55* (1963), p. 291 : "Therefore in this age of ours, which prides itself on its atomic power, it is irrational to think that war is a proper way to obtain justice for violated rights."

3. Cf. Pius XII, *Allocution*, 30 Sept. 1954 : *AAS 46* (1954), p. 589; *Christmas Message* 1954 : *AAS 47* (1955), pp. 15 ff.; John XXIII, Litt. Encycl. *Pacem in Terris : AAS 55* (1963), pp. 286-291; Paul VI, *Address to the United Nations,* 4 Oct. 1965 : *AAS 57* (1965), pp. 877-885.

directed to the indiscriminate destruction of whole cities or vast areas with their inhabitants is a crime against God and man, which merits firm and unequivocal condemnation.

The hazards peculiar to modern warfare consist in the fact they expose those possessing recently developed weapons to the risk of perpetrating crimes like these and, by an inexorable chain of events, of urging men to even worse acts of atrocity. To obviate the possibility of this happening at any time in the future, the bishops of the world gathered together to implore all men, especially government leaders and military advisers, to give unceasing consideration to their immense responsibilities before God and before the whole human race.

THE ARMS RACE

81. Undoubtedly, armaments are not amassed merely for use in wartime. Since the defensive strength of any nation is thought to depend on its capacity for immediate retaliation, the stockpiling of arms which grows from year to year serves, in a way hitherto unthought of, as a deterrent to potential attackers. Many people look upon this as the most effective way known at the present time for maintaining some sort of peace among nations.

Whatever one may think of this form of deterrent, people are convinced that the arms race, which quite a few countries have entered, is no infallible way of maintaining real peace and that the resulting so-called balance of power is no sure and genuine path to achieving it. Rather than eliminate the causes of war, the arms race serves only to aggravate the position. As long as extravagant sums of money are poured into the development of new weapons, it is impossible to devote adequate aid in tackling the misery which prevails at the present day in the world. Instead of eradicating international conflict once and for all, the contagion is spreading to other parts of the world. New approaches, based on reformed attitudes, will have to be chosen in order to remove this stumbling block, to free the earth from its pressing anxieties, and give back to the world a genuine peace.

Therefore, we declare once again : the arms race is one of the greatest curses on the human race and the harm it inflicts on the poor is more than can be endured. And there is every reason to fear if it continues it will bring forth those lethal disasters which are already in preparation. Warned by the possibility of the catastrophes that man has created, let us profit by the respite we now enjoy, thanks to the divine favour, to take stock of our responsibilities and find ways of resolving controversies in a manner worthy of human beings. Providence urgently demands of us that we free ourselves from the age-old slavery of war. If we refuse to make this effort, there is no knowing where we will be led on the fatal path we have taken.

TOTAL OUTLAWING OF WAR : INTERNATIONAL ACTION TO PREVENT WAR

82. It is our clear duty to spare no effort in order to work for the moment when all war will be completely outlawed by international agreement. This goal, of course, requires the establishment of a universally acknowledged public authority vested with the effective power to ensure security for all, regard for justice, and respect for law. But before this desirable authority can be constituted, it is necessary for existing international bodies to devote themselves resolutely to the exploration of better means for obtaining common security. But since peace must be born of mutual trust between peoples instead of being forced on nations through dread of arms, all must work to put an end to the arms race and make a real beginning of disarmament, not unilaterally indeed but at an equal rate on all sides, on the basis of agreements and backed up by genuine and effective guarantees. 4

In the meantime one must not underestimate the efforts already made or now under way to eliminate the danger of war. On the contrary, support should be given to the good will of numerous individuals who are making every effort to eliminate the havoc of war; these men, although burdened by the weighty responsibilities of their high office, are motivated by a consciousness of their very grave obligations, even if they cannot ignore the complexity of the situation as it stands. We must beseech the Lord to give them the strength to tackle with perseverance and carry out with courage this task of supreme love for man which is the building up of a lasting peace in a true spirit of manhood. In our times this work demands that they enlarge their thoughts and their spirit beyond the confines of their own country, that they put aside nationalistic selfishness and ambitions to dominate other nations, and that they cultivate deep reverence for the whole of mankind which is painstakingly advancing towards greater maturity.

The problems of peace and disarmament have been treated at length with courage and untiring consultation at negotiations and international meetings; these are to be considered as the first steps towards the solutions of such im-

---

4. Cf. John XXIII, Litt. Encycl. *Pacem in Terris*, where the reduction of arms is treated : *AAS 55* (1963), p. 287.

portant questions and must be further pursued with even greater insistence, with a view to obtaining concrete results in the future. But people should beware of leaving these problems to the efforts of a few men without putting their own attitudes in order. For state leaders, who are at once the guardians of their own people and the promoters of the welfare of the whole world, rely to a large extent on public opinion and public attitudes. Their peace-making efforts will be in vain, as long as men are divided and warring among themselves through hostility, contempt, and distrust, as well as through racial hatred and uncompromising hostilities. Hence there is a very urgent need of re-education and a new orientation of public opinion. Those engaged in the work of education, especially youth education, and the people who mold public opinion, should regard it as their most important task to educate the minds of men to renewed sentiments of peace. Every one of us needs a change of heart; we must see our gaze on the whole world and look to those tasks we can all perform together in order to bring about the betterment of our race.

But let us not be buoyed up with false hope. For unless animosity and hatred are put aside, and firm, honest agreements about world peace are concluded, humanity may, in spite of the wonders of modern science, go from the grave crisis of the present day to that dismal hour, when the only peace it will experience will be the dread peace of death. The Church, however, living in the midst of these anxieties, even as it makes these statements, has not lost hope. The Church intends to propose to our age over and over again, in season and out of season, the apostle's message : "Behold, now is the acceptable time" for a change of heart; "behold, now is the day of salvation" (cf. 2 Cor. 6:2).

(Flannery, pp. 986-993)

JOHN PAUL II

ENCYCLICAL LETTER "REDEMPTOR HOMINIS"
4 March 1979

... This eschatological scene must always be "applied" to man's history; it must always be made the "measure" for human acts as an essential outline for an examination of conscience by each and every one : "I was hungry and you gave me no food... naked and you did not clothe me... in prison and you did not visit me." (Mt. 25:42-43). These words become charged with even stronger warning, when we think that, instead of bread and cultural aid, the new States and nations awakening to independent life are being offered, sometimes in abundance, modern weapons and means of destruction placed at the service of armed conflicts and wars that are not so much a requirement for defending their just rights and their sovereignty but rather a form of chauvinism, imperialism, and neocolonialism of one kind or another. We all know well that the areas of misery and hunger on our globe could have been made fertile in a short time, if the gigantic investments for armaments at the service of war and destruction had been changed into investments for food at the service of life.

This consideration will perhaps remain in part an "abstract" one. It will perhaps offer both "sides" an occasion for mutual accusation, each forgetting its own faults. It will perhaps provoke new accusations against the Church. The Church, however, which has no weapons at her disposal apart from those of the spirit, of the word and of love, cannot renounce her proclamation of "the word... in season and out of season." (2 Tim. 4:2). For this reason she does not cease to implore each side of the two and to beg everybody in the name of God and in the name of man : Do not kill ! Do not prepare destruction and extermination for men ! Think of your brothers and sisters who are suffering hunger and misery ! Respect each one's dignity and freedom ! (No. 16)

(L'Osservatore Romano, English edition, No. 12, 1979, p. 9)

ADDRESS TO THE GENERAL ASSEMBLY
OF THE UNITED NATIONS ORGANIZATION
2 October 1979

... We are troubled also by reports of the development of weaponry exceeding in quality and size the means of war and destruction ever known before. In this field also we applaud the decisions and agreements aimed at reducing the arms race. Nevertheless, the life of humanity today is seriously .endangered by the threat of destruction and by the risk arising even from accepting certain "tranquillizing" reports. And the resistance to actual concrete proposals of real disarmament, such as those called for by this Assembly in a special session last year, shows that together with the will for peace that all profess and that most desire there is also in existence — perhaps in latent or conditional form but nonetheless real — the contrary and the negation of this will. The continual *preparations for war* demonstrated by the production of ever more numerous, powerful and sophisticated weapons in various countries show that there is a desire to be ready for war, and *being ready* means *being able to start it*; it also means taking the risk that sometime, somewhere, somehow, someone can set in motion the terrible mechanism of general destruction. (No. 10) ...

(L'Osservatore Romano, English edition, No. 42, 1979, p. 9)

ADDRESS TO THE PRESIDENT OF THE UNITED STATES,
Mr. CARTER
6 October 1979

... I know and appreciate this country's efforts for arms limitation, especially of nuclear weapons. Everyone is aware of the terrible risk that the stockpiling of such weapons brings upon humanity. Since it is one of the greatest nations on earth, the United States plays a particularly important part in the quest for greater security in the world and for closer international collaboration. With all my heart I hope that there will be no relaxing of its efforts both to reduce the risk of a fatal and disastrous worldwide conflagration, and to secure a prudent and progressive reduction of the destructive capacity of military arsenals. At the same time, by reason of its special position, may the United States succeed in influencing the other nations to join in a continuing commitment for disarmament. Without wholeheartedly accepting such a commitment how can any nation effectively serve humanity, whose deepest desire is true peace ?...

(L'Osservatore Romano, English edition, No. 44, 1979, p. 13)

ADDRESS TO THE ORGANIZATION
OF AMERICAN STATES
6 October 1979

... 2. Peace is a most precious blessing that you seek to preserve for your peoples. You are in agreement with me that it is not by accumulating arms that this peace can be ensured in a stable way. Apart from the fact that such accumulation increases in practice the danger of having recourse to arms to settle the disputes that may arise, it takes away considerable material and human resources from the great peaceful tasks of development that are so urgent. It can also tempt some to think that the order built on arms is sufficient to ensure internal peace in the single countries.

I solemnly call on you to do everything in your power to restrain the arms race on this continent. There are no differences between your countries that cannot be peacefully overcome. What a relief it would be to your peoples, what new opportunities it would provide for their economic, social and cultural progress, and how contagious an example it would give the world, if the difficult enterprise of disarmament were here to find a realistic and resolute solution !...

(L'Osservatore Romano, English edition, No. 44, 1979, p. 13)

HOMILY ON THE WORLD DAY OF PEACE
1 January 1980

... 4. Recalling all that already today, on the first day of the Benedictine jubilee, we must address an ardent message to all men and all nations, particularly those who live on our continent. The subjects that have shaken European public opinion in the course of the last few weeks of the year that has just ended, require us *to think of the future with solicitude*. This solicitude is forced upon us by the news about so many means of destruction, of which the fruits of this rich civilization, produced with the toil of so many generations beginning from St Benedict's times, could be a victim. We are thinking of the cities and villages — in the West and at the same time in the East — which with the means of destruction already known could be completely reduced to heaps of rubble. In this case, who could protect those marvellous nests of history and centres of the life and culture of every nation, which are the source and support for whole populations in their march, sometimes a difficult one, towards the future ?

I have recently received from some scientists a concise forecast of the immediate and terrible consequences of a nuclear war. Here are the principal ones :

- Death, by direct or delayed action of the explosions, of a population that might range from 50 to 200 million persons;
- A drastic reduction of food resources, caused by residual radioactivity over a wide extent of arable land;
- Dangerous genetic mutations, occurring in human beings, fauna and flora;
- Considerable changes in the ozone layer in the atmosphere, which would expose man to major risks, harmful for his life;
- In a city stricken by a nuclear explosion the destruction of all urban services and the terror caused by the disaster would make it impossible to offer the inhabitants the slightest aid, creating a nightmarish apocalypse.

Just two hundred of the fifty thousand nuclear bombs which it is estimated already exist, would be enough to destroy most of the large cities in the world. It is urgent, those scientists say, that the peoples should not close their eyes to what an atomic war can represent for mankind.

5. These few reflections are enough to raise the question : can we continue along this way ? The answer is clear.

The Pope discusses the subject of the danger of war and the necessity of saving peace with many men and on various occasions. The way to safeguard peace lies through bilateral or multilateral negotiations. However, at their basis we must find again and reconstruct a principal factor, without which they will not yield fruit in themselves and will not ensure peace. We must *find again and reconstruct mutual trust*! And this is a difficult problem. Trust cannot be acquired by means of force. Nor can it be obtained with declarations alone. Trust must be won with concrete acts and facts.

"Peace to men of *goodwill*". These words once uttered, at the moment of Christ's birth, continue to be the key to the great cause of peace in the world. Those in particular on whom peace depends most, must remember them...

(L'Osservatore Romano, English edition, No. 3, 1980, p. 9)

ADDRESS TO UNESCO
2 June 1980

... 21. We realize it, Ladies and Gentlemen, *the future of man and of the world is threatened*, radically threatened, in spite of the intentions, certainly noble ones, of men of learning, men of science. It is threatened because the marvellous results of their researches and their discoveries, especially in the field of the sciences of nature, have been and continue to be exploited — to the detriment of the ethical imperative — for purposes that have nothing to do with the requirements of science, and even for *purposes of destruction and death*, and that to a degree never known hitherto, causing really unimaginable damage. Whereas science is called to be in the service of man's life, it is too often a fact that it is subjected to purposes that destroy the real dignity of man and of human life. That is the case when scientific research itself is directed towards these purposes or when its results are applied to purposes contrary to the good of mankind. That happens in the field of genetic manipulations and biological experimentations as well as in that of chemical, bacteriological or nuclear armaments.

Two considerations lead me to submit particularly to your reflection the nuclear threat which is weighing upon the world today and which, if it is not staved off, could lead to the destruction of the fruits of culture, the products of civilization elaborated throughout the centuries by successive generations of

227

men who believed in the primacy of the spirit and who did not spare either their efforts or their fatigue. The first consideration is the following. Geopolitical reasons, economic problems of world dimension, terrible incomprehension, wounded national pride, the materialism of our age and the decadence of moral values have led our world to a situation of instability, to a frail balance which runs the risk of being destroyed any moment as a result of errors of judgment, information or interpretation.

Another consideration is added to this disquieting perspective. Can we be sure, nowadays, that the upsetting of the balance would not lead to war, and to a war that would not hesitate to have recourse to nuclear arms? Up to now it has been said that nuclear arms have constituted a force of dissuasion which has prevented a major war from breaking out, and it is probably true. But we may wonder at the same time if it will always be so. Nuclear arms, of whatever order of magnitude or of whatever type they may be, are being perfected more and more every year, and they are being added to the arsenal of a growing number of countries. How can we be sure that the use of nuclear arms, even for purposes of national defence or in limited conflicts, will not lead to *an inevitable escalation*, leading to a destruction that mankind can never envisage or accept? But it is not you, men of science and culture, that I must ask not to close your eyes to what a nuclear war can represent for the whole of humanity (cf. *Homily for the World Day of Peace*, 1 January 1980). ...

(L'Osservatore Romano, English edition, No. 25, 1980, p. 12)

ADDRESS TO THE DIPLOMATIC CORPS
ACCREDITED TO THE HOLY SEE
12 January 1981

... As regards the defence of peace, *the role of the Holy See is exercised in tensions and in crises of international life.* There again, it wishes to be inspired always by an overall view of the common good. That is not done without difficulties, due to the contrary positions held by the parties. On the one hand, the Holy See wishes to be full of attention and respect for the subjective reasons claimed or put forward by each of the parties; then, too, there is also the complexity of highly technical aspects, or the lack of real data. As a result of all that, the Holy See has quite often to abstain from expressing a concrete judgment on the conflicting theses. This is the case, among other things, of *disarmament.*

The Holy See is deeply convinced — and it has been able to repeat it on many occasions — that the arms race is ruinous for mankind, and that far from reducing the threat that weighs on security and world peace, it increases it. It emphasizes the fundamental elements that make possible and realistic an agreement that would put an end to the race for ever new and more powerful means of destruction. These elements are particularly *a climate of greater trustfulness,* which can spring from real and global détente in international relations; respect for the *prerogatives of all peoples,* even if they are small and disarmed, prerogatives based on their cultural identity; sincere collaboration to improve "the human component of peace", represented above all by respect for human rights. (No. 10) ...

(L'Osservatore Romano, English edition, No. 4, 1981, p. 4)

ADDRESS TO THE REPRESENTATIVES
OF THE UNITED NATIONS' UNIVERSITY
IN HIROSHIMA
25 February 1981

... 2. Ladies and gentlemen, we have gathered here today at Hiroshima : and I would like you to know that I am deeply convinced that we have been given an historic occasion for reflecting together on the responsibility of science and technology at this period, marked as it is by so much hope and so many anxieties. At Hiroshima, the facts speak for themselves, in a way that is dramatic, unforgettable and unique. In the face of an unforgettable tragedy, which touches us all as human beings, how can we fail to express our brotherhood and our deep sympathy at the frightful wound inflicted on the cities of Japan that bear the names of Hiroshima and Nagasaki ?

That wound affected the whole of the human family. Hiroshima and Nagasaki : few events in history have had such an effect on man's conscience. The representatives of the world of science were not the ones least affected by the moral crisis caused throughout the world by the explosion of the first atomic bomb. The human mind had in fact made a terrible discovery. We realized with horror that nuclear energy would henceforth be available as a weapon of devastation; then we learned that this terrible weapon had in fact been used, for the first time, for military purposes. And then there arose the question that will never leave us again : Will this weapon, perfected and multiplied beyond measure, be used tomorrow ? If so, would it not probably destroy the human family, its members and all the achievements of civilization ?

3. Ladies and gentlemen, you who devote your lives to the modern sciences, you are the first to be able to evaluate the disaster that a nuclear war would inflict on the human family. And I know that, ever since the explosion of the first atomic bomb, many of you have been anxiously wondering about the responsibility of modern science and the technology that is the fruit of that science. In a number of countries, associations of scholars and research-workers express the anxiety of the scientific world in the face of an irresponsible use of science, which too often does grievous damage to the balance of nature, or brings with it the ruin and oppression of man by man. One thinks in the first place of physics, chemistry, biology and the genetical sciences, of which you rightly condemn those applications or experimentations which are detrimental to humanity. But one also has in mind the social sciences and the human behavioural sciences when

they are utilized to manipulate people, to crush their minds, souls, dignity and freedom. Criticism of science and technology is sometimes so severe that it comes close to condemning science itself. On the contrary, science and technology are a wonderful product of a God-given human creativity, since they have provided us with wonderful possibilities, and we all gratefully benefit from them. But we know that this potential is not a neutral one : it can be used either for man's progress or for his degradation. Like you, I have lived through this period, which I would call the "post-Hiroshima period", and I share your anxieties. And today I feel inspired to say this to you : surely the time has come for our society, and especially for the world of science, to realize that the future of humanity depends, as never before, on our collective moral choices.

4. In the past, it was possible to destroy a village, a town, a region, even a country. Now, it is the whole planet that has come under threat. This fact should finally compel everyone to face a basic moral consideration : from now on, it is only through a conscious choice and through a deliberate policy that humanity can survive. The moral and political choice that faces us is that of putting all the resources of mind, science and culture at the service of peace and of the building up of a new society, a society that will succeed in eliminating the causes of fratricidal wars by generously pursuing the total progress of each individual and of all humanity. Of course, individuals and societies are always exposed to the passions of greed and hate; but, as far as within us lies, let us try effectively to correct the social situations and structures that cause injustice and conflict. We shall build peace by building a more humane world. In the light of this hope, the scientific, cultural and university world has an eminent part to play. Peace is one of the loftiest achievements of culture, and for this reason it deserves all our intellectual and spiritual energy...

_____

(L'Osservatore Romano, English edition, No. 10, 1981, pp. 15-16)

APPEAL FOR PEACE AT THE PEACE MEMORIAL
IN HIROSHIMA
25 February 1981

War is the work of man. War is destruction of human life. War is death.

Nowhere do these truths impose themselves upon us more forcefully than in this city of Hiroshima, at this Peace Memorial. Two cities will forever have their names linked together, two Japanese cities, Hiroshima and Nagasaki, as the only cities in the world that have had the ill fortune to be a reminder that man is capable of destruction beyond belief. Their names will forever stand out as the names of the only cities in our time that have been singled out as a warning to future generations that war can destroy human efforts to build a world of peace.

1. Mr Mayor,

Dear friends here present, and all of you who are listening to my voice, and whom my message will reach :

It is with deep emotion that I have come here today as a pilgrim of peace. I wanted to make this visit to the Hiroshima Peace Memorial out of a deep personal conviction that to remember the past is to commit oneself to the future.

Together we recall that it is one of humanity's sad achievements that all across the face of the earth the names of very many — too many — places are remember- ed mainly because they have witnessed the horror and suffering produced by war : war-memorials, that with the victory of one side also recall the suffering and death of countless human beings, cemeteries where rest those who sacrified their very lives in the service of their country or in the service of a noble cause, and cemeteries where lie the innocent civilian victims of war's destructive fury; the remains of concentration and extermination camps, where contempt for man and for his inviolable rights reached its most base and cruel expression; battle- fields, where nature has mercifully healed the earth's scars, but without being able to blot out past human history of hate and enmity. Hiroshima and Nagasaki stand out from all those other places and monuments, as the first victims of nuclear war.

I bow my head as I recall the memory of thousands of men, women and children who lost their lives in that one terrible moment, or who for long years carried in their bodies and minds those seeds of death which inexorably pursued their process of destruction. The final balance of the human suffering that began here has not been fully drawn up, nor has the total human cost been tallied, especially when one sees what nuclear war has done — and could still do — to our ideas, our attitudes and our civilization.

2. To remember the past is to commit oneself to the future, I cannot but honour and applaud the wise decision of the authorities of this city that the memorial recalling the first nuclear bombing should be a monument to peace. By so doing, the City of Hiroshima and the whole People of Japan have forcefully expressed their hope for a peaceful world and their conviction that man who wages war can also successfully make peace. From this City, and from the event its name recalls, there has originated a new worldwide consciousness against war, and a fresh determination to work for peace.

Some people, even among those who were alive at the time of the events that we commemorate today, might prefer not to think about the horror of nuclear war and its dire consequences. Among those who have never personally experienced the reality of armed conflict between nations, some might wish to abandon the very possibility of nuclear war. Others might wish to regard nuclear capacity as an unavoidable means of maintaining a balance of power through a balance of terror. But there is no justification for not raising the question of the responsibility of each nation and each individual in the face of possible wars and of the nuclear threat.

3. To remember the past is to commit oneself to the future. I evoke before you the memory of 6 August 1945, so that we may better grasp the meaning of the present challenge. Since that fateful day, nuclear stockpiles have grown in quantity and in destructive power. Nuclear weaponry continues to be built, tested and deployed. The total consequences of full-scale nuclear war are impossible to predict, but even if a mere fraction of the available weapons were to be used, one has to ask whether the inevitable escalation can be imagined, and whether the very destruction of humanity is not a real possibility. I wish to repeat here what I said to the United Nations General Assembly : "The continual preparations for war demonstrated by the production of ever more numerous, powerful and sophisticated weapons in various countries show that there is a desire to be ready for war, and being ready means being able to start it; it also means taking the risk that sometime, somewhere, somehow, someone can set in motion the terrible mechanism of general destruction" (No. 10).

4. To remember the past is to commit oneself to the future. To remember Hiroshima is to abhor nuclear war. To remember Hiroshima is to commit one-

self to peace. To remember what the people of this city suffered is to renew our faith in man, in his capacity to do what is good, in his freedom to choose what is right, in his determination to turn disaster into a new beginning. In the face of the man-made calamity that every war is, one must affirm and reaffirm, again and again, that the waging of war is not inevitable or unchangeable. Humanity is not destined to self-destruction. Clashes of ideologies, aspirations and needs can and must be settled and resolved by means other than war and violence. Humanity owes it to itself to settle differences and conflicts by peaceful means. The great spectrum of problems facing the many peoples in varying stages of cultural, social, economic and political development gives rise to international tension and conflict. It is vital for humanity that these problems should be solved in accordance with ethical principles of equity and justice enshrined in meaningful agreements and institutions. The international community should thus give itself a system of law that will regulate international relations and maintain peace, just as the rule of law protects national order.

5. Those who cherish life on earth must encourage governments and decision-makers in the economic and social fields to act in harmony with the demands of peace rather than out of narrow self-interest. Peace must always be the aim : peace pursued and protected in all circumstances. Let us not repeat the past, a past of violence and destruction. Let us embark upon the steep and difficult path of peace, the only path that befits human dignity, the only path that leads to the true fulfillment of the human destiny, the only path to a future in which equity, justice and solidarity are realities and not just distant dreams.

And so, on this very spot where, 35 years ago, the life of so many people was snuffed out in one fiery moment, I wish to appeal to the whole world on behalf of life, on behalf of humanity, on behalf of the future.

To the Heads of State and of Government, to those who hold political and economic power, I say : let us pledge ourselves to peace through justice; let us take a solemn decision, now, that war will never be tolerated or sought as a means of resolving differences; let us promise our fellow human beings that we will work untiringly for disarmament and the banishing of all nuclear weapons : let us replace violence and hate with confidence and caring.

To every man and woman in this land and in the world, I say : let us assume responsibility for each other and for the future without being limited by frontiers and social distinctions; let us educate ourselves and educate others in the ways of peace; let humanity never become the victim of a struggle between competing systems; let there never be another war.

To young people everywhere, I say : let us together create a new future of fraternity and solidarity; let us reach out towards our brothers and sisters in need, feed the hungry, shelter the homeless, free the downtrodden, bring justice where injustice reigns and peace where only weapons speak. Your young hearts have an extraordinary capacity for goodness and love : put them at the service of your fellow human beings.

To everyone I repeat the words of the Prophet : "They shall beat their swords into ploughshares and their spears into pruning hooks; nation shall not lift up sword against nation, neither shall they learn war any more" (Is. 2:4).

To those who believe in God, I say : let us be strong in his strength that infinitely surpasses our own; let us be united in the knowledge that he calls us to unity; let us be aware that love and sharing are not faraway ideals but the road to enduring peace — the peace of God.

And to the Creator of nature and man, of truth and beauty I pray :
Hear my voice, for it is the voice of the victims of all wars and violence among individuals and nations;
Hear my voice, for it is the voice of all children who suffer and will suffer when people put their faith in weapons and war;
Hear my voice when I beg you to instill into the hearts of all human beings the wisdom of peace, the strength of justice and the joy of fellowship;
Hear my voice, for I speak for the multitudes in every country and in every period of history who do not want war and are ready to walk the road of peace;
Hear my voice and grant insight and strength so that we may always respond to hatred with love, to injustice with total dedication to justice, to need with the sharing of self, to war with peace.
O God, hear my voice and grant unto the world your everlasting peace.

(L'Osservatore Romano, English edition, No. 10, 1981, p. 14)

ANGELUS MESSAGE
30 August 1981

1. Today is the last Sunday of August.

Consequently, the first day of September is approaching, with which is associated the painful, tragic memory of the outbreak of the terrible Second World War. We can not forget this anniversary.

On 25 February of this year, in the framework of my visit to Japan, it was granted me to go on pilgrimage to Hiroshima and Nagasaki. Precisely there — with the explosion of the first atomic bomb — the war which was then nearing its end left to humanity the grave warning of what could become a new war with the use of nuclear energy.

And so we refer the memory of that first of September of forty-two years ago not only to the past, which year by year grows more distant, but we also apply it with the thought always directed to the future of all nations and of the whole human family.

2. I repeat today with the same sorrowful concern the words that I spoke at Hiroshima : "War is destruction of human life. War is death... Hiroshima and Nagasaki are distinguished from all the other places and monuments as the first victims of nuclear war. I bow my head at the memory of thousands of men, women and children who lost their lives in one terrible moment, and those who for long years have borne in their bodies and minds the seeds of death... To recall the past is to commit ourselves to the future... From this city and from the event that its name recalls, there has been arising a new world consciousness against war and a renewed determination to work in favour of peace... To recall Hiroshima is to abhor nuclear war. To recall Hiroshima is to commit ourselves for peace."

3. Unfortunately, since that fatal day nuclear arms have increased in quantity and destructive power.

At this moment it is necessary yet again to emphasize vigourously the need to exert every effort aimed at securing peace. In Hiroshima I always invited all those in positions of responsibility to loyal and harmonious action : "Let us commit ourselves", I said, "for peace in justice; let us make a solemn decision, now, that war will never be tolerated and seen as a means for resolving differences; let us promise our fellow-men that we will tirelessly do our utmost for disarmament and abolition of all nuclear weapons; let us replace violence and hatred with trust and concern."

This invitation I repeat today with all my strength, in the conviction that it will be heard. It is the whole world that is waiting. It is Christ himself who calls us, all of us, to be "peacemakers" (Mt. 5:9), so that the spirit of this beatitude may ever more permeate the life of peoples and international society.

4. The prayer for peace is never lessened by the lips of the Church. We repeat it in every Mass, first of all in the Communion rite, referring to the words of the Our Father, which Jesus Christ taught us : "Deliver us, Lord, from every evil, and grant us peace in our day."

We pray again for peace, which is a gift of God and at the same time a fruit of men's good will, when we say, "Lord Jesus Christ, who said to your Apostles : 'Peace I leave you, my peace I give you', look not on our sins but on the faith of your Church, and grant us unity and peace..." We pray that the Church be also the refuge of peace for the world, for all men, for every man and for every society.

And finally, a little before Communion, the priest says, "The peace of the Lord be with you always."

5. Today we wish to include this invocation with particular fervour in our Angelus, addressing it to the whole world, to all nations, and to all systems and ideologies, to all statesmen and heads of military forces : "PEACE BE WITH YOU".

(L'Osservatore Romano, English edition, No. 36, 1981, p. 1)

ANGELUS MESSAGE
29 November 1981

... 3. On this first Sunday of Advent, on which the Church begins to prepare for the coming of the Prince of Peace, I wish to recall an intention which is certainly close to the hearts of a great many men and women of our time.

Tomorrow two delegations of the United States and of the Soviet Union will begin talks in Geneva to discuss the reduction of nuclear armaments in Europe. On the eve of this meeting I sent to the two highest authorities of the two countries a personal message to express deep interest in the outcome of the talks, to which the attention of millions of men all over the world is directed in anxious expectation. With that wish, I expressed also an encouragement in order that — thanks to common efforts of good will — this opportunity will not pass without results being reached such as to consolidate the hope of a future no longer threatened by the spectre of a possible nuclear conflict.

Let us recite the Angelus now for this intention...

(L'Osservatore Romano, English edition, No. 49, 1981, p. 1)

MESSAGE FOR THE WORLD DAY OF PEACE, 1982
8 December 1981

... Only God the giver of life, when he unites all things in Christ (cf. Eph. 1:10), will fulfil our ardent hope by himself bringing to accomplishment everything that he has undertaken in history to his Spirit in the matter of justice and peace.

Although Christians put all their best energies into preventing war or stopping it, they do not deceive themselves about their ability to cause peace to triumph, nor about the effect of their efforts to this end. They therefore concern themselves with all human initiatives in favour of peace and very often take part in them; but they regard them with realism and humility. One could almost say that they "relativize" them in two senses : they relate them both to the sinful condition of humanity and to God's saving plan. In the first place, Christians are aware that plans based on aggression, domination and the manipulation of others lurk in human hearts, and sometimes even secretly nourish human intentions, in spite of certain declarations or manifestations of a pacifist nature. For Christians know that in this world a totally and permanently peaceful human society is unfortunately a utopia, and that ideologies that hold up that prospect as easily attainable are based on hopes that cannot be realized, whatever the reason behind them. It is a question of a mistaken view of the human condition, a lack of application in considering the question as a whole; or it may be a case of evasion in order to calm fear, or in still other cases a matter of calculated self-interest. Christians are convinced, if only because they have learned from personal experience, that these deceptive hopes lead straight to the false peace of totalitarian regimes. But this realistic view in no way prevents Christians from working for peace; instead, it stirs up their ardour, for they also know that Christ's victory over deception, hate and death gives those in love with peace a more decisive motive for action than what the most generous theories about man have to offer; Christ's victory likewise gives a hope more surely based than any hope held out by the most audacious dreams.

This is why Christians, even as they strive to resist and prevent every form of warfare, have no hesitation in recalling that, in the name of an elementary requirement of justice, peoples have a right and even a duty to protect their existence and freedom by proportionate means against an unjust aggressor (cf. Constitution *Gaudium et Spes*, 79). However, in view of the difference between classical warfare and nuclear or bacteriological war — a difference so to speak of nature — and in view of the scandal of the arms race seen against the background of the needs of the Third World, this right, which is very real in principle, only underlines the urgency for world society to equip itself with effective means of negotiation. In this way the nuclear terror that haunts our time can encourage us to enrich our common heritage with a very simple discovery that is within our reach, namely that war is the most barbarous and least effective way of resolving conflicts. More than ever before, human society is forced to provide itself with the means of consultation and dialogue which it needs in order to survive, and therefore with the institutions necessary for building up justice and peace.

May it also realize that this work is something beyond human powers ! (No. 12) ...

(L'Osservatore Romano, English edition, No. 1, 1982, p. 7)

ANGELUS MESSAGE AND STATEMENT ON THE CONSEQUENCES OF THE USE OF NUCLEAR WEAPONS

13 December 1981

5. On Sunday, 29 November, I referred to the message I sent to the Heads of State of the United States and of the Soviet Union, on the eve of the Geneva negotiation for the reduction of nuclear armaments in Europe.

In the same spirit of deep concern before the terrifying hypothesis of an atomic war, I asked the same High Authorities and those of Great Britain and France, as well as the President of the General Assembly of the United Nations, kindly to receive in the next few days delegations of the Pontifical Academy of Sciences, charged with the task of illustrating a scientific document, the fruit of a careful study carried out by the same Academy with the collaboration also of other eminent scholars, on the consequences of the use of these armaments.

I have, in fact, the deep conviction that, in the light of a nuclear war's effects, which can be scientifically foreseen as certain, the only choice that is morally and humanly valid, is represented by the reduction of nuclear armaments, while waiting for their future complete elimination, carried out simultaneously by all the parties, by means of explicit agreements and with the commitment of accepting effective controls.

In our Angelus prayer let us now recommend to Our Lady also the cause of peace.

*　　*　　*

On 7-8 October 1981, under the chairmanship of Professor Carlos Chagas, President of the Pontifical Academy of Sciences, at the headquarters of the Academy (Casina Pius IV, Vatican City), a group of fourteen specialized scientists (Carlos Chagas, Rio de Janeiro; E. Amaldi, Rome; N. Bochkov, Moscow; L. Caldas, Rio de Janeiro; H. Hiatt, Boston; R. Latarjet, Paris; A. Leaf, Boston; J. Lejeune, Paris; L. Leprince-Ringuet, Paris; G.B. Marini-Bettòlo, Rome; C. Pavan, São Paulo; A. Rich, Cambridge, Mass.; A. Serra, Rome; V. Weisskopf, Cambridge, Mass.) from various parts of the world assembled to examine the problem of the consequences of the use of nuclear weapons on the survival and health of humanity.

Although most of these consequences would appear obvious, it seems that they are not adequately appreciated. The conditions of life following a nuclear attack would be so severe that the only hope for humanity is prevention of any form of nuclear war. Universal dissemination and acceptance of this knowledge would make it apparent that nuclear weapons must not be used at all in warfare and that their number should be progressively reduced in a balanced way.

The above-mentioned group discussed and unanimously approved a number of fundamental points, which have been further developed in the following statement.

Recent talk about winning or even surviving a nuclear war must reflect a failure to appreciate a medical reality : any nuclear war would inevitably cause death, disease and suffering of pandemic proportions and without the possibility of effective medical intervention. That reality leads to the same conclusion physicians have reached for life-threatening epidemics throughout history : prevention is essential for control.

In contrast to widespread belief, much is known about the catastrophe that would follow the use of nuclear weapons. Much is known too about the limitations of medical assistance. If this knowledge is presented to people and their leaders everywhere, it might help interrupt the nuclear arms race. This in turn would help prevent what could be the last epidemic our civilization will know.

The devastation wrought by an atomic weapon on Hiroshima and Nagasaki provides direct evidence of the consequences of nuclear warfare, but there are many theoretical appraisals on which we may also draw. Two years ago, an assessment undertaken by a responsible official agency described the effect of nuclear attacks on cities of about 2 million inhabitants. If a one-million ton nuclear weapon (the Hiroshima bomb approximated 15,000 tons of explosive power) exploded in the central area of such cities, it would result, as calculated, in 180 km^2 of property destruction, 250,000 fatalities and 500,000 severely injured. These would include blast injuries, such as fractures and severe lacerations of soft tissues, thermal injuries such as surface burns, retinal burns and respiratory tract damage, and radiation injuries, both acute radiation syndrome and delayed effects.

Even under optimal conditions, care of such casualities would present a medical task of unimaginable magnitude. The study projected that if 18,000 hospital beds were available in and around one of these cities, no more than 5,000 would remain relatively undamaged. These would accommodate only 1 per cent of the human beings injured, but it must be stressed that in any case no one could deliver the medical service required by even a few of the severely burned, the crushed and the radiated victims.

The hopelessness of the medical task is readily apparent if we consider what is required for the care of severely injured patients. We shall cite one case history, that of a severely burned twenty year old man who was taken to the burn unit of a Boston Hospital after an automobile accident in which the gasoline tank had exploded. During his hospitalization he received 140 litres of fresh-frozen plasma, 147 litres of fresh-frozen red blood cells, 180 millilitres of platelets and 180 millilitres of albumin. He underwent six operative procedures during which wounds involving 85 per cent of his body surface were closed with various types of grafts, including artificial skin. Throughout his hospitalization, he required mechanical ventilation. Despite these and many other heroic measures, which stretched the resources of one of the world's most comprehensive institutions, he died on his 33rd hospital day. His injuries were likened by the doctor who supervised his care, to those described for many of the victims of Hiroshima. Had twenty score of such patients been presented at the same time to all of Boston's hospitals the medical capabilities of the city would have been overwhelmed. Now, consider the situation if, along with the injuries to many thousands of people, most of the medical emergency facilities had been destroyed.

A Japanese physician, Professor M. Ichimaru, published an eyewitness account of the effects of the Nagasaki bomb. He reported : "I tried to go to my medical school in Urakami which was 500 metres from the hypocentre. I met many people coming back from Urakami. Their clothes were in rags and shreds of skin hung from their bodies. They looked like ghosts with vacant stares. The next day I was able to enter Urakami on foot and all that I knew had disappeared. Only the concrete and iron skeletons of the buildings remained. There were dead bodies everywhere. On each street corner, we had tubs of water used for putting out fires after air raids. In one of these small tubs, scarcely large enough for one person, was the body of a desperate man who sought cool water. There was foam coming from his mouth, but he was not alive. I cannot get rid of the sounds of the crying women in the destroyed fields. As I got nearer to the school there were black, charred bodies with the white edges of bones showing in the arms and legs. When I arrived some were still alive. They were unable to move their bodies. The strongest were so weak that they were slumped over on the ground. I talked with them and they thought that they would be O.K. but all of them would eventually die within two weeks. I cannot forget the way their eyes looked at me and their voices spoke to me forever...".

It should be noted that the bomb dropped on Nagasaki had a power of about 20,000 tons of TNT, not much larger than the so-called "tactical bombs" designed for battlefield use.

But even these grim pictures are inadequate to describe the human disaster that would result from an attack on a country by today's stockpiles of nuclear weapons, which contain thousands of bombs with the force of one-million tons of TNT or greater.

The suffering of the surviving population would be without parallel. There would be complete interruption of communications, of food supplies and of water. Help would be given only at the risk of mortal danger from radiation for those venturing outside of buildings in the first days. The social disruption following such an attack would be unimaginable.

The exposure to large doses of radiation would lower immunity to bacteria and viruses and could, therefore, open the way for widespread infection. Radiation would cause irreversible brain damage and mental deficiency in many of the exposed in utero. It would greatly increase the incidence of many forms of cancer in survivors. Genetic damage would be passed on to future generations, should there be any.

In addition, large areas of soil and forests, as well as livestock, would be contaminated, reducing food resources. Many other harmful biological and even geophysical effects would be likely, but we do not have enough knowledge to predict with confidence what they would be.

Even a nuclear attack directed only at military facilities would be devastating to the country as a whole. This is because military facilities are widespread rather than concentrated at only a few points. Thus, many nuclear weapons would be exploded. Furthermore, the spread of radiation due to the natural winds and atmospheric mixing would kill vast numbers of people and contaminate large areas. The medical facilities of any nation would be inadequate to care for the survivors. An objective examination of the medical situation that would follow a nuclear war leads to but one conclusion : prevention is our only recourse.

The consequences of nuclear war are not, of course, only medical in nature. But those that are compel us to pay heed to the inescapable lesson of contemporary medicine : where treatment of a given disease is ineffective or where costs are insupportable, attention must be turned to prevention. Both conditions apply to the effects of nuclear war. Treatment would be virtually impossible and the costs would be staggering. Can any stronger argument be marshalled for a preventive strategy ?

Prevention of any disease requires an effective prescription. We recognize that such a prescription must both prevent nuclear war and safeguard security.

Our knowledge and credentials as scientists and physicians do not, of course, permit us to discuss security issues with expertise. However, if political and military leaders have based their strategic planning on mistaken assumptions concerning the medical aspects of a nuclear war, we feel that we do have a responsibility. We must inform them and people everywhere of the full-blown clinical picture that would follow a nuclear attack and of the impotence of the medical community to offer a meaningful response. If we remain silent, we risk betraying ourselves and our civilization.

(L'Osservatore Romano, English edition, No. 51-52, 1981, p. 19)

HOMILY ON THE WORLD DAY OF PEACE
1 January 1982

... 4. The Apostle writes : "God has sent the Spirit of his Son into our hearts, crying, 'Abba ! Father !' So through God you are no longer a slave but a son, and if a son then an heir" (Gal. 4:6-7).

In the depths of human heart *a great struggle* is going on : *the "son" fights the "slave"*. This struggle takes place at the same time in the history of man on earth.

Man can become a "slave" in various ways. He can be a "slave" when his freedom is restricted, when he is deprived of objective human rights : but he can also become a slave due to an abuse of the freedom which is specifically his.

Modern man is threatened by a "*slavery*" derived *from the products of his own thought* and his will, products which may serve mankind, but can also be turned against man.

As I wrote in the Encyclical *Redemptor Hominis*, "this seems to make up the main chapter of the drama of present-day existence... Man therefore lives increasingly in fear. He is afraid that what he produces — not all of it, of course, or even most of it, but part of it and precisely that part contains a special share of his genius and initiative — can radically turn against himself" (No. 15).

This is what would happen, in particular, in the hypothesis of a nuclear conflict. As can be seen, in fact, from the document prepared by the Pontifical

Academy of Sciences and presented by special delegations, which I sent to four Heads of State and to the President of the Assembly of the United Nations, "any nuclear war would inevitably cause death, disease and suffering of pandemic proportions and without the possibility of effective medical intervention." Apart, in fact, from the mass destruction of human lives, "the suffering of the surviving population would be without parallel. There would be complete interruption of communications, of food supplies and of water. Help would be given only at the risk of mortal danger from radiation for those venturing outside of buildings in the first days. The social disruption following such an attack would be unimaginable.

The exposure to large doses of radiation would lower immunity to bacteria and viruses and could, therefore, open the way for widespread infection. Radiation would cause irreversible brain damage and mental deficiency in many of the exposed in utero. It would greatly increase the incidence of many forms of cancer in survivors. Genetic damage would be passed on to future generations, should there be any."

An objective assessment of the sanitary situation following a nuclear war leads to but one conclusion : "prevention is our only way out".

On the first day of the new year we pray that in this struggle of the "son" with the "slave" — a struggle that persists in the hearts and the history of man — the "son" will be victorious...

(L'Osservatore Romano, English edition, No. 2, 1982, pp. 1-16)

ADDRESS TO THE DIPLOMATIC CORPS
ACCREDITED TO THE HOLY SEE
16 January 1982

... This See of Peter remains faithful to its mission : that of promoting rightful understanding among peoples and of safeguarding the good of peace, which is the most precious heritage, the indispensable heritage for man's complete development, even in the framework of the earthly city. The Church carries out this task *for the good of man*, taking up its position *above parties*, as it testified particularly by the recent initiative carried out, according to my express desire, under the sponsorship of the Pontifical Academy of Sciences. To the Heads of State of Nuclear powers and to the President of the General Assembly of the United Nations, a study was presented on the terrible and irreversible consequences of a nuclear conflict. In the perspective of the Holy See, the initiative does not intend to deal with technical details of the negotiations in course or of other possible negotiations; it wants to show clearly, from the human and moral point of view, and appealing to men of science to make their contribution to the great cause of peace, that the only solution possible, in face of the hypothesis of a nuclear war, is to reduce at once, and subsequently to eliminate completely, nuclear armaments, by means of specific agreements and effective controls. (No. 2) ...

(L'Osservatore Romano, English edition, No. 4, 1982, p. 1)

TABLE OF CONTENTS

PREFACE

THE FOURTH ASSEMBLY PERIOD

249

THE HOLY SEE ON
DISARMAMENT AND PEACE

PIUS XII

251